Books by Evan S. Connell

The Anatomy Lesson
   and Other Stories
Mrs. Bridge
The Patriot
Notes from a Bottle
   Found on the Beach at Carmel
At the Crossroads
The Diary of a Rapist
Mr. Bridge
Points for a Compass Rose
The Connoisseur
Double Honeymoon
A Long Desire
The White Lantern
Saint Augustine's Pigeon
Son of the Morning Star

THE
WHITE
LANTERN

Evan S. Connell

NORTH POINT PRESS
San Francisco *1989*

Originally published by Holt, Rinehart and Winston,
New York; reprinted by arrangement.
Portions of this book first appeared in *The North American
Review* and *The Carleton Miscellany*, to whom
acknowledgment is made.
Passages from *The Etruscans*, by Massimo Pallottino,
translation copyright © 1955, 1975 by Penguin Books,
are reprinted by permission of Indiana University Press.

LIBRARY OF CONGRESS CATALOGING-IN-PUBLICATION DATA
Connell, Evan S., 1924–
    The white lantern / Evan S. Connell.
      p.   cm.
    Reprint. Originally published: New York : Holt, Rinehart,
    and Winston, c1980.
    Bibliography: p.
    ISBN 0–86547–364–1
    1. Antiquities—Miscellanea.   2. Astronomy—Miscellanea.
    3. Writing—Miscellanea.   I. Title.
CC175.C66   1989
930.1—dc19   88–34554

North Point Press
850 Talbot Avenue
Berkeley, California
94706

To William Abrahams

Que sçais-je?

　　　—*Montaigne*

Contents

The White Lantern

1

Olduvai & All That

J ames Ussher, born in 1581, attended Trinity College,
Dublin, where he was ordained at the age of twenty.
Four years later he became chancellor of Saint Patrick's
Cathedral. Ten years after that he drafted the articles of
doctrine and discipline for the Irish Protestant Church. At
forty he was appointed bishop of Meath. Soon he became
archbishop of Armagh. He visited England frequently and
after his death he was buried, by Cromwell's order, in
Westminster Abbey. Widely honored and respected, not
merely because of his ecclesiastic eminence but for prodigious scholarship, he was the first to distinguish between
the genuine and spurious epistles of Saint Ignatius of Anti-
och. He wrote as fluently in Latin as in English, and
among his most celebrated works is *Annales Veteris et
Novi Tentamenti*, a tremendous article of faith which
proves that God created the universe in 4004 B.C.

Considering Archbishop Ussher's erudition and prestige, nobody should have challenged his date for the Creation, but the devil's disciples seldom rest. So we come
upon Isaac de La Peyrère who, after examining some

oddly chipped stones gathered from the French countryside, wrote a little book in which he asserted that these
stones had been chipped by human beings who lived before the time of Adam. The year A.D. 1655 was not a good
year to make such observations: M. de La Peyrère's blas-
phemous monograph was publicly incinerated.

You might think this warning would be sufficient, enabling Christians to sleep comfortably through another millennium; but the Western world had begun to awaken and
strict guardians of the status quo could not prevent imper-
tinent questions from blossoming like daffodils in spring.

The Ark, for instance. How big was it? How many animals shuffled up the gangplank?

This problem, although not new, had been complicated
by the voyages of Columbus and other explorers who reported seeing strange birds and beasts. In 1559 a monk
named Johann Buteo had tried to clear up the matter with
a learned disquisition titled *Noah's Ark, its Form and its
Capacity.* Alas, Brother Buteo's statement did not assuage
certain doubts.

Theologians then explained that these previously unknown creatures came into existence after the Flood just
as domestic animals crossbreed and evolve, just as the
mating of a cat with a wolf produces a lynx, or a camel
with a leopard produces a giraffe.

Sir Walter Raleigh had something to say, as usual. New
species might emerge not only through crossbreeding but
also because of different surroundings. The European
wildcat, when its home is India, grows up to become the
panther. The European blackbird changes color and size
in Virginia.

Nevertheless, despite every explanation, new and more
odious questions bloomed, nourished by such infernal ad-
vocates as a French diplomat named Benoît de Maillet

who wrote that germs of the first living organisms could have arrived from outer space—an idea considered preposterous until quite recently. These germs inevitably dropped into the ocean because a long time ago there was no land, and here they commenced to evolve. Hence it must follow that Man's ancestors were aquatic: "maritime people who spend part of their life under water and who often have fins instead of feet, scales instead of bare skin." About ninety such creatures had been sighted, we are told, and several females were delivered to the king of Portugal who, wanting to preserve these curious beings, graciously allowed them to spend three hours a day in the sea—secured by a long line. And it is said that they submerged at once and never came up for air. The king kept these maritime women for several years, hoping to communicate with them, "but they never learnt to speak at all."

Maillet also reflected upon the metamorphosis of fish into birds:

> There can be no doubt that fish, in the course of hunting or being hunted, were thrown up on the shore. There they could find food, but were unable to return to the water. Subsequently their fins were enlarged by the action of the water, the radial structures supporting the fins turned to quills, the dried scales became feathers, the skin assumed a coating of down, the belly-fins changed into feet, the entire body was reshaped, the neck and beak became prolonged, and at last the fish was transformed into a bird. Yet the new configuration corresponded in a general way to the old. The latter will always remain readily recognizable.

However bold he may have been imaginatively, Benoît de Maillet in person was altogether discreet. Rather than identify himself as the author of these intellectual flights, he contrived the anagram Telliamed, and further protected himself by attributing his theory to an Indian philosopher who had revealed it to a French missionary. "I confess to you," says the missionary to the philosopher, prudently separating himself from the Indian's outrageous ideas, "that notwithstanding the small Foundation I find in your system, I am charmed to hear you speak. . . ."

Maillet also stipulated that the manuscript should not be published until eleven years after his death, as though there were a statute of limitations on the digging up of heretics in order to burn or otherwise abuse their corpses.

Despite these precautions, copies of *Telliamed ou Entretien d'un Philosophe Indien avec un Missionnaire Français* were circulating through Paris salons during his lifetime; and the great naturalist Georges Louis Leclerc, Comte de Buffon, seems to have been much impressed by the startling essay.

Buffon, we should note, admitted to being one of history's five supreme figures—the others being Newton, Bacon, Leibniz, and Montesquieu. The earth, said he, had been thrown from the sun and congealed until it attained a temperature suitable for life. That being so, the earth's exact age could be deduced without resorting to biblical texts. One needed only to heat some iron spheres, observe how long they required to cool, and correlate this information, taking into account the earth's dimensions. Buffon then announced that he had found our planet to be 74,832 years old. It had sustained life for the past 40,062 years, but because the temperature would continue falling it would become uninhabitable after another 93,291 years, a globe forever sheathed in ice.

Along with these facts, which have not weathered very well, he came close to anticipating Darwin: "It may be assumed that all animals arise from a single form of life which in the course of time produced the rest by processes of perfection and degeneration." And he went on to say that the organic structure of each natural thing illustrates the following truth: life on earth developed gradually.

However, discretion may at times be advisable, and Buffon could appreciate the monumental power of the Church. No, he wrote somewhat hastily at one point, "no, it is certain—certain by revelation—that all animals have shared equally the grace of creation, each has emerged from the hands of the Creator as it appears to us today."

One of Buffon's pupils, Jean-Baptiste Pierre de Monet, Chevalier de Lamarck, encouraged the attack on biblical dogma. He wrote that species cannot be absolutely distinguished from each other; species pass into one another, proceeding from simple infusoria to the magnificent complexity of Man.

Immanuel Kant had similar thoughts: "It is possible for a chimpanzee or an orangutan, by perfecting its organs, to change at some future date into a human being. Radical alterations in natural conditions may force the ape to walk upright, accustom its hands to the use of tools, and learn to talk."

Schopenhauer wrote in 1851: "We must imagine the first human beings as having been born in Asia of orangutans and in Africa of chimpanzees. . . ."

James Hutton, a Scottish geologist and farmer, a gentleman of numerous parts—philosopher, chemist, jurist, Quaker, inventor, physicist—Hutton found the world not in a grain of sand but in a brook gently transporting sediment to the sea. Only one portrait of this extraordinary man survives, revealing a long, sad face. The face of somebody who has looked so far, comments Loren Eiseley, that mortals do not interest him. For the lesson of the industrious brook was this: mountains, plains, rivers, and oceans must be the result of slow topographical changes. The earth's surface must have been lifted and then eroded, which would take a while. Indeed, Hutton wrote, "we find no vestige of a beginning, no prospect of an end." Apparently he did not think this contradicted the Bible because he is said to have been gravely shocked when charged by the Royal Irish Academy with atheism; so shocked that he became physically ill and never quite recovered.

Then along came Sir Charles Lyell who demonstrated in three stout volumes, *Principles of Geology,* how the earth had been modified in the past and how this process continues. If, let us say, you watch some pebbles tumble from a crag you are watching a mountain disintegrate. Furthermore, he said, any catastrophic flooding in the past had resulted not from a stupendous rain but from glaciers melting.

This latter argument especially troubled the faithful because the Bible was explicit: forty days, forty nights. Rain rain rain rain. Fifteen cubits of water. We had God's Word. Besides, look at the evidence.

In 1726, for example, the city doctor of Zurich, Johann Jakob Scheuchzer, had unearthed a fossilized skeleton near the village of Oeningen. This ancient sinner, according to Scheuchzer's calculations, went down for the last time in 2306 B.C.

"You will like to know, my learned friend," wrote Scheuchzer to the prominent British physician and naturalist, Sir Hans Sloane, "that we have obtained some relics of the race of man drowned in the Flood. . . . What we have here is no vision of the mere imagination, but the well-preserved bones, and much in number, of a human skull, quite clearly distinguishable. . . ."

Dr. Scheuchzer then wrote an uncompromising pamphlet titled *A Most Rare Memorial of That Accursed Generation of Men of the First World, the Skeleton of a Man Drowned in the Flood,* which informs us that together with the infallible testimony of the Divine Word we have other proofs of a Deluge: various plants, fishes, insects, snails, quadrupeds, et cetera. Of human beings drowned on that occasion, however, few traces survive because their corpses floated on the surface of the waters and soon decayed. How fortunate that Oeningen Man should be preserved.

Dr. Scheuchzer provided an illustration of his remarkable find: "a carefully executed woodcut now offered for the consideration of the learned and inquiring world. . . . It does not merely present certain features in which a vivid imagination could detect something approximating to the human shape. On the contrary, it corresponds completely with all the parts and proportions of a human skeleton. Even the bones embedded in the stone, and some of the softer components too, are identifiable as genuine. . . ."

And there was the testimony of a German pastor, Johann Friederich Esper, who had uncovered the shoulder blade and jaw of another Flood victim in a cave near Bamberg.

During the nineteenth century additional proof turned up. William Buckland, Dean of Westminster and author of *Reliquiae Diluvianae*, reported a unique burial in South Wales—a female skeleton which became known as the Red Lady because her bones were stained with red ocher. Such mortal deposits, Buckland wrote, "by affording the strongest evidence of a universal deluge, leads us to hope that it will no longer be asserted as it has been by high authorities, that geology supplies no proofs of an event in the reality of which the truth of the Mosaic records is so materially involved."

Just the same, renegade Christians continued boring holes in the Ark:

Scheuchzer's rare memorial, upon close examination,

proved to be all that was left of a giant salamander.

Esper's fossils could not be reexamined because they had somehow disappeared, but on the basis of contemporary drawings it would seem that what he picked up were the bones of a cave bear.

Buckland's so-called Red Lady was indeed human—though male instead of female—but nothing about the discolored scraps indicated that this person had drowned. Apart from sex, in fact, all that could be scientifically determined was that his bones, which had been discovered in association with Paleolithic tools, were older than the date of Scheuchzer's flood, perhaps older than the date established by Archbishop Ussher for the creation of the universe. Just how old Dean Buckland's masculine lady might be—ah, that would be hard to say. One can scarcely estimate how long men and women have been going about their affairs. To resolve such questions quite a lot more information would be necessary.

Then, in 1857, while the Neander valley near Düsseldorf was being quarried for limestone, workmen blasted open a cave and the shattering reverberations have not yet died away. Within this cave lay a wondrously complete skeleton. Laborers shoveled it aside because they were after something more valuable; but the owner of the quarry, Herr Beckershoff, either noticed these bones or was told about them and decided to save them. By this time, however, all that could be collected were some bits of arm and leg, part of the pelvis, a few ribs, and the skullcap. Herr Beckershoff thought these might be fragments of a bear, and after keeping them awhile he gave them to the president of the Elberfield Natural Science Society, J. C. Fuhlrott.

Fuhlrott realized that the bones were human. The slanted brow of the skullcap and the thick, bent limbs convinced him that this individual must have lived a long time ago. Possibly he had been washed into the cave while Noah was riding out the storm. In any event somebody important ought to be notified, so Fuhlrott called on Professor Schaaffhausen who taught anatomy at the University of Bonn.

Schaaffhausen carefully appraised and measured Fuhlrott's treasure: "The cranium is of unusual size, and of a long, elliptical form. A most remarkable peculiarity is at once obvious in the extraordinary development of the frontal sinuses. . . . The cavity holds 16,876 grains of water, whence its cubical contents may be estimated at 57.64 inches, or 1033.24 cubic centimeters." Or, in dried millet seed, "the contents equalled 31 ounces, Prussian Apothecaries' weight." This skull and the attendant bones, Professor Schaaffhausen deduced, probably belonged to one of the "barbarous, aboriginal people" who inhabited northern Europe before the Germans arrived.

Not so, replied other experts. The bones of a forest-dwelling hydrocephalic, said one. A cannibal somehow transported to Europe, said another.

Probably a Dutch sailor, said Professor Andreas Wagner of Göttingen.

An old Celt who perished during a tribal migration, said Dr. Pruner-Bey of Paris.

A Mongolian Cossack killed in 1814 while the Russians were chasing Napoleon across the Rhine, said a colleague of Schaaffhausen's, Professor Robert Mayer. Unmistakably a Cossack because, if you will be good enough to observe, the femur is bent inward, which is characteristic of a man accustomed to riding horses. No doubt this soldier had been wounded and crawled into the cave to die.

T. H. Huxley, soon to be Darwin's champion, also thought the skeleton was recent. An odd specimen, granted, but still a member of *Homo sapiens.*

Darwin himself would not comment; he seldom did unless he could be absolutely sure.

The great panjandrum of the era was Rudolf Virchow, director of the Berlin Pathological Institute. In his opinion the bones Fuhlrott displayed were not prehistoric but merely diseased. The bent legs were a consequence of rickets. The bony ridge above the eyes, together with other apparent malformations, were the result of arthritis. What could be more obvious? Also, this individual had suffered a number of blows on the head. Yet in spite of injury and disease he had lived to a ripe old age, which would be conceivable only in a settled community; and as there were no settled communities thousands of years ago it must be self-evident that the Neander valley bones were recent.

Nobody cared to debate Virchow. There is a portrait of him seated tensely in an armchair. A long sharp nose supports thin spectacles; he looks acutely intelligent, crisp, impatient, and merciless.

Years later these bones would be unpacked and scrutinized again, compared with similar finds, and subjected to a variety of microscopic, electronic, and chemical tests, with the result that we now know quite a lot about Fuhlrott's caveman. It has even been determined that he was unable to raise his left hand to his mouth because of an elbow injury.

And we have learned enough from other Neanderthal remnants to make a few tentative generalizations. For instance, it could be deduced from an Iraqi skeleton that the owner was arthritic, blind in one eye, and had a birth defect limiting the use of his right side. Now what this means is that he would have been unable to hunt, which in turn means that somebody had to provide his food.

Care of the infirm and elderly is not what comes to mind when the word *Neanderthal* is mentioned.

Something else we don't think of in relation to these people is a concept of life after death; yet the Neanderthals buried their dead, which implies concern. Furthermore, the characteristics of a burial may tell us what the survivors were thinking. At least that is the assumption we make. Fires had been kindled on the graves of two Belgian Neanderthals, presumably to lessen the chill of death. And in France, at La Chapelle-aux-Saints, a hunter was interred with a bison leg—food for his long journey.

Another French site held bits and pieces of a man, a woman, two children about five years old, and two babies. Flint chips and bone splinters were discovered in the man's grave and a flat stone lay on his head, either to protect him or to prevent him from coming back. The woman was buried in a tight fetal position, as though she had been bound with cords. Perhaps, like the stone slab, this was meant to confine her. Or maybe it saved work by reducing the size of the grave.

On a gentle slope near this family plot another child had been buried—its head separated from its body. The head lay almost a yard higher on the slope. Why this child did not lie with the others, and why the head was detached, is not known.

Quite a few Neanderthal graves were found at the Shanidar cave in northern Iraq. Several of these people appeared to have been killed by rocks falling from the roof, possibly during an earthquake. In one trench lay a hunter with a fractured skull, and when the surrounding soil was analyzed it disclosed pollen from a number of brightly colored wildflowers related to the hollyhock, bachelor's button, grape hyacinth, and groundsel. The existence of so much pollen could not be attributed to wind or to the feces of animals and birds. The only other explanation is that flowers were scattered on his grave by somebody who loved him.

A less agreeable picture came into focus at Monte Circeo, fifty miles south of Rome. Laborers at a tourist resort were widening a terrace when they exposed the entrance to a cave that had been sealed long ago by a landslide. The owner of the resort, accompanied by some friends, crept on hands and knees through a tunnel leading deep into the hillside and finally they entered a chamber that had not been visited for perhaps 60,000 years. By lantern light they saw a human skull, face to the earth, within a circle of stones. Anthropologists suspect the skull may have been mounted on a stick and dropped in that position when the wood decayed; but the unforgettable part of this ceremony must have occurred before the skull was mounted, because the aperture at the base had been enlarged—almost certainly in order to extract and eat the brain.

Neanderthal rituals in Switzerland clearly focused on the bear. A number of boxlike stone structures found in Alpine caves contain bear skulls. One of these crude chests held seven skulls arranged so that the muzzles pointed to the chamber entrance, while farther back in the cave six more skulls had been set in niches along the wall—one with a bone thrust through the arch of the cheek.

What this bear business means, nobody knows. Maybe the earliest human pageantry involved a bear. Even today a few Stone Age tribes conduct ceremonies whose principal figure is a bear, and some ethnologists regard this as the last glint of light from Neanderthal times.

Says Herbert Wendt: "It was in the time of cave bears that the first cultural and religious ideas arose, that the first magicians appeared, that Man achieved dominion over Nature and began to believe in the support of super-natural powers."

What did they look like?—these people we faintly ab-hor and seldom think about, yet who seem always to be not far away.

Museum dioramas are familiar: shambling, hairy, ape-faced monstrosities wearing animal pelts, the males hold-ing spears or clubs, the females usually crouched beside a fire. This is the image, but it may not be accurate. Our impression is based on a skeleton reconstructed and stud-ied in 1908. The relatively uncorrugated inner surface of the skull suggested that the brain had been simple, with convolutions resembling those of apes. The 1908 exam-iners also deduced a "simian arrangement" of spinal ver-tebrae and concluded that Neanderthal man slumped along with knees bent, on feet very much like the feet of a gorilla.

In 1957 this skeleton, which was that of a male, was reexamined. The gentleman was not exactly typical. He might have been fifty years old, which in those days was very old indeed. He suffered from arthritis of the jaws and spine, and perhaps of the lower limbs. The 1957 inspectors issued this statement: "There is no valid reason for the assumption that the posture of Neanderthal man . . . dif-fered significantly from that of present-day man."

And in museum displays their faces are never painted because it was assumed that Neanderthals had not crossed that threshold of humanity where the idea of decorating something—a wall, or themselves—would occur to them. Well, maybe. But powdered black manganese, yellow ocher, and various red pigments are found at their camp-sites, frequently in stick-shaped pieces that appear to have been rubbed on a soft surface.

As for other artistic efforts, probably there were none.

No sculpture has been found, nothing but tantalizing hints. A bone with a hole drilled in it. An ox rib with a collection of unnatural streaks. A bit of ivory polished and artificially stained.

Yet these same people, struggling toward a new plateau, seemed unable or unwilling to distinguish between animal meat and the carcasses of their neighbors. Twenty mutilated skeletons were discovered in a Yugoslav cave, skulls bashed, arm and leg bones split lengthwise to get at the marrow. And in France another grisly accumulation turned up—some of the bones charred, implying a barbecue.

Neanderthal front teeth, when examined under a microscope, often show a number of parallel scratches, the result of an eating habit. Even today certain primitive people stuff big chunks of meat into their mouths and use a knife to hack off what they are not able to chew, which leaves scratches on their teeth. These scratches almost always run diagonally from upper left to lower right, proving that the gourmets in question are right-handed—as you will see if you act out the scene. Now this information is not as useless as you might think, because man is the only animal that prefers one hand to another, and neurologists suspect there may be some kind of relationship between this preference and the development of speech. If that is correct, those minuscule marks on Neanderthal teeth could help to solve one of the most fascinating questions about our predecessors—whether or not they could speak.

The answer would seem to be: Yes.

Yes, but only a little. So say linguist Philip Lieberman and anatomist Edmund Crelin who reconstructed the vocal tracts of some fossilized men. They concluded that European Neanderthals did not have much of a pharynx, and without a decent pharynx it is impossible to articulate

g or k or several vowel sounds. Consequently a Neanderthal's power of speech would be limited. Furthermore,
say Lieberman and Crelin, he could not have pronounced
his few sounds in quick succession. He spoke slowly, about
one-tenth as fast as we do, perhaps one-twentieth as fast as
a Spaniard.

It is alleged that Pharaoh Psamtik in the seventh century B.C. had two infants reared beyond the sound of
human voices on the theory that when they began to talk
they would necessarily resort to man's earliest language.
One child finally said "bekos"—which is the Phrygian
word for bread. But that k would seem to preclude Phrygian as the Neanderthal language.

James IV of Scotland conducted an almost identical experiment. He gave two babies to a mute woman who lived
alone on Inchkeith Island, and we are told that the children grew up speaking perfect Hebrew. However, with a
stunted pharynx it would be exceptionally difficult to
speak Hebrew. At the moment, therefore, all we can do is
speculate.

But the absorbing question about Neanderthals is not
what they spoke; it is what became of them.

Did they vanish because of some inability to meet a
changing climate?

Could they have been slaughtered, liquidated, ter-
minated with extreme prejudice, by the Cro-Magnon
people?

Or could these two supposedly distinct races be, in fact,
the same?

Present wisdom holds that the last unadulterated Neanderthal died 40,000 years ago. However, one April evening in 1907 some Russian explorers led by Porshnyev
Baradiin were setting up camp in an Asian desert when
they noticed a shaggy human figure silhouetted against the

late sun on a ridge just ahead. Whatever the thing was, it appeared to be watching them. After a while the creature turned and lumbered away, so they ran after it but were quickly outdistanced. This was the first meeting between Westerners and Yeti, or Sasquatch as the beast is called in the Pacific Northwest of the United States.

Soviets do not treat these encounters with as much levity as do Americans; there are Soviet anthropologists who believe that a few Neanderthals have survived in the deserts and mountains. European and American scientists doubt this. More significant than such reports, they say, are the features of people around us. In other words, although the race is extinct, Neanderthal characteristics have endured.

So they are among us at least in a vestigial sense, and just possibly as an isolated race that exists like the giant condor in remote pockets of the earth. Frequent reports of midnight brushes with humanoid monsters indicate a certain tremulous anticipation—which is to say, an abiding belief—but thus far no hairy pelts have been tacked to the wall.

In any event, while Rudolf Virchow and his nineteenth-century colleagues were disparaging Fuhlrott's caveman, a most outrageous book was published. Its author—a tall, bald, white-bearded gentleman—subsequently became known as the Shy Giant. He read so slowly, wrote so slowly, even thought so slowly, remarks biographer William Irvine, "that he always felt desperately behindhand, like a tortoise concentrating every energy on the next step, as he creeps in frantic haste toward impossible horizons. . . ."

This sounds exactly like a living Neanderthal, but of course it was Charles Darwin. And twenty-eight years earlier he almost did not get to sail on the *Beagle* because Captain Fitzroy, who believed one could pretty well judge a man by his features, mistrusted the shape of Darwin's nose. He thought the young man looked indecisive. We can only guess what might have happened, or failed to happen, had Fitzroy himself been more decisive and stamped his foot and lifted the gangplank so Darwin could not slip aboard.

Then the Scopes trial, that little masterpiece of idiocy, might never have been staged.

Nor should we have had that immortal debate between Thomas Huxley, on behalf of Darwin, and Bishop Wilberforce, known unkindly as Soapy Sam, on behalf of God:

"It would be interesting to know," said the bishop, "whether the ape in question was on your grandfather's or your grandmother's side."

But it is not a sound idea to prick a man as intelligent as Huxley, who whispered, "The Lord hath delivered him into my hands." And getting to his feet he answered aloud: "If you ask me whether I would rather have a miserable ape for a grandfather or a man highly endowed by nature and possessed of great means of influence and yet who employs those faculties and that influence for the mere purpose of introducing ridicule into a grave scientific discussion, then I unhesitatingly affirm my preference for the ape."

Whereupon, we are told, a lady in the audience fainted. And good Captain Fitzroy, trembling with honorable Christian rage, picked up a Bible and was just prevented from throwing it at Huxley. Fitzroy later was promoted to vice-admiral, which seems to be the natural course of events.

One is tempted to caricature Fitzroy. Still, whatever his faults, the man was not a simpleton. He came from a distinguished family, which perhaps proves nothing, but he had traveled around the world on the survey ship *Beagle* once before, and had been appointed a captain at the age

of twenty-three. His surveys were accurate and highly val-
ued, and he was a Fellow of the Royal Society. It is said,
too, that after getting to know Darwin he changed his
opinion. All the same, no matter how hard you try to look
without prejudice upon Captain Fitzroy, it seems best to
admit that this is an individual you cannot love.

However, the important thing is the debate, not the
audience, and those traditional opponents Science and Religion once again entered the arena when Thomas Huxley
challenged Soapy Sam.

It is the scientist, of course, armed with some imperti-
nent fact, who attacks first—though the maneuver may be
oblique or heavily veiled. Then the ecclesiastic must coun-
terattack, for the very good reason that he perceives a
threat to his office and to his life's work. The status quo
must be protected, the heretical march of knowledge ob-
structed, whether it be the development of anesthetics,
the experiments of Galileo, or the deductions of infamous
bulb-nosed naturalists.

Both attitudes are easy to understand. Science feels ob-
ligated to inquire, whereas the Church comes armed with
infallible dogma.

Thus we have Dr. John Lightfoot, Vice-Chancellor of
Cambridge and Master of Saint Catherine's, nailing down
the particulars in Archbishop Ussher's article of faith:
"Heaven and earth, center and circumference were created all together and in the same instant, clouds full of
water. This took place, and Man was created by the Trinity on the 23rd October, 4004 B.C. at 9 o'clock in the
morning."

Gilgamesh the Sumerian may have been eating ham and
eggs at that hour, but never mind; what impresses us is Dr.
Lightfoot's stately assurance.

By contrast, old Darwin frets about each mistake he
makes, telling us he is ready to weep with vexation, refer-

ring to himself as "the most miserable, bemuddled, stupid dog in all England." He goes then, we are informed, and walks through the winter morning—this aloof old genius—walking by himself and meditating, so early that he startles foxes trotting to their lairs at dawn.

Accompanying these famous champions we now and again meet an individual who, like some overexcited spectator at a wrestling match, resolves to assert himself by clambering into the ring. Consider a certain Denis or Didier Henrion, a seventeenth-century French engineer, who measured various bones that probably came from a brontosaurus and then announced without qualification that our progenitor Adam stood 123 feet, 9 inches tall. Eve, he said, had been five feet shorter. M. Henrion did not calculate their weight, which is too bad, nor Eve's other measurements, which must have been formidable; but what we would like to know most of all is why he positioned himself so awkwardly in the path of common sense.

Then we have the case of a respected historian named von Eckhart.

Early in the eighteenth century Professor Johannes Bartolomäus Beringer who taught natural history at the University of Würzburg, and who collected fossils, dug up hundreds of stones containing the imprint of fruits, flowers, spiders, turtles, snakes, frogs, and so forth. He studied them carefully because he had never seen anything like them and he therefore assumed that his report would have unusual scientific value. He published his conclusions in a handsome book titled *Lithographiae Wirceburgensis*, illustrated with twenty-two plates of the finest specimens. Unfortunately, von Eckart had persuaded some boys to carve and bury these fakes where Professor Beringer would be sure to find them.

It was a practical joke born of petulant dislike for

Beringer, yet something beyond malice seems to have been involved: there is an undertone of hostility toward science.

This brings up the American Goliath, born of animosity toward hard-shell Protestants. An Iowa cigar manufacturer named Hull and a preacher named Turk argued about giants in the earth. Reverend Turk of course defended the Bible. Hull, choking with disgust, resolved to mock him as viciously as Eckhart had mocked Beringer.

In the summer of 1868 Hull bought a five-ton block of gypsum at a quarry near Fort Dodge and sent it by rail to Chicago where a stonemason was hired to sculpt a proper giant. The monster was then aged with acid and shipped to the New York village of Cardiff where Hull had a relative—William Newell—who buried it on his farm.

A year later Newell employed some laborers on the pretext of digging a well. Very soon their picks struck a stony ten-foot corpse, and considering that they knew nothing of the plot their fright does not seem unreasonable.

Thousands of sightseers arrived, so many that the town of Syracuse put a horse-drawn omnibus in service to Newell's farm. Among these visitors was Ralph Waldo Emerson who judged the slumbering colossus to be "undoubtedly ancient." The curator of the New York State Museum called it "the most remarkable object yet brought to light in this country"—a comment that might be variously interpreted. Dr. Oliver Wendell Holmes also paid a visit. Dr. Holmes drilled a hole behind one ear in order to inspect the substance, which suggests that at the very least he was uncertain. Most people thought it was a fossilized antediluvian man.

Whether or not Reverend Turk made a pilgrimage to Newell's farm, we don't know; but it would be safe to assume that when he heard about this giant in the earth he fairly quivered with satisfaction. How vindicated he must have felt. How joyous. How proud. Maybe a little complacent. Even a bit pontifical. If only we knew what he said to the diabolic cigar manufacturer.

And when Hull at last decided to crucify the gullible pastor how did Reverend Turk respond? Did he pray? Did he forgive? Did he foam at the mouth? Furthermore, one can't help wondering if the experience taught him anything. Probably not. Fundamentalists are apt to be so fundamental.

More sophisticated, more enigmatic, and infinitely more knowledgeable than our cranky American atheist was the British sponsor of Piltdown Man—that veritable missing link with a human cranium and the jaw of an ape.

"Several years ago I was walking along a farm-road close to Piltdown Common, Fletching, when I noticed that the road had been mended with some peculiar brown flints not usual in the district. On enquiry I was astonished to learn that they were dug from a gravel-bed on the farm, and shortly afterwards I visited the place, where two labourers were at work. . . ."

So begins the account of Mr. Charles Dawson, a rotund Uckfield lawyer and amateur antiquarian who discovered the famous skull. He told his story in 1912 at a meeting of the London Geological Society, to which he had been invited by Dr. Arthur Smith-Woodward of the British Museum, and his remarks later were printed in the society's journal. Several renowned scientists were present when Dawson spoke, and for many years a painting titled *Discussing the Piltdown Man* hung on the staircase of the society's headquarters.

Dawson said that after coming upon fragments of a skullcap he got in touch with Smith-Woodward, who examined the bones and considered them so important that he joined the search. Together they turned up quite a lot. According to Dawson: "Besides the human remains, we found two small broken pieces of a molar tooth of a rather early Pliocene type of elephant, also a much-rolled cusp of a molar of *Mastodon*, portions of two teeth of *Hippopotamus*, and two molar teeth of a Pleistocene beaver."

From an adjacent field they recovered bits of deer antler and the tooth of a Pleistocene horse. All the specimens, including those of Piltdown Man, were highly mineralized with iron oxide.

The Piltdown cranium did not quite fit the Piltdown jaw, which made a few scientists uneasy. Yet they had been excavated at the same level, and despite the apelike lower jaw the molars were flat—indicating that the jaw worked with an acceptably human rotary motion. Then too, it would be exceedingly strange if, side by side, a prehistoric man had left only his skullcap while a prehistoric ape left only its jaw. Therefore they must belong to the same beast.

So excited was Dr. Smith-Woodward that he built a little house near the gravel bed, and when visitors arrived he could talk about nothing else.

A few more specimens were picked up: small bones from the nasal bridge and some delicate turbinal bones which support the membrane inside the nasal cavity. These turbinal bones were quite fragile; they fell apart when lifted out, but the shards were collected and glued together. And one hot August day Father Teilhard de Chardin, who had become interested in the project, was seated on a dump heap beside the pit idly running his fingers through the gravel when he noticed a canine tooth.

This tooth caused further debate at the Geological Society. It was very large, perhaps too large, and it appeared to be the tooth of a relatively old man whereas the jaw was that of a young man. Did this tooth come from another skull?

Piltdown Man eventually was accepted by English scientists, not without discomfort, as certain applicants for a social club may be accepted; but among friends and relatives, so to speak, he was admitted to the evolutionary tree. Elsewhere his credentials were not approved. Giuffrida-Ruggeri in Italy, Mollison in Germany, and Boule in France all thought the jaw belonged to an ape. American experts, too, looked skeptically at the reconstruction.

Against their doubts stood the simple argument of the discovery: fossil remains taken from Pleistocene gravel, much of it excavated under the meticulous supervision of Dr. Smith-Woodward of the British Museum.

Year after year the dispute simmered.

Then in 1953 the skull got a new custodian, Dr. Kenneth Oakley, who subjected it to a fluorine test. Buried bones gradually absorb fluorine from water in the earth; the longer the burial, the more fluorine.

Results of Oakley's tests were astonishing and puzzling. On the basis of fluorine content the jaw and skullcap did indeed belong together, yet they held less fluorine than animal bones taken from the same stratum. The contradiction so exasperated Dr. Oakley that he abruptly told a colleague: "This thing is bogus!" But his intuitive thrust was ignored, perhaps because the skull had been in the museum such a long time—almost forty years. One hesitates to denounce an old acquaintance.

A few months later an Oxford anthropologist named J. S. Weiner was driving home at night when he clearly understood that Piltdown Man was a fake. And it is curious how often an insight such as Weiner's is accompanied by actual physical movement. The astronomer Kepler, while drawing a figure on the blackboard for his students, was seized by an idea which led to our modern concept of the universe. The mathematician Poincaré reported that just as he was getting aboard an omnibus, just as his foot touched the step, a brilliant realization unfolded: "that the transformations I had used to define the Fuchsian functions were identical with those of non-Euclidean geometry." Beethoven, writing to his friend Tobias von Haslinger: "On my way to Vienna yesterday, sleep overtook me in my carriage. . . . Now during my sleep-journey, the following canon came into my head. . . ." A.E. Houseman: "Two of the stanzas . . . came into my head, just as they are printed, while I was crossing Hampstead Heath. . . ." And we have the testimony of Bertrand Russell who says that while walking toward Cambridge, capriciously tossing a tin of pipe tobacco and catching it—at the exact instant a ray of sunlight reflected from the metal surface of the tin he understood the basis of a certain philosophical argument. Goethe, too, experienced a swift flowering of knowledge while out for a walk, just as he noticed the whitened skull of a sheep on a hillside.

So it happened with the anthropologist, driving alone at night from London.

Weiner mentioned his startling thought to Sir Wilfred Le Gros Clark at Oxford. Then he took a chimpanzee jaw and spent a while filing down the molars. He was surprised by how quickly the teeth could be redesigned to look like human teeth. He dipped the chimp's jaw in permanganate until it acquired a suitable brownish hue and when it was dry he laid his new fossil on the desk of Le Gros Clark. He is said to have remarked with a look of innocence: "I got this out of the collections. What do you suppose it is?" And Sir Wilfrid, who knew immediately, exclaimed: "You can't mean it!"

They decided to have a conference with Oakley.

Soon after that conference Piltdown Man started falling apart. Those distinctively human molars had been artificially flattened; close inspection revealed that their surfaces were not quite on the same plane—as though the counterfeiter had altered his grip when he moved from one tooth to the next. The delicate turbinal bones were not what previous investigators had presumed them to be; they were merely a few bone splinters of indeterminate origin. The canine tooth found by Teilhard de Chardin was X-rayed and discovered to be a young tooth that had been ground down until the pulp chamber was almost exposed, which would not happen to a living tooth.

New chemical tests showed a nitrogen concentration of 3.9 percent in the jaw, 1.4 percent in the skullcap. There was also, on this occasion, a discrepancy in the fluorine content.

Details were noticed that should have been noticed earlier. Stone "tools" from the pit had been superficially stained with iron salts—except for one which had been colored with bichromate of potash. An elephant-bone pick, when examined under a glass, revealed uncharacteristic marks. This implement, said Oakley, was probably obtained from a Middle Pleistocene brick-earth or sandy formation: "The ends were whittled with a steel knife. . . ."

Various bones taken from the pit were given a newly developed test for uranium salts. If the bones had come naturally to their ultimate resting place the Geiger counter should have clicked along at more or less the same speed, but Oakley noted a wide spectrum, including one "fossil" so radioactive that when left on a photographic plate it took its own picture.

Thus, after forty years, the walls came tumbling down. The pit had been salted from top to bottom. The skullcap was old, perhaps even Neolithic; the jaw was recent and apparently belonged to a female orangutan. Of eighteen specimens collected by Dawson and Smith-Woodward ten unquestionably were fraudulent. As to the other eight, they are not held in high esteem.

Punch ran a cartoon showing Piltdown Man in a dentist's chair with the dentist saying, "This may hurt, but I'm afraid I'll have to remove the whole jaw."

And a motion was put before the House of Commons: "That the House has no confidence in the Trustees of the British Museum. . . ."

Among those trustees were some rather celebrated personages including Winston Churchill, Anthony Eden, the Archbishop of Canterbury, and a member of the royal family.

Many scientists regarded the great Piltdown farce as not only an embarrassment but a waste of time. Others disagreed. It did stimulate public interest in anthropology; it did remind professionals of the need for accurate data and improved analytical procedures.

One is entitled to ask, of course, how so many eminent scientists could have been fooled for such a long while. There's no satisfactory answer. Dr. Louis Leakey suggested that the Piltdown bones were accepted as genuine because they fitted the pattern of what a very early human skull *ought* to look like. And this preconceived image must have been known to whoever contrived the hoax. Leakey himself had been dissatisfied with the skull, yet the idea of a forgery never occurred to him.

Asking himself how he could have been duped, he recalled a day in 1933 when he went to the British Museum. After explaining to the curator that he was writing a textbook on early man he was escorted to the basement where the Piltdown fossils were kept in a safe. They were removed from the safe and placed on a table, together with reproductions. "I was not allowed to handle the originals in any way," said Leakey, "but merely to look at them and satisfy myself that the casts were really good replicas." The originals were then locked up, leaving him with only the casts to study. "It is my belief now that it was under these conditions that all visiting scientists were permitted to examine the Piltdown specimens. . . ."

Two other important questions cannot be answered. First, who was responsible? Second, what was the motive?

Charles Dawson, who died in 1916, is thought to have been the villain. Whoever concocted the fake had known quite a lot about anatomy, geology, and paleontology. Dawson qualified. There were no other suspects. "It is certainly not nice to accuse a dead man who cannot defend himself," wrote the Dutch geologist von Koenigswald, "but everything points quite clearly to his responsibility for the forgery."

Besides, Dawson once claimed to have observed a sea serpent in the Channel—although one must admit this is not impossible. Another time he was sure he had found a petrified toad. And he seems to have been fascinated by the concept of missing links. He picked up a tooth that he thought must be intermediate between reptile and mammal. He attempted to cross a carp with a goldfish in order to create a golden carp. He said he had unearthed a strange boat—half coracle, half canoe. Furthermore, he is known to have washed old bones with potassium bichromate.

Very well, suppose we ascribe the forgery to Dawson. Next, why did he do it? Why would Dawson, or anybody, go to all that trouble? For the pleasure of humiliating the authorities? To stir up a drowsy neighborhood? To make money? To obstruct and detour the search for knowledge?

And did he plan to reveal the hoax?

Fictional crimes are more gratifying: the author keeps you writhing in suspense, which is his job, but at last he tells you.

So much for cranks, fakes, jongleurs, and fanatics. Dawson, Hull, von Eckhart, M. Denis Henrion—no matter how diverting these testy eccentrics might be, they contributed nothing. They acted out their compulsions, that was all.

At the same time, offstage, a number of earnest men had been at work.

Eugène Dubois, following Darwin's conjecture that originally we lived in a "warm, forest-clad land," left Holland for the Dutch East Indies where he served with the colonial military forces as health officer, second class. In 1891 on the island of Java he unearthed some extremely heavy, chocolate-brown bones, harder than marble—remnants of a 700,000-year-old creature whose low skull resembled that of an ape, yet whose legs were adapted to walking erect. That the bones were ancient could not be disputed, but Dubois' claim that they represented a transitional form of life was not greeted with much enthusiasm. Most professionals who examined these bones in Europe thought he had brought back the top of an ape and the bottom of a man.

A few years later a fossil-collecting German naturalist who was traveling through China noticed a human tooth in a druggist's shop, where it was regarded as a dragon's tooth and would soon have been ground up for medicine. This tooth, along with other fossilized scraps of humanity, led paleontologists to a hillside near the village of Choukoutien, southwest of Peking, which yielded the remains of some exceptionally old Chinese. But by now the Second World War was gathering and archaeological work became difficult, especially after Japanese forces occupied

Choukoutien in 1939. Chinese scientists grew increasingly concerned, and in 1941 they asked that the fossils be taken to America.

It is known that the Choukoutien fossils were packed in two white wooden boxes, labeled A and B, destined for the port of Chingwangtao where they were to be put aboard the S.S. *President Harrison*. A detachment of U.S. Marines was assigned to guard them.

Almost certainly these boxes left the Peking Union Medical College in a car which was going either to the U.S. Embassy or to the Marine barracks.

Beyond this point the journey of the prehistoric Chinese is obscured by swirling mist. Their bones are said to have been scattered and lost when Japanese soldiers stopped a train carrying the Marines. They are said to have disappeared from a warehouse in Chingwangtao which was twice ransacked by the Japanese. They are said to have been aboard a barge that capsized before reaching the *President Harrison*—although this sounds unbelievable because the *President Harrison* ran aground at the mouth of the Yangtze, quite a long distance from Chingwangtao. Then there is the possibility that an enterprising chemist may have gotten hold of them, in which case we must assume they were pulverized and swallowed.

Even now, decades later, the search for these bones goes on. Considering how much evolutionary evidence has accumulated since 1941, we might ask why anthropologists are so anxious to locate one particular batch of fossils.

There has never been a loss of such magnitude, says Dr. Harry Shapiro of the American Museum of Natural History, "for these ancient bones represented a veritable population of at least forty individuals—men, women and children—from a stage of human evolution previously unknown. . . . Although a few additional representatives of this ancient population have recently been discovered as a result of renewed exploration by the Chinese, it is unlikely that anything approaching the original sample will ever be restored."

Conceivably a few men might still be alive who know exactly what happened. If so, the inscrutable old Chinese could reappear. But more probably, somewhere between Peking and Chingwangtao, they passed from the hands of those who knew their scientific value into the hands of those who either didn't know or didn't care. And it is this last thought that appalls Dr. Shapiro, who reflects upon the dismay and sadness we would feel if we heard that Shakespeare's manuscripts had been found, only to be burned by a maid who looked at them without comprehension.

In Africa it's a different story, less tragic but more incredible because here we are concerned with men who supposedly knew what they were doing. The first important fossil turned up in Africa was contemptuously dismissed.

Momentous news is greeted like this more often than you would suspect. Einstein's germinal bolt of lightning did not attract much notice for eight years. Francis Bacon anticipated Newton's law of gravity by half a century, but the times were out of joint. The linguist Grotefend correctly deciphered an obscure cuneiform script and published his evidence in three reports, all of them ignored. Olaus Roemer, a seventeenth-century astronomer, discovered that light traveled at a fixed rate instead of propagating instantaneously, yet academic scientists rejected this idea for fifty years.

It happened again in 1924 when a Johannesburg anatomy professor named Raymond Dart reported on a miniature skull found in a limestone quarry near a railroad station called Taungs.

Two crates of fossil-bearing rock had been delivered to Professor Dart while he was getting dressed for the wedding of his friend Christo Beyers—"past international footballer and now senior lecturer in applied anatomy and operative surgery at the University of Witwatersrand." Dart immediately opened both crates. The first was a disappointment; he saw nothing but petrified eggshells and turtle shells.

The second crate held a gem: nearly enclosed by rock was the skull.

Dart returned to it as soon as Beyers had been legally committed. With a hammer, a chisel, and one of Mrs. Dart's knitting needles he set to work—delicately, because the little creature he meant to release had been imprisoned for almost a million years.

"No diamond cutter ever worked more lovingly or with such care on a priceless jewel," he later wrote, "nor, I am sure, with such inadequate tools. But on the seventy-third day, December 23, the rock parted. I could view the face from the front, although the right side was still embedded. . . . What emerged was a baby's face, an infant with a full set of milk teeth and its permanent molars just in the process of erupting. I doubt if there was ever any parent prouder of his offspring than I was of my 'Taungs baby' on that Christmas."

The skull seemed to be that of a young ape, yet its cranium was too large—implying a large brain, a brain in which for the first time intellect might outweigh instinct—and its roundness suggested that the creature had walked erect. Dart estimated that when fully grown the baby would have been perhaps four feet tall and would have weighed about ninety pounds.

Cautiously he named it *Australopithecus,* Ape of the South; but in a paper for the British scientific journal *Nature* he pointed out certain human characteristics and indicated that his baby belonged in the family somewhere between Pongidae and Hominidae: "The specimen is of importance because it exhibits an extinct race of apes intermediate between living anthropoids and man."

Not so! Not so in the least! cried European authorities, none of whom had examined the South African infant.

"Professor Dart is not likely to be led astray," commented the British anatomist Sir Arthur Keith. "If he has thoroughly examined the skull we are prepared to accept his decision." But presently Sir Arthur changed his mind: ". . . one is inclined to place *Australopithecus* in the same group or sub-family as the chimpanzee and gorilla. It is an allied genus. It seems to be near akin to both."

"There are serious doubts. . . ." wrote Smith-Woodward of Piltdown fame.

". . . the distorted skull of a chimpanzee just over four years old, probably a female," said Professor Arthur Robinson.

Not a hominid but an anthropoid ape, said Hans Weinert. Not a member of the human gallery, said Wilhelm Gieseler. Related to the gorilla, said Wolfgang Abel. And there were others. The consensus being that Dart's child was a chimpanzee.

Only one ranking professional agreed with Dart. This was Dr. Robert Broom, who looked like everybody's grandfather, who spoke with a Scottish burr, and who had become widely known—however implausible it may sound—for studying reptiles in the Great Karoo. He is described as a small, elderly gentleman who invariably wore a business suit with a high, starched collar, a black necktie, and a black hat. This was his uniform no matter where he happened to be, even in the bush. He was a medical doctor and part-time paleontologist who liked to collect things. In Ardrey's eloquent phrase: "fossils,

Rembrandt etchings, postage stamps, susceptible girls."

A couple of weeks after Dr. Broom heard about the Taungs skull he came marching into Dart's laboratory unannounced, ignored everybody, strode to the bench on which the skull rested, and dropped to his knees. He remained for the weekend as Dart's houseguest and spent almost the entire time inspecting *Australopithecus*. He agreed that it was an intermediate form of life.

Because of Dr. Broom's reputation the skull became famous, so famous that witty young men would ask: "Who was that girl I saw you with last night?—is she from Taungs?"

But along with the simpletons, as usually happens, a few intelligent people spoke up. An editorial in the London *Observer* concluded with these lines:

> There must needs be some who will say that the discovery of a damaged skull in sub-tropical Africa makes no difference. Admittedly it does not affect us materially like the discovery of wireless or electric light. The difference is in outlook. The stimulus to all progress is man's innate belief that he can grasp the scheme of things or his place therein. But this stimulus compels him to track his career backward to its first beginnings as well as to carry it forward to its ultimate end. The more clearly he sees whence he has come the more clearly he will discern whither he is bound. Hence it is not an accident that an age of immense scientific advance produced Darwin with his Theory of Origins, or that a later period of social unrest has stimulated archaeologists to reveal the strength of the social tradition. Viewed in some such intellectual context as this, the Taungs skull is at once a reminder of limitations and an encouragement to further endeavour. Its impor-

tance, significant in itself, is enhanced by the fact that its message has been preserved through unimaginable ages for discovery here and now.

The *Observer*'s thoughtful opinion did not convince everybody. Letters from around the world arrived at Dart's office, warning him vociferously, emphatically, with magisterial certainty, that he would roast in Hell. The London *Times* printed a sharp rebuke, addressed to Dart, from a woman who signed herself "Plain but Sane": "How can you, with such a wonderful gift of God-given genius—not the gift of a monkey, but a trust from the Almighty—become a traitor to your Creator by making yourself the active agent of Satan and his ready tool? What does your Master pay you for trying to undermine God's word? . . . What will it profit you? The wages of the master you serve is death. Why not change over? What will evolution do for you when dissolution overtakes you?"

And, regardless of evolution or dissolution, Profit was much on the mind of a gentleman who owned property in Sterkfontein, northeast of Taungs, for he issued a pamphlet with this invitation:

"Come to Sterkfontein and find the missing link!"

Given any conversation about men, apes, evolution, and all that, somebody inevitably will use the phrase *missing link*, often as a derisive question: "Why can't they find it?"—followed by hostile laughter. The unmistakable inference being that the link can't be found because it never existed, which proves that Archbishop Ussher must have been right. Oh, not 4004 B.C. exactly, but once upon a time the clouds split with a blinding flash, a huge Anglo-Saxon finger pointed down, and immediately the earth was populated with dinosaurs and cavemen. And if, let's say, a bona fide living breathing furry link could in fact be produced—a specimen undeniably half-and-half—you may be sure it would be angrily rejected, identified either as a peculiar chimpanzee or as a hairy little man with rickets.

The skull seems to be the determining factor. If the skull looks reasonably human—well then, the owner must have been human. Otherwise it was some sort of ape.

Consider the brow, the jaw, the dome. Especially the dome. Is it high, capacious, handsomely rounded?—a suitable receptacle for a human brain? If so, we have Man. Hominidae. Glory of the universe.

Does it resemble a football?—flattened, unimposing, diminutive? Then we have Pongidae, brute keeper of the forest.

The problem with such attractive and shapely logic may be illustrated by the fact that Lord Byron's brain measured 2,350 cubic centimeters while that of Anatole France measured just 1,100. It should follow, therefore, that Lord Byron was at least twice as intelligent as Anatole France. You see the brambles on this path.

Besides, the average cranial capacity of Cro-Magnon skulls is 1,650 cubic centimeters while that of modern Europeans is about 1,400—which implies that the human brain is shrinking. It could be. And perhaps for the best.

But this leads in another direction, so let's return to the Transvaal, to Professor Dart patiently sifting the earth for additional scraps of *Australopithecus*.

In the Makapan valley he discovered where a troop of these "chimpanzees" had stopped, and the campsite revealed gruesome proof of human behavior—an assortment of baboon skulls together with that of another *Australopithecus* child. The jaw of each baboon skull, as well as that of the child, had been broken in such a way as to suggest a feast. Chimpanzees customarily eat plants and fruit, not baboons, nor do adult chimps eat their own children. So, Dart reasoned, these creatures a million years ago were evolving rapidly.

He showed his skull collection to an expert in forensic medicine who told him that the *Australo* infant and forty-two baboons had been dispatched by powerful blows with a hard object. Dart suspected that the hard object, or objects, might still be around. Presently he found them: antelope leg bones. In some instances a particular bone could be fitted to the break in a particular skull. The fragile, porcelain-thin skulls of infant baboons had been emptied of their brains, then crushed and tossed aside, says Dart, just as a human child might crush and throw away a breakfast eggshell.

He published an article about these carnivorous Transvaal citizens in 1949, and being a scientist he gave it an appropriate title: "The Predatory Implemental Techniques of Australopithecus." Very few people who read it liked it.

Six years later a scientific congress met at the town of Livingstone near Victoria Falls. Dart was allotted twenty minutes, which meant he scarcely had time to summarize what he had learned. His talk seems to have been ignored. Many of the scientists did not bother to look at the exhibit he had prepared. Those skulls could not have been fractured by our ancestors. Probably a band of hyenas killed the baboons. Or some leopards. Or it could be that porcupines, which occasionally collect bones to chew on—porcupines might be responsible.

Said von Koenigswald, speaking for most of the Establishment: "It is easy to take such bones for implements, and this is in fact often done. But a comparison of the picture produced by Dart shows without any doubt that these bones have been gnawed and split by hyenas."

However, a British paleontologist named Sutcliffe who

had spent a great deal of time studying hyenas did not
agree. He said it would be uncharacteristic of hyenas to
leave all those skulls around. Hyenas pulverize everything.
Then, too, some rudimentary "tools" were unearthed in
the *Australo* encampment—and the shaping of implements
for a specific purpose is a trait that distinguishes *Homo
sapiens* from beasts.

Rather cautiously the professionals began revising their
opinion of Dart's exhibit.

Meanwhile, Dr. Broom had been attracted to the Sterkfontein limeworks where some fossils were turning up.
The plant manager, Mr. Barlow, previously had worked at
Taungs and he now understood that there were commodities other than lime; he was gathering fossils and sell-
ing them to tourists. Through him Dr. Broom got a few
interesting bones, though nothing important. Then one
day Mr. Barlow said, "I've something nice for you this
morning." And he produced a jaw with recently broken
teeth which Broom bought for two pounds. However, because the matrix looked different, Broom suspected it had
not been dug out of the quarry. When asked about this,
Barlow grew evasive. Dr. Broom therefore returned to the
limeworks on the manager's day off and showed the jaw to
some workmen. None of them recognized it.

Broom then had a serious talk with the plant manager,
who admitted he had gotten the jaw from a boy named
Gert Terblanche. Broom drove to the Terblanche home.
Gert was at school. Broom drove immediately to the
school. He arrived just after noon, during playtime, and
spoke to the headmaster. The boy was located and took
out of his pocket "four of the most wonderful teeth ever
seen in the world's history." These teeth, says Broom, "I
promptly purchased from Gert, and transferred to my own
pocket."

The boy had noticed the jaw protruding from a ledge. He had worked it loose by beating it with a rock, which accounted for the broken teeth.

In 1939 the price of lime dropped, closing the Sterkfontein quarry, and the Second World War further restricted archaeological work.

After the war Prime Minister Jan Smuts asked Dr. Broom to see what else he could find at Sterkfontein. Barlow was now dead, but from him Dr. Broom had learned to appreciate dynamite, so that very soon the vast African silence was being thunderously violated. And almost at once, remarks William Howells, first-rate fossils began describing small arcs in the air to the tune of his blasts.

The most startling find was an immensely powerful jaw—a jaw so massive that its owner came to be known as the Nutcracker Man. Further bits and pieces of these robust nutcracker people, or near-people, revealed the significant fact that their skulls had been crested like the skulls of orangutans or gorillas.

Dart and Broom now were convinced that East Africa was where it all began, but very few professionals agreed with them. Africa seemed rather distant. One would expect humanity's cradle to be nearer the center of things. Not that our first squiggly tracks ought to show up on Thames mud or the Champs-Élysées, but Africa did seem remote. A more familiar setting—Italy or Greece, let's say—would be perfect. The Dutch East Indies, possibly. Java might be acceptable. Perhaps China.

Louis Leakey then clambered out of the Olduvai Gorge where he had been prospecting for eighteen years, and he brought undeniable news.

Olduvai is a Masai word for the sansevieria plant which grows wild in that area. The gorge is about 25 miles long and 300 feet deep: a parched canyon where anthropologists, rhinos, cobras, and black-maned lions go about their business in dignified solitude, except for an occasional truckload of apprehensive tourists from Nairobi. It is a splendid place to study human evolution because quite a lot was happening here and because erosion has made it possible for scientists to get at the remains.

Archaeologist Hans Reck commented in 1913: "It is rare for strata to be so clearly distinguishable from one another as they are at Olduvai, the oldest at the bottom, the most recent at the top, undisturbed by a single gap, and never indurated or distorted by mountain-building forces."

Leakey, with his wife Mary, camped season after season at the edge, walked down into the gorge looking for bones, and shared a water hole with various large animals. "We could never get rid of the taste of rhino urine," he said, "even after filtering the water through charcoal and boiling it and using it in tea with lemon."

He sounds like the natural descendant of those nineteenth-century British explorers, men and women both, who marched presumptuously in when common sense should have kept them out. Eighty years ago one of his aunts arrived at Mombasa with the idea of touring the continental interior. Local officials, aghast at such madness, told her to go home; instead, she took a firm grip on her umbrella, hired a string of porters, and walked to Uganda. No doubt she approved of a nephew who chose to spend his life associating with dangerous animals and fever-laden mosquitos in the serene conviction that none of them would dare interrupt his work.

Leakey's first diamond in the rough was, as we might expect, a chunk of somebody's skull. It looked human—if compared to Dart's semihuman *Australopithecus*—and was about 750,000 years old. This, as professionals say, hardened the evidence that the African evolutionary line had continued. Leakey's man fitted nicely between ourselves and Dart's bone-wielding cannibalistic baboon killers.

Between 1961 and 1964 the Leakeys uncovered some two-million-year-old bones. The skulls indicated a large brain and the reconstructed hands looked altogether human. But we have trouble granting the existence of humans two million years ago—humans of any sort—not to mention those who may have been sophisticated enough to invent a device still used by various people around the world. By Argentine cowboys, for example, and by Eskimos who use it to capture geese and ptarmigan. That is, the bola. For there is evidence in the form of stone spheres from Bed II at Olduvai that those people used bolas to hunt animals. The spheres, which have been deliberately worked, are the size of baseballs. They might have been nothing more than hammers or clubheads, or balls meant to be thrown individually, though it would be strange to spend so much time shaping an object that could be lost. The reason Leakey suspected they were bolas—the stones encased in hide and connected by thongs—is that they often are found in pairs, or in sets of three.

It's a bit staggering to think that bolas may have been whirling across the earth for two million years.

A number of occupied sites have been located. At one of them the debris forms a curious pattern: a dense concentration within a rectangular area fifteen feet long by thirty feet wide. Outside this rectangle practically nothing can be found for three or four feet in any direction. The ground is bare. Then, beyond this vacant area, the artifacts show up again, though not as many. The explanation is simple. The littered rectangle was their home, surrounded by a protective thorn fence. Trash was tossed over the fence.

At another site there is a ring, about fifteen feet in diameter, consisting of several hundred stones. Occasionally
the stones form a mound. The Okombambi tribe con-
structs shelters like this. For two million years they've
been doing it. The mounds of rock support upright poles
over which grass mats or hides are stretched to break
the wind.

So the chronicle of humanity continues to lengthen.
Now and again this record is frankly reassuring. In 1966
on the French Riviera, while a hillside was being excavated to make way for some luxurious apartments, the
site of an ancient encampment was revealed. And there,
400,000 years old, lay a human footprint. It tells as much
as anything. The footprint proves that we have tenure on
earth as certainly as the whale and the crocodile. We, too,
have taken part in the grand scheme.

Flipper-bearing lungfish moved ashore in East Africa—
in East Africa or some other warm forest-clad land—where
they turned into tree shrews which turned into apes.
Then, fifteen or twenty million years ago, presumably
when forests were dwindling because of a change in climate, some adventurous or desperate apes moved from
the trees to the savannas. Here, anxious to see what was
happening, because it could mean life or death, they spent
most of their time upright.

And on the plain, unprotected, they learned the value
of tools and the use of fire.

After that it was downhill all the way, or uphill—depending on your estimate of mankind—from omnivorous
thighbone-wielding assassins to those erect Ice Age people
with whom we can sympathize, who felt a previously unknown need to worship, to make music, to dance, and
paint pictures.

Evidence that our Ice Age ancestors could appreciate

music is tentative, unlike the vividly painted animals that register their love of graphic art, yet what seems to be a musical instrument still exists in southern France. In a cave at Peche Merle a set of stalactites appears to have been worn down unnaturally, and when struck with a chamois-covered stick each column produces a different note. Ascribe this to chance or not, as you like.

At Le Tuc d'Audoubert, half a mile inside the cave, a pair of bison were modeled in high relief on a clay bank— the bull ready to mount the cow. The clay is now dry and deeply cracked, otherwise the animals seem unaffected by the millennia that have passed since they were formed. They surge with vitality. But the arresting thing about this tableau is not the elemental vigor of the bison or the skill with which they have been realized; more startling is the fact that the mud floor of the cave shows a ring of little heelprints—as though children had been dancing. In other words, these two animals were the central images of a ritual, a bison dance. And it is possible that the young dancers wore bison horns and pelts, just as in the eagle dance American Indians wear eagle feathers and represent themselves as eagles—circling, sweeping, fluttering.

Prehistorians agree that this grotto was the scene of a ritual, though some of them are not sure about the dancing; they favor a kind of backward march, a goose step in reverse—which is such an ugly concept that it may well be correct. Neither theory has been certified, however, so let's assume the children were dancing.

In either case, why should this performance have been limited to children? The answer is fairly obvious. At an appropriate age each child was admitted to tribal membership, just as today the Church observes a rite of confirmation. Deep inside Le Tuc d'Audoubert these novitiates danced around a male and female bison, dancing from childhood toward the mysteries of adult life.

Not far away, in the cave known as Les Trois Frères, an entire wall is covered with snowy owls, rabbits, fish, musk-oxen, mammoths, and so on—with arrows flying toward them from every direction. This complicated mural may very well illustrate something of profound mystic significance. The numinous spirit of life, for instance. But probably what it represents is more immediate and understandable: Hunger. Meat for the table.

Sex and the stomach, remarks one anthropologist, such are the dominant themes of most philosophy.

Still, in this same cave, cut into the rock twelve feet above the ground with a stone knife, we find a very different philosopher—a prancing round-eyed antlered Wizard who gazes emptily down upon today. Something about the position of his hands is strangely terrible and important, but what does the gesture signify? What is he telling us? If only we knew. All we can be sure of is that he has dominated this wall for thousands of years, dressed in a stag's pelt with the tail of a horse.

Less enigmatic and threatening than the Wizard of Les Trois Frères is the ivory Venus of Lespugue, who now holds court not in her original cave but in a glass cabinet at the Musée de l'Homme in Paris, just a step from the Trocadéro métro. She is flanked by mirrors so that after pressing the minuterie button you have sixty seconds to contemplate her prodigious feminine melons, north and south. Unspeakably poised, tranquil as a water lily, this stained and fractured Aurignacian princess waits, more beguiling than your favorite movie actress. Modern sculpture seldom says as much.

Further evidence of man's complex artistic roots turned up at La Genière, near Serrières-sur-Ain. Excavators came across a limestone plaque tucked into a layer of the Middle Stone Age, and on this limestone scrap had been engraved that popular subject the bison—engraved decisively, powerfully. Most unusual, however, was the fact that this one resembled a polychrome bison on a wall painting at Font-de-Gaume some 300 kilometers distant. So close indeed was the resemblance between these animals that the famous abbé-archaeologist Henri Breuil wrote: ". . . one is forced to consider the possibility that both are by the same hand. Who knows whether that small limestone plaque from Serrières could not have been a sketch for the wall painting. Or was the drawing of La Genière, on the other hand, just a souvenir of a pilgrimage."

Did the artist who painted the wall at Font-de-Gaume carry his preliminary sketch all the way to La Genière? Or did a prehistoric tourist so greatly admire the mural that he, or she, bought or stole the sketch in order to take it home?

Both thoughts are surprising. Who could have imagined such artistic concern during the Stone Age?

Alas, regardless of ancient aesthetics, we are here confronted by a fake. Professor Viret of Lyon observed suspiciously: "On ne saurait pas manquer d'être frappé de la profondeur et de la régularité du sillon de la gravure." In other words, authentic Stone Age engravings almost always are drawn softly, delicately, whereas the beast at La Genière had been delineated with deep regular strokes.

Professor Viret, troubled by this discrepancy, submitted the limestone bison for laboratory analysis, and beneath ultraviolet light one could see that the fluorescence of the line sharply differed from the fluorescence of the surface. This meant the engraving must be recent. Quite recent. And here, too, just as in the case of Charles Dawson, although the faker cannot be positively identified, circumstantial evidence does point to somebody: one of the workmen at La Genière. It's been learned that he was familiar with the Font-de-Gaume wall painting, and he is known to have made an engraving of a deer in the same style. The deer is not as good, probably because he didn't have a model. Forgers are better at copying than at creating.

So, regrettably, the limestone plaque cannot persuade us that our ancestors would travel 300 kilometers to view the latest chef d'oeuvre.

However, when sifting evidence one must be careful. Consider the engravings of mammoths discovered at Les Eyzies. In 1885 these were denounced as fakes. Modern investigators, though, have doubts about the nineteenth-century doubts. For example, certain anatomical peculiarities of a mammoth—which are clearly represented at Les Eyzies—were unknown even to scientists in 1885.

And the Altamira paintings were ridiculed for a long time, mostly because nineteenth-century scholars were able to perceive a "slightly mediocre air of modernity."

All of which should remind us that one can be not only too gullible, but too skeptical.

Besides, as the twentieth-century scholar Luis Pericot-Garcia has remarked: "Without aesthetic ability, the experience gained by apprenticeship in a school, and the background of a tradition, no artist would spontaneously paint a bison such as those at Altamira."

Herbert Kühn, who examined the work at Lascaux, discovered that the figures had been outlined with knives before they were painted, and these outlines first had been delineated with a brush—perhaps made from the plume of a snipe—because such fragile drawing could not be rendered any other way. Parenthetically it may be noted that in German the snipe's plume is *die Malerfeder*, the artist's feather, and when equipped with a bone handle it becomes a perfectly adequate little brush. The Lascaux art work, however, does not seem to have been brushed on; almost certainly the paint was squirted, very much as we spray-paint automobiles. The surface was prepared with oil and fat, then powdered colors were blown onto the sticky background through bone tubes. Now this is quite a sophisticated technique, which clearly supports Pericot-Garcia's theory. There must indeed have been schools.

Ice Age pigments are genuine oil colors, not much different from those used by artists today, says Kühn. "The ochres would have been pounded fine in mortars, and in many caves ochre-crayons have been found. . . ."

On a rock bench at Altamira lay a supply of crayons, sharpened and neatly arranged, resembling women's lipstick displayed on a cosmetics counter, just as the artist left them 12,000 years ago. Or perhaps long before that. Say 15,000. The mere existence of these crayons seems astonishing, yet still more so is the arrangement—the fact that it was not a disorderly collection but a coherent spectrum from which the artist could select whatever he thought appropriate. It is this evidence of planning which truly surprises us because we assume that those spear-carrying fur-clad hunters did not shrewdly organize their thoughts, did not quite bring their minds into focus. Not unless it concerned survival. Organizing for a mammoth hunt, yes. But one man, a cave muralist, reflectively choosing his palette?

And if you still think Ice Age artists lacked sophistication, it might be observed that a grasshopper incised on a bone at Les Trois Frères was portrayed with such fidelity that the insect's species has been determined.

They seem to have been modern enough in other ways. One engraved bone depicts a man who is either watching or following a voluptuous nude woman—a picture that bluntly points out, with little equivocation, how you and I happen to be here.

Professor Magín Berenguer suggests that man entered the world of art by way of these adipose Venuses, where the entire expressive force is concentrated on fecundity. Then, through his art, man established the immense distance which separates him from all other created things.

So be it.

Lungfish to shrew to ape to man. For better or worse that was the sequence; at least it's a sequence acceptable to many anthropologists. As always, however, there are creepers of dissent pushing in every direction.

According to Richard Leakey, who has continued the work started by his father: "Early man was a hunter, but I think the concept of aggressiveness—the killer-ape syndrome—is wrong. I am quite sure that the willingness of modern aggressive man to kill his own kind is a very recent cultural development. . . ."

Says George Schaller: "Man is a primate by inheritance but a carnivore by profession. . . ."

David Pilbeam: "I have grown increasingly skeptical of the view that hominids differentiated as weapon-wielding savanna bipeds. I am as inclined to think that changes in a predominantly vegetarian diet provided the initial impetus. Also I believe that too little emphasis has been placed on the role of language and communication. . . ."

F. Clark Howell: "We still do not know the source of the hominids, but it is possible that their origin may lie between seven and fifteen million years ago, and perhaps not only in Africa. . . ."

Von Koenigswald: "I definitely believe man's earliest ancestors came from Asia. . . ."

Or you may choose to go along with paleontologist Bjurn Kurten, who thinks man did not evolve from the ape but vice versa. He considers it possible to draw a direct line of ancestry from ourselves to a small-jawed animal called *Propliopithecus* that lived thirty or forty million years ago.

If none of this sounds appealing you can always return to the comfortable certitude of Archbishop Ussher.

The ultimate question, though, toward which all inquiries bend, and which carries a hint of menace, is not where or when or why we came to be as we are, but how the future will unfold.

2

Eca Suthi...

In 1828 a peasant who was plowing on the Italian estate of Lucien Bonaparte, Napoleon's brother, crashed through the roof of an Etruscan burial vault. A bailiff was ordered to investigate, and what he saw underground promptly caused Lucien to start raking the countryside for more tombs. Hundreds were found and looted, yielding thousands of painted dishes, statuettes, jewels, rings, bracelets, and so on. The Vulci necropolis, from which Bonaparte recovered most of this treasure, is thought to have given up more valuables than any other ancient site with the exception of Pompeii.

News of the Vulci bonanza whistled through Italy and across Europe while Lucien Bonaparte's neighbors began to contemplate their own fields with deep interest. As a result, more tombs were ripped open and stripped of marketable merchandise, and Prosper Mérimée felt inspired to write *The Etruscan Vase*. The vase that excited him was not Etruscan, it happened to be Greek, either imported or manufactured in a south Italian Greek pottery shop; but Mérimée did not know this, for which we may be mildly grateful. *Le Vase Étrusque* is not classified as a masterpiece but we need all the literature we can get, even if it's written under a misapprehension.

One by one the sites and the important relics were catalogued, scholarly papers rustled, and archaeologists took to quarreling over the debris. They still quarrel, mostly because the language cannot quite be understood and because nobody has proved beyond doubt where the Etruscans came from.

At present we have two legitimate theories concerning their homeland, and a third theory which once was greeted with respect but now is not. Wherever they originated, these people dominated the central Mediterranean for several centuries. We are told by Livy that Etruria's renown "filled the lands and the waters from one end of Italy to the other, from the Alps to the Straits of Messina."

Herodotus thought they emigrated from Asia Minor: "During the reign of Atys, son of Manes, there was famine throughout Lydia. For a while the Lydians persisted in living as they always had, but when the famine lengthened they looked for a way to alleviate their misery—some suggesting one thing, some another. At this time they invented dice games, knuckle-bone games, handball games, and other games—except draughts, which they did not invent. They would play all day for two days in order to distract themselves and on the third day they would eat. For eighteen years they lived like this. . . ."

At last, continues Herodotus, the king divided his subjects into two groups and chose by lot which would remain in Lydia and which must go in search of a new home. The king himself remained, while those who were to leave he put in charge of his son Tyrsenos. Then all those who were departing went down to Smyrna where they built ships, and after loading the ships with their possessions they sailed away and "passed by many nations in turn" until they reached the land of the Umbrians.

Summarizing the exodus in this manner makes it sound like a ten-day cruise. The reality—if we are discussing reality—must have been quite different. Assuming a degree of truth in the legend, it seems unlikely that there could have been one vast embarkation; more probably there would be numerous small embarkations over a period of years, just as bands of Crusaders straggled toward the Holy Land for 200 years—in contrast to the popular view of seven Christian armies one after another clanking through Syria. And Herodotus' remark about passing many nations in turn could mean that the emigrants settled here and there, then some of their descendants drifted along, and theirs wandered farther, until at last—centuries after Tyrsenos left home—people with Lydian blood and Lydian traditions reached Italy.

That there was famine in Asia Minor during the thirteenth century B.C. cannot be doubted. Pharaoh Merneptah shipped grain to "Kheta," land of the Hittites, and a communiqué from one Hittite ruler alludes to starvation. There is also the account of a provincial king with an unpronounceable name who led his famished subjects to the court of the Hittite emperor.

Egyptian hieroglyphs speak of an attempted invasion by "Peoples of the Sea" during the reign of Pharaohs Merneptah and Ramses III, between 1230 and 1170 B.C., and it's possible that among these half-identified sea people were some Lydians. Whether or not this is so, the course of the emigrants is reasonably clear: they sailed past Malta and Sicily, at which point a few might have continued west to the famous city of Tartessus in Spain. A majority, however, must have turned north to the Italian mainland where they settled along the coast between the Tiber and the Arno, north of the marsh that eventually would become Rome. Here, in Tuscany, among a Bronze Age people called Villanovans, they built those cities we dimly remember from school—Cerveteri, Tarquinia, Populonium, and the others—and here they became known to the Greeks as Tyrsenoi, to the Latins as Etrusci.

The evidence for such a theory is persuasive. In the first place, Herodotus was not the only historian to describe an ancient Lydian migration. Secondly, it is a fact, with little disagreement among archaeologists, that during the eighth and ninth centuries B.C. a noticeable change occurred in the Tuscan way of life. This commonly is called the "Orientalizing" period. It included the substitution of burial for cremation and the appearance of chambered tombs beneath a *dromo,* or mound, very similar to the earliest tombs in Asia Minor. Religion, too, assumed a different form, apparently related to the eastern Mediterranean. Even the Tuscan devils evolved into first cousins of Assyrian and Chaldean devils. And the livers of sacrificed animals were examined for signs, a Babylonian practice.

Furthermore, the social organization began to display Eastern characteristics, particularly the attitude toward women. The Greeks, in fact, were shocked to learn that Etruscan men treated women as equals. To the Greeks, and later to the Romans, this seemed degenerate.

The style of dress became Eastern. Fashionable ladies wore the round or pointed cap that had been popular with Hittite women. Men wore a belted jerkin with a cloak thrown across one shoulder—which developed into the Roman toga. Men and women both wore pointed shoes with turned-up toes, very much like Hittite shoes.

Then there are linguistic arguments for supposing that these people came from Asia Minor, because Etruscan is not one of the Indo-European languages. Its alphabet is Greek, but the words and sentence construction are not. Nobody has been able to relate Etruscan to any other language, though just about everything has been tried: Sanskrit, Albanian, Hebrew, Basque, Hungarian, and various Anatolian languages. That it should still be indecipherable is not just curious but rather outrageous, because Etruscan was spoken in Tuscany right up to the opening of the Christian era and was used by Etruscan priests as late as the fifth century A.D. This being so, how could it absolutely disappear? We have no explanation, although there are reasons for thinking that the Christian Church obliterated it, just as the Church attempted to silence Aztec, Mayan, and other such ungodly tongues.

However, remnants of a lost civilization tend to be as durable as pottery shards. The archbishop's staff, for instance, developed from the coiled wand of an Etruscan soothsayer. And the mallet used by Charun to smash the skulls of Etruscan dead is employed whenever a pope dies. Not long ago, you may remember, the Vatican secretary of state, Cardinal Villot, tapped John Paul's forehead three times with a silver hammer, calling him by his given name: "Albino, Albino, Albino. Are you dead?" People everywhere, including many who are not Catholic, must have prayed that the elfish little pontiff would smile and sit up. Alas, there was no response; the September pope was gone. Cardinal Villot grasped John Paul's hand, withdrew the gold ring of the fisherman, and smashed it.

And occasionally we speak or write an Etruscan word: *tavern, cistern, letter, person, ceremony, lantern.* But except for these, only about 100 Etruscan words have been deciphered, mostly funeral announcements which occur again and again so that their meaning is not much in doubt. *Eca suthi,* let us say, followed by a name.

One of the strongest linguistic pillars supporting the Eastern theory is a stela from the seventh century B.C. which was uncovered in 1885 on the island of Lemnos in the Aegean. It depicts a warrior holding a lance and it bears two inscriptions using the Greek alphabet. The language, though, is not Greek; it is Etruscoid. Other fragments of this language have since been found on Lemnos, which does away with the idea that the stela might have been imported. What all of this suggests is that Etruscan-speaking Lydians might have settled there.

Take a narrow look at the statues, pots, tripods, jewelry, sword hilts, murals. So much hints at Oriental ancestry.

If you study the Cerveteri sarcophagus which is now in Rome's Villa Giulia it becomes very difficult to think of these people as primitive Italians: the husband's tilted eyes and stiff Turkish beard, the wife's little cap and pointed slippers, the languorous sensuality surging like a wave between them.

And in the Louvre, not fifty yards from the Winged Victory in her stone nightgown, rests another Etruscan sarcophagus—less erotic than the Italian, a bit more crisp, more architectonic, although they were produced at about the same time in the same city, perhaps in the same workshop. Once again you meet those tilted eyes, the complacent wife's up-curled slippers, the mild husband's carefully shaped beard. And, if you walk around behind the sarcophagus, you see how the hair has been styled in tight Babylonian ringlets.

New York's Metropolitan used to display three impressively sculpted Etruscans with somewhat Asiatic features: a gigantic helmeted head; a six-foot, eight-inch warrior; and the "Big Warrior" who stood eight feet tall. They turned out to be fakes, manufactured sixty years ago by a quartet of young entrepreneurs in Orvieto, but that's not the point; the point is that even a fraudulent Etruscan seems less Italian than Eastern.

I remember the big warrior. I looked at him a number of times when he was considered authentic, and I always felt surprised that such an enormous antique could be in such good condition. When I heard he was a fake I felt incredulous, but only for an instant. Almost at once I heard myself muttering "Of course! Yes, of course! Anybody could see that!"

And what puzzled me then, as it does today, is why the experts were deceived. Because if somebody with no particular knowledge of Etruscan art could half suspect the truth, as I did—well then, how could professionals be so blind? But for twenty-eight years most of them saw nothing wrong. One or two had doubts. One or two called these giants bogus. As for the rest: they came to marvel, to offer learned praise.

Now in Copenhagen, in the basement of that peculiar Edwardian museum known as the Glyptothek, are several bona fide Etruscan figures: a shattered frieze of black-bearded warriors wearing Trojan helmets and carrying circular shields embellished with a mysterious red, white, and black whirlpool. These thick-legged businesslike fighting men are the real McCoy, and everything about them points east.

So often with Etruscan artifacts one does apprehend these long reverberations from Asia. Nevertheless, a good many prominent archaeologists refuse to buy Herodotus' account; they consider it a fable. They reject the idea of an immense migration—half a nation sailing into the sunset—and insist unromantically that the Etruscans were natural descendants of some Italian farmers. What a gray thought. It's like being told the Kensington runestone is a fake—that the bloody tale of a battle between Indians and

Vikings in upper Minnesota never took place. One wants to imagine.

Among the cold-blooded exponents of this autochthonous theory none is chillier than Massimo Pallottino, professor of Etruscology and Italic archaeology at the University of Rome. Indeed, Professor Pallottino sounds exasperated that other professionals could be wrongheaded enough even to contemplate the migration hypothesis, which he goes about dissecting with meticulous disdain and a glittering assortment of scalpels:

> Edoardo Brizio in 1885 was the first to put this theory on a scientific footing: he identified the Etruscan invaders with the bearers of Orientalizing (and later Hellenizing) civilization into Tuscany and Emilia, and he saw the Umbrians of Herodotus—i.e. Indo-European Italic peoples—in the cremating Villanovans. Among the most convinced followers of Brizio's thesis were O. Montelius, B. Modestov, G. Körte, G. Ghirardini, L. Mariani. . . . Herodotus may have been attracted by the similarity of the name Tyrrhenian (*Tyrrhenoi, Tyrsenoi*) with that of the city of Tyrrha or Torrhebus in Lydia. . . .

Nor was there an abrupt change in burial rites from the practice of cremation, typical of the Villanovan period, to Oriental inhumation. Both were characteristic of early Villanovan ceremonies, he tells us, notably in southern Etruria where the idea of cremation predominated. Later, during the eighth century B.C., the practice of inhumation gradually became established—not only in Etruria but in Latium where no Etruscan "arrival" has been postulated.

"We should now examine the linguistic data. In spite of assertions to the contrary made by Lattes, Pareti and others, a close relationship unites Etruscan with the dialect spoken at Lemnos before the Athenian conquest of the island by Miltiades in the second half of the sixth century B.C. . . . This does not mean, however, that Lemnian and Etruscan were the same language. . . . Further, the onomastic agreements between the Etruscan and eastern languages carry no great weight (as E. Fiesel correctly pointed out) when we consider that they are based upon . . ."

Obviously this is not the stuff of which best-sellers are made, even in light doses, and with Pallottino one is forced to swallow page after page of it. The result is tedium sinking inexorably toward stupefaction, together with a dull realization that whatever the man says probably is correct. To read him is appalling. No dreams, my friend, just facts. Facts and deductions. Deductions followed by occasional impeccable qualifications. One is reminded of those medieval ecclesiastics wondering how many angels could dance on the head of a pin, it is all so academic. The difference, of course, being that these churchmen had not the least idea what they were talking about, while Professor Pallottino knows precisely.

Along the way, before telling us how it actually was, he takes a few pages to demolish that third theory, the illegitimate one. In this version, highly regarded during the nineteenth century, the Etruscans came down from the north. The reason for thinking so was linguistic: traces of an Etruscan dialect had been found among the Rhaetian Alps. But it seems that this material dates from the fourth century B.C., long after Etruscans had staked a claim in Italy.

An additional argument against it, says Pallottino, is the relationship of Etruscan to pre-Hellenic languages throughout the Aegean: "This could only be explained by accepting Kretschmer's thesis of a parallel overland immigration into Greece and Italy originating from the Danube basin. We would then still have to explain those elements in the 'Tyrrhenian' toponymy. . . ."

In other words, let such nonsense be forgotten.

What remains, then, is the not particularly exciting thought that our sensuous, artistic, enigmatic Etruscans were the natural children of Villanova peasants. The name *Villanova*, if anybody asks, comes from a suburb of Bologna where vestiges of a previously unknown culture turned up: hut-shaped urns filled with human ashes, bronze weapons, amber jewelry, pins and combs. Apparently these ancestors of the Etruscans, if that is what they were, drifted south into Tuscany about the eleventh or tenth century before Christ and overwhelmed whatever inhabitants they encountered.

Perhaps 300 years later the Orientalizing began. This was the time of a Dark Age in Greece, between the decay of Mycenaean civilization and the emergence of those wise marble Pericleans against whom we half-consciously measure ourselves. It was a time when that templed colossus, Egypt, was beginning to crumble. Assyrian armor glinted ominously. Phrygian trumpets bellowed. Phoenician traders drove westward, dipping their sails at Carthage and Tartessus. Fresh currents rippled the length of the Mediterranean.

So, inevitably, the rude Villanova culture was affected. Greek vase painters moved to Cerveteri, bringing the alphabet and other such radical concepts. Pallottino believes that these various intellectual and artistic transfusions have given the impression of Etrurian dependence on the East, an impression to which the ancients—notably Herodotus—succumbed, and which still inhibits the thinking of twentieth-century investigators.

D. H. Lawrence, faced with the cool reason of Pallottino, might have been impatient or just disgusted. His own exploration of the subject, *Etruscan Places,* did not precede the professor's *Etruscologia* by much more than ten years, but Lawrence illuminated a region fully ten light-years away. He was a breast-fed romantic, the Italian a most assiduous scholar. Lawrence plunged into Etruria; Pallottino picks and brushes and trowels away at it.

The experience! cried Lawrence. The *experience*—that was what mattered. Live! Empathize! Feel!

When he visited Tuscany in 1927, three years before he died, he was quite sick; yet the book gives no hint of it, except indirectly. "Ease, naturalness, and an abundance of life," he wrote. "The things they did, in their easy centuries, are as natural and easy as breathing." No need to twist the mind or soul. Death was simply a pleasant continuance of life, with jewels and wine and flutes playing for the dance. Neither an ecstasy of bliss, a heaven, nor a purgatory of torment.

"From the shadow of the prehistoric world emerge dying religions that have not yet invented gods or goddesses, but live by the mystery of the elemental powers in the Universe, the complex vitalities of what we feebly call Nature."

"The goat says: let me breed for ever, till the world is one reeking goat. But then the lion roars from the other blood-stream, which is also in man, and he lifts his paw to strike. . . ."

This sort of thing annoys Pallottino, who has no time for mystics. Painted tombs littered with jewelry and elegant vases have created around his specialty "a peculiar aura of romantic suggestion, which the books of Dennis and Noël des Vergers helped to spread, never to disappear again. Scholarly uncertainties and polemics on the interpretation of Etruscan inscriptions, on the classification of the language, on the problem of Etruscan origins, gave birth to the notion of an 'Etruscan mystery'; and this notion, rather than describing, more or less aptly, a scientific situation . . ."

On and on he goes in his oddly dry, convincing prose— so much less gratifying than the rainbows whipped up by Lawrence. And what he is insisting is that these people twenty-five centuries ago were neither more nor less enigmatic than you and I; which is to say that they are interesting by themselves, never mind the blather.

Physically they were small, judged by skeletal remains. The man averaged five feet, four inches. The women just above five feet. On the basis of tomb information their life expectancy was about forty.

Early historians denounced them as decadent and drunken, promiscuous lovers intoxicated by comfort, a reputation they shared with the Sybarites. Theopompus wrote in the fourth century B.C. that they copulated publicly and did not consider it shameful. "They all do the thing, some watching one another. . . . The men approach the women with great delight, but obtain as much pleasure from young men and adolescents. They grow up, in fact, to be very beautiful, for they live luxuriously and shave their bodies. . . ."

Posidonius, a Stoic author of the second century B.C., after observing that the Etruscans once were valorous, attributes their degeneration to the richness of the land—its minerals, timber, and so on. Later critics explained the decline with equal facility. Victorians, for example, thought they collapsed because of a perverse religion. Our twentieth century is less positive: we aren't sure just what happened to their world. From our balcony they appear to be at once naïve and sophisticated, artistic and mate-

rialistic, radical, conservative, industrious, indolent, foolish, clever, ad infinitum. That is to say, a disorganized
bellowing parade of contradictory mortals.

Despite meager evidence we do know a little about
their activities and concerns.

Etruscan women liked to bleach their hair—a fancy that
has been entertained, it seems, from the female prototype
to the latest model. And depilatories were popular. Try
this: boil a yellow tree frog until it has shrunk to half its
natural size, then rub the shriveled frog on the unsightly
area. Now, it's too bad we have no testimonials from satisfied beauties of Vetluna or Caere, but that does not mean
the treatment is useless. These people sometimes equaled
or surpassed us in the most unexpected ways.

Etruscan hunters understood the compelling power of
music far better than we do. Aelian, who wrote in the
third century, reveals that after the nets and traps had
been set a piper would come forth playing his sweetest
tunes. Wild pigs, stags, and other beasts at first would be
terrified. But after a while, seduced, they draw closer, be-
witched by these dulcet sounds, "until they fall, over-
powered, into the snares." And we have the word of
Polybius, five centuries earlier, who asserts that Etruscan
swineherds walk their charges up and down the beach, not
driving them as we would expect, but leading them by
blowing a trumpet.

In dentistry, too, one must salute these creative sons of
Villanova. Skulls found at Tarquinia contain teeth neatly
bridged and capped with gold.

Insecticides, which we regard as a small miracle of our
century, were commonplace. The agronomist Saserna rec-
ommends an aromatic vine called serpentaria. Soak the
root of this vine in a tub of water, then empty the tub on
the infested earth. Or let's say you become conscious of

ravenous little guests in your bed at night. Should that be the case, dampen your bed with a potion of ox gall and vinegar.

Take an ordinary business such as the production of cheese. Here again the Etruscan surprises us. Do you know those great wheels made in Holland and Denmark? Listen, my friend, Etruscans in the village of Luni fashioned wheels of goat cheese weighing 1,000 pounds.

Yet right along with such innovations they clung obstinately to the mindless beliefs of their fathers. Even the Romans, who are not celebrated for a liberal imagination, had begun to grasp the nature of things more clearly. Seneca, commenting on the difference between Romans and Etruscans, offers this example: "Whereas we believe lightning to be released when clouds collide, they believe that clouds collide so as to release lightning."

Another difference, more curious, which has not yet been explained, is that the Greeks and Romans and everybody else in that part of the world faced north when attempting to determine celestial influences. Only the Etruscans, those perverse, contradictory individuals, faced south. Why? Tomorrow, if the gods so ordain, we'll dig up the answer.

You can see them as they were, just as they were, on the ragged stone sarcophagus lids. You see the rich and powerful, of course, rather than the poor, because nobody commemorates the poor; but the features of affluent Etruscans have been studiously registered on their coffins. And there can be little doubt that these sculpted effigies are portraits of unique men and women, not blind symbols.

At least so it seems to an impressionable observer. However, one must be cautious. When making little terra cotta votive heads the Etruscan coroplasts often used molds, then a touch or two with a modeling tool could give an effect of individuality. In other words, a mass-produced standardized face with a few singular characteristics—let's say a bobbed nose, a couple of warts, and a triple chin—is not the same as a portrait. Therefore one should regard the sarcophagus sculpture with mild distrust; maybe these figures, too, were only impersonations of life.

Yet no matter how they were done they do give the sense of being particular people. They are quickly recognizable and somehow appalling, like faces on the society page, and they tell quite a lot.

For instance, toward the end—while Etruscan civilization deteriorates—the sarcophagus men and women grow flabbily plump. They project an air of self-indulgence, of commercial success. And they seem strangely resigned or dissatisfied, as though they could anticipate the falling curtain. Yet if you look back a few centuries, not at these phlegmatic inheritors but at the pioneers who lived seven or six centuries before Christ, you notice a quality of strength or assurance like that found on prehistoric terra cotta statues from India and Thailand and Mexico. It is surprising and alarming to perceive what happens to a nation.

The despair these people felt has been reflected also in the late tomb paintings. Gone are the joyous leaping dolphins, the pipers and dancers. Instead, the hereafter looks grim. Mournful processions of the dead are escorted by gray-green putrescent demons with pointed ears and snakes in their hair. Ghoulish underworld heralds brandish tongs, ropes, and torches; they carry hammers and clubs with which to smash the skulls of the newly deceased. Everything seems to prefigure medieval Christianity.

Perhaps the *Libri Fatales* were responsible, not the minerals and timber, nor a degenerate religion—though it is true that the *Fatales* were religious texts. These books concerned the division of time, with limitations on the lives of men and women, and they placed a limit of ten saecula on the life of the Etruscan nation. A saeculum was a variable period, averaging about 100 years, and it was up to the priests to determine when each had ended. During the eighth and ninth saecula, while their city-states gradually were being absorbed by Rome, the people must have realized that the end was near, that nothing could save Etruria from extinction. Thus the prophecy became self-fulfilling.

In 44 B.C. when Julius Caesar was murdered a comet gleamed overhead, sheeted corpses gibbered in the street, and the Etruscan seer Vulcatius proclaimed an end to the ninth saeculum.

Claudius died 98 years later—the last high Roman to understand the Etruscan language. His wife Plautia Urgulanilla was Etruscan, and Claudius had written a twenty-book history of them, *Tyrrhenica,* which has been lost. At his death, we are told, another brilliant comet appeared and lightning struck his father's tomb, marking the end of the final saeculum. Archaeologists find no evidence of what might properly be called Etruscan civilization after that date.

These ominous books, the *Fatales,* were part of a complex prescription covering rules of worship, life beyond the grave, civil and military ordinances, the founding of cities, interpretation of miracles, et cetera. Much of it has vanished, but some was transcribed by Greek, Roman, and Byzantine chroniclers, so we have—along with the *Fatales*—the *Libri Fulgurales* and *Haruspicini.*

Because it derives from the verb "to lighten," *fulgurale,* the first of these books naturally had to do with divination from objects hit by lightning. According to the sound and color of the bolt, and by the direction from which it came, a soothsayer would deduce which god had ordered the stroke and what it meant. The next step was to consult the

Libri in order to learn what should be done. This was not easy. Any of nine gods might have thrown it, and Jupiter himself could hurl three different kinds of lightning. Etruscan skill at interpretation seems to have impressed the Romans; they themselves could recognize only one bolt from Jupiter's hand. If the regnant god was enraged he struck, and that was that. Consequently they would call for an Etruscan whenever they wanted a truly subtle reading. It was an Etruscan, Spurinna, who advised Caesar against the Ides of March.

In 1878 near Piacenza in the Po valley a unique object turned up: a bronze model of a sheep liver. The surface was divided into forty compartments enclosing the names of various gods such as Cilens, Ani, Hercle, Thuflthas, Muantras, and Satres. Without a Rosetta stone it has been necessary to proceed inchwise, as Mayan linguists do, but still there has been progress and several of these names have been correlated with familiar Latin gods. Others remain incomprehensible. But the significance of the bronze object is understood. The liver, being the seat of life, was a rich source of information. A priest would examine the liver of a sacrificed animal for blemishes or deformity, and after interpreting what he saw he would consult the *Libri Haruspicini* for an appropriate ritual. The bronze liver unearthed at Piacenza might have been used to instruct apprentices.

How remote it sounds—interpreting divine will through lightning bolts and sheep livers—like something from Stonehenge or the labyrinths of Crete. Yet as late as the fifth century A.D. these services were ordered in Christian Rome: Pope Innocent I, frightened by the approach of Alaric's Visigoths, consulted Etruscan *fulgiatores* and *haruspices*.

How remote, psychically, is Etruria? Well, my neighbor knocks on wood, millions consult the horoscope, and I myself don't much care for room 13. Interpret that as you please. Now back to the facts.

This incomplete collection of sacred books is just about all the Etruscan literature we have. Otherwise there are only scraps, threads, allusions, and those brief monotonous remarks on funerary items, on mirrors, weapons, and little boxes:

I BELONG TO LARTHIA.

TARCHUNIES HAD ME MADE.

VEL PARTUNU, SON OF VELTHUR AND RAMTHA SATLNEI, DIED AGED TWENTY-EIGHT.

ASKA MI ELEIVANA, MINI, MULVANIKE MAMARCE VELCHANA, which of course means: "I am an oil bottle donated by Mamarce Velchana."

A contemporary of Cicero mentions some tragedies written by Velna, or Volnius, but that is all we know, not the titles, not even the century. Indeed, there may not have been much Etruscan literature. If there was, it failed to excite the Romans.

In 1964 three rectangular sheets of gold were discovered near the port of Santa Severa. All were inscribed—one in Phoenician, two in Etruscan—perhaps telling a wonderful story, perhaps describing a voyage from Lydia. So, as you might imagine, there was whooping and dancing among Etruscologists. Unfortunately the Phoenician is not a translation of the Etruscan; linguists are convinced of that. Still, the plates have been helpful because the messages are similar: the king of Caere, Thefarie Velianas, is dedicating a shrine to the Lady Astarte in the month of the Sacrifice of the Sun. This ceremony, which must have been widely proclaimed, occurred about 500 B.C.

Latin inscriptions from the period of Roman hegemony often are found on monuments or on the pedestals of statues. One speaks of a military commander who led an army against "C," which would mean Caere. He led another force against Sicily, thus becoming the first Etruscan general to cross the water, and when he returned from this punitive expedition he was rewarded with an eagle and a golden crown. Clearly he was a great general. His name, almost obliterated, appears to be "Vel X, son of Lars."

What seems to resist oblivion, outlasting all other created things, including the greatest plays and the most exquisite poems, outlasting murals, statues, bronze mirrors, and stone sarcophagi, is pottery, the humble craftsman's daily product. It is just about indestructible. Certain plastics may last until the end of the world—maybe longer, if anybody cares—but pottery shards are practically as durable, which is a bit of luck. They are easily glued together, very often they fit to perfection although the object may have been shattered millennia ago, and the most ordinary scraps reveal quite a lot because, almost from the beginning, potters have decorated their pots. Changes of taste, form, and technique accurately measure the passing years. The examination of pots and cups and plates, therefore, becomes a fundamental discipline of the archaeologist.

Kylix, alabastron, rhyton, hydria—Etruscan potters, often adapting Greek forms, steadily manufactured them, century upon century. Thousands have survived intact, or faintly chipped, and we can only guess how many would be around if grave robbers were more considerate.

For instance, the famous blackware called bucchero. Lawrence described these vases and dishes as opening out "like strange flowers, black flowers with all the softness and the rebellion of life." Another Englishman, George Dennis—the same Dennis of whom Professor Pallottino disapproves—tells of being present during an excavation at Vulci in 1843. Under orders from Lucien Bonaparte's widow, the workmen divided whatever they found into two groups: jewelry, richly painted Greek vases and so forth, which fetched a good price, on one side; everything of slight commercial value, such as bucchero dishes, on the other side. Whereupon, says Dennis, everything of little or no value was deliberately smashed. Widow Bonaparte did not want to dilute the market. "At the mouth of the pit in which they were at work, sat the *capo*, or overseer—his gun by his side. . . ."

One is reminded of Genghis Khan destroying what he was unable to use because he could not imagine what else should be done with it. Or Diego de Landa burning the elegant Mayan codices. Or those Mohammedan soldiers who broke into the library at Alexandria and helped themselves to 700,000 books—fuel enough to heat the public baths for six months.

Today what remains of Etruria?

A stone leopard. Dice. Chariot fragments. Several lead discs. An ivory writing tablet. Those three sheets of gold. Odd, mysterious items such as the bronze handle picked up at Fabbrecce, near Città di Castello, which shows a man wearing a crown of leaves, arms raised, with a dog or a lion on the ring above his head—with a human arm issuing from the animal's mouth! What does it mean? Or the engraved ostrich egg from Quinto Fiorentino. An ostrich egg with Etruscan lettering. What about that?

And the Capitoline wolf—emblem of Rome. We have this wild bronze mother, which probably was cast at Veii during the fifth century before Christ. Romulus and Remus, the sucklings, who crawled beneath her sometime during the sixteenth century, are meant to symbolize how Rome drew nourishment from Etruria.

So we have all this and more. Quite a lot more. But if one item alone testifies to the fugitive existence of these people it must be the ivory writing tablet. On its surface are traces of wax and some very old scratches; therefore we assume that an Etruscan stylus scratched the tablet.

Professor Luisa Banti, terse and formidable, says no. Without qualification: No.

We assume the tablet belonged to a child because of its small size and because an alphabet has been cut into the rim, just as you see our alphabet printed in bold letters on the cover or first page of a child's tablet.

Professor Banti does not waste time on this sentimental hypothesis. Instead, she offers two explanations, not mutually exclusive, for the small size and for the presence of an alphabet. First, the tablet may have been symbolic. Writing was then a new art in Etruria and the personage with whom it was buried wanted everybody to know that he could write. Second, the tablet might have been used for practice. If you have trouble forming letters you need a model.

The argument that Etruscan adults needed a model abecedary is tenuous but convincing: the alphabet was engraved also on quite a few miniature vases and these vases are thought to have been "inkpots"—containers for the red or black liquid that served as ink when writing on papyrus.

Regardless of who owned this tablet or how it was used, it must have been a delightful possession because one could magically erase the letters by waving a baton of hot metal over the wax. A hole drilled through the handle implies that there was a string, meaning it probably was worn like a necklace.

Such things—objects accompanying a funeral—are the most reliable guide to Etruria, as long as they are studied without preconceived theories. They are the one true Etruscan source, says Banti, "the only one unaltered by personal ideas, or by the interpretations and prejudices of the ancient writers whose works we use as historical sources. Archaeological finds are the archive documents of antiquity, documents that have to be studied patiently in museums and in excavation diaries. They are safer and more credible than the scant information handed down by ancient Greek and Latin historians."

We could almost fill a railroad train with Etruscan bric-a-brac. Corroded swords, dented bronze helmets, pots, plates, boxes, flasks, cinerary urns, mirrors, figurines, antefixes, cylinders, and so on. And yet, paradoxically, we don't seem to have nearly enough. We hunt for more and more, perhaps because it's easy to imagine how much has been lost.

What else remains?

Inside those odd funerary beehives that dot the Tuscan hillsides we come upon stained murals whose colors evoke memories of Crete and Egypt—pink, green, black, white, red, yellow—though the sensibility is Etruscan. Some of them cross the centuries between us like a bolt of lightning. A mural at Chiusi shows a charioteer who has just been pitched out of his vehicle: a moment from now he will land on his head. We can understand this. We appreciate and comprehend his problem. One can empathize with him more easily than with a Cretan acrobat somersaulting over the horns of a bull.

All right, we have these disintegrating murals. What else?

Sundry goods. Everyday merchandise. Scraps of apparel. Here and there a tantalizing curiosity.

In the National Museum of Yugoslavia stands a rigid female mummy shaped like a cudgel, or a Giacometti sculpture, or one of those elongated prehistoric Sardinian bronzes; and what is unique about this mummy is that, although it turned up in Egypt, the linen wrappings are covered with Etruscan liturgical formulas. Furthermore, what was written on the bandages has no connection with the burial. The linen contains 1,185 words, evenly spaced, written in red. Allowing for repetitions and illegible areas, there are 530 different Etruscan words, only a few of which can be translated. *Vinum* is obvious, and some others are not difficult for philologists: *fler* meaning an offering or sacrifice, *tur* meaning to give, *ais* or *eis* being the word for god. But most of the text is indecipherable: "cilths spurestres enas ethrse tinsi tiurim avils chis . . ."

Now the red-haired young woman stands naked in Zagreb, her leathery brown body stripped of its last garment—the one thing about her that excited professionals. Nobody knows her name or where she came from. *Eca suthi* . . . But then what? She could have been Egyptian, she could have been Etruscan. The linen roll probably was brought to Egypt by Etruscan colonists during their migration from Lydia about the ninth century B.C.—assuming such a migration did take place—or brought by a wealthy Etruscan family fleeing the Roman encroachment.

So much for scholarship.

You can visit Etruria with no trouble. Every morning the tourist buses leave Rome, air-conditioned buses with multilingual guides. They will take you to Cerveteri and Tarquinia and other famous sites. Or you can go by yourself and walk along the dusty paths, which may well be those the Etruscans used—because paths, like pots, last indefinitely. And you get the feeling that not much has changed. In midsummer the bloated purplish flies have no fear; they believe they are entitled to stick to your face. Pale blue blossoms of rosemary decorate the low hills, thick with prickly shrubs, and there is a sense of the Tyrrhenian Sea not far off.

You can visit the places where they lived and search the hills and enter the caves and burrows overgrown with trees. Uneasily you look at the *cippi*—stone symbols outside their tombs, a phallus to show that a man lies within, a house with a triangular roof to indicate a woman. That is to say, you can find the Etruscans—if you pretend. Because of the murals and painted ceramics, because of what you have been told or have read, you dimly perceive them. Almost. But it doesn't quite work. Imagination fails. There is no authentic Etruscan sound, no touch of an Etruscan hand, nor the odor of a plump Etruscan body. They seem to be present, yet they are not.

At last you return comfortably to Rome on the bus, having been told about Etruscans; or you return by yourself, exhausted and sweaty and confused, knowing no more, the past unrecaptured.

A Roman art dealer named Augusto Jandolo got a little closer. When he was a boy in Tuscany he watched as the sarcophagus of a Tarquinian nobleman was opened. The great stone cover was difficult to lift; but finally it rose, stood on end for a moment, and fell heavily aside. Then, says Jandolo, he saw something that he would remember until his dying day:

> Inside the sarcophagus I saw resting the body of a young warrior in full accoutrements, with helmet, spear, shield, and greaves. Let me stress that it was not a skeleton I saw; I saw a body, with all its limbs in place, stiffly outstretched as though the dead man had just been laid in the grave. It was the appearance of but a moment. Then, by the light of the torches, everything seemed to dissolve. The helmet rolled to the right, the round shield fell into the collapsed breastplate of the armor, the greaves flattened out at the bottom of the sarcophagus, one on the right, the other on the left. At the first contact with air the body which had lain inviolate for centuries suddenly dissolved into dust. . . In the air, however, and around the torches, a golden powder seemed to be hovering.

3

Vinland Vínland

The most complete accounts of early Norse voyages to America are "The Greenlanders' Saga" and "Eirik's Saga." Both were written long after the events they describe and both are copies or variations of earlier accounts that have been lost.

"The Greenlanders' Saga" is part of a large vellum codex known as the *Flateyjarbók*, which was commissioned sometime between 1382 and 1395 by a wealthy Icelandic farmer named Jon Hakonarson who lived—as the title indicates—on a flat island. The book was carefully preserved by his descendants until one of them gave it to an Icelandic bishop, who gave it to the king of Denmark. It is now in the Royal Library.

There are two versions of Eirik's saga. One occurs in *Hauksbók*, which dates from about 1334 and was written by a certain Hauk Erlendsson "the Lawman" with the help of two secretaries. Erlendsson was descended from one of the first Norsemen to visit America, he was quite proud of this fact, and scholars believe he revised history somewhat in order to make his family seem still more illustrious. The other version appears in *Skálholtsbók*, probably written during the second half of the fifteenth century, and because it is later than Erlendsson's version it was at first assumed to be less accurate. But apparently the opposite is true; the *Skálholtsbók* copyist, no doubt descended from a long line of impoverished and lusterless clerks, did not care about history. He only wanted to produce a satisfactory duplicate so that he could get paid. At any rate, if you read medieval Norse and wish to compare them, both are in Copenhagen's Arnamagnaean Library.

"The Greenlanders' Saga" and "Eirik's Saga" recount many of the same events, though not all, and occasionally they contradict each other, which makes historical detective work just that much more difficult. Considering this, as well as the sparse evidence from other sources, and the obscurities, and the centuries that have elapsed since Leif and his half sister Freydis and Thorfinn and the others went adventuring, and the fact that both sagas are either variants or perhaps inaccurate copies of lost manuscripts—considering these handicaps, only an arrogant and simpleminded historian would claim to have deduced the truth absolutely.

Even so, the sagas are not fiction.

It is well known that scholars fight like spiders in a bottle over the interpretation of artifacts and crumbling parchment, and medieval Norse explorations have particularly excited their testiness, making it almost impossible for an ignorant reader to know which gray eminence to believe. All the same, this seems to be more or less what happened:

In A.D. 985 or 986 a young Icelandic trader named Bjarni Herjolfsson returned from Norway to spend the winter with his father, as he customarily did every second year. But when he got to the farm it was deserted, and neighbors told him that his father had accompanied Eirik Raude, Eirik the Red, to Greenland. Bjarni, according to one translation, was "taken heavily aback" by this news, and instead of unloading his cargo he decided to sail on to Greenland. Having never been there, he asked where it was to be found and what it looked like; and after being told that it lay somewhere to the west Bjarni asked his crewmen if they were prepared to go there with him, because Greenland was where he meant to spend this winter.

They said they would go with him.

He told them that the trip might be considered foolhardy, since none of them had been to the Greenland Sea. But they told him they would go, if that was what he had in mind.

After taking aboard supplies they left Iceland, not in one of those classic dragonships with brightly painted shields overlapping the rail but in a broad-beamed wallowing merchant ship called a knarr. They sailed west "until the land sank into the sea." Then, we are told, "the fair wind dropped, and there was a north wind and fog, and they did not know where they were going. Day after day passed like this. Then the sun came out again, and they were able to get their bearings from the sky."

Presently they saw land. They asked each other if this could be Greenland. Bjarni did not think it was, but they sailed closer. The country was low, with many trees and small hills.

They turned away and sailed north.

Two days later they sighted another coast. The crew asked if this might be Greenland. Bjarni did not think it was, for there were said to be huge glaciers in that country while this was flat and heavily forested. The crew wanted to put ashore because they needed water, but he refused.

They continued sailing north.

After several more days they sighted land for a third time. They saw mountains and glaciers, but again Bjarni refused to stop, saying the country had an inhospitable look. So, once more: ". . . they turned their prow from the land and held out to sea with the same following wind."

The wind freshened. They sailed four days and nights until they saw yet another coast.

"From what I have been told," said Bjarni, "this most resembles Greenland. Here we will go ashore."

They put in that evening at a cape and found a boat nearby. Bjarni's father, Herjolf Bardsson, was living on this cape, which has been known ever since as Herjolfsnes.

"The next thing that happened," says the narrator of "The Greenlanders' Saga," "was that Bjarni Herjolfsson came from Greenland to see Earl Eirik"—which refers not to Eirik the Red but to Earl Eirik Hakonarsson who ruled Norway from A.D. 1000 to 1014. During this visit Bjarni described the lands he had seen when he was blown off course fifteen years earlier and people at the court rebuked him for his lack of curiosity, telling him that he should have gone ashore.

The following summer he was back in Greenland. His embarrassment at court must have been the subject of considerable gossip; but more important, the sagas tell us that "there was now great talk of discovering new countries." Eirik the Red's son, Leif, then bought Bjarni's ship and signed up a crew of thirty-five.

Old Eirik was asked to lead this voyage of exploration, just as he had led the colonists from Iceland to Greenland. He consented reluctantly, observing that he was not able to stand bad weather as he used to. But on the day they were to embark, while they were riding horseback to the ship, he was thrown and injured his foot.

"It is not fated that I shall discover more lands than Greenland, on which I live," he said. "We can go no further together."

Eirik Raude then returned to his farm, called Brattahlid, or Steep Slope, while Leif and the crew went
aboard. Among the crew was a southerner, probably a
German, named Tyrkir, who is identified in some accounts
as Leif's godfather.

They followed Bjarni's route backward, coming first to
the inhospitable country. "They made for land, lowered
the boat and rowed ashore; but they saw no grass there.
The uplands were covered with glaciers, and from the
glaciers to the shore it was like one great slab of rock."
Leif called this barren plateau Helluland. The leading
candidates for Helluland seem to be Baffin Island and
Newfoundland.

Next they came to the forest land, which they named
Markland. It sounds agreeable, "with white sandy beaches
shelving gently toward the sea," yet according to the sagas
Leif and his men stayed only a short time before hurrying
back to their ship as fast as they could. The sagas do not
explain why they were anxious to leave. Nor do we know
exactly where they were, though it must have been either
Labrador or Nova Scotia.

Two days later they reached an island and went ashore.
The weather was fine. They saw dew on the grass, which
they tasted, "and they thought that never had they tasted
anything as sweet." After this they returned to the ship
and entered the sound which lay between the island and a
cape projecting northward from the mainland.

They sailed westward past this cape. The water was
very shallow. At low tide the ship touched bottom, "and it
was a long way from the ship to the sea. But they were so
impatient to get to land that they did not want to wait for
the tide to rise under their ship but ran ashore at a place
where a river flowed out of a lake."

As soon as the tide refloated their ship they brought it

up into the lake. Here they anchored, unloaded some sacks of hide, and built stone-and-turf huts. Later, after deciding to winter at this place, they built houses. The lake and river were full of huge salmon and they thought cattle would be able to survive without fodder. There was no frost and the grass scarcely withered.

When the house-building had been completed Leif divided his men. Each day one group went out to explore the countryside, with orders that they should not become separated and that they return by dusk. At first things went well, but one evening Tyrkir was missing. Leif was very much disturbed because Tyrkir had been one of his father's companions for a long time.

"Leif spoke harsh words. . . ."

Twelve men set out to find Tyrkir. They had not gone far when he showed up. He was obviously in a good mood, rolling his eyes and laughing and talking in German so that nobody understood what he was saying. "The Greenlanders' Saga" describes him as being small, dark, and seedy in appearance, with a sloping forehead and an unsteady eye, but good at all kinds of odd jobs.

"Why are you so late, foster-father?" asked Leif. "And why did you leave your comrades?"

Tyrkir continued laughing, grimacing, and talking in German. Finally he spoke in Norse. "I have some news for you," he said. "I have found vines with grapes."

"Is that true, foster-father?" Leif asked.

"Of course it's true," said Tyrkir, "because where I was born there are plenty of vines and grapes."

Next morning Leif instructed his men to pick grapes and cut vines and to begin felling trees so that when they returned to Greenland they would have a good cargo. And when they embarked in the spring their ship carried a load of grapes, vines, and timber. Leif named the place Vinland.

All right, where was this lush country?

The sagas give many clues, several quite pointed, others too general to be of much help. That sweet-tasting dew, for instance, has been identified by some investigators as the sweet excreta of certain plant lice and flies—yet this could be found any number of places. Others who have studied the problem say it might have been only the dew which normally collects overnight, and the men had been aboard ship so long that they were eager for a taste of fresh water. Then there's a third possibility: the incident might be a fabrication which should be disregarded.

As for grapes, about thirty varieties grow wild in the northeastern United States and Nova Scotia. Along the coast at the present time they grow no farther north than Massachusetts, which would seem to establish Vinland's northern limit. However, in Leif's day the climate might have been different, which would extend that boundary. In the 1530s, for example, Jacques Cartier saw grapevines on both banks of the Saint Lawrence where none grow today. And botanists who examined pollen found in the ruins of Greenland Viking settlements have concluded that eleventh-century weather was not bad, certainly no worse than it is now, perhaps a little warmer.

The big argument about grapes, though, is not how far north they might have been growing during the Middle Ages but whether Leif's men actually found any. The quarrel hangs like a sword over the syllable *vin* or *vín*. In the original manuscript—long lost—did that syllable, or did it not, have a diacritical mark? Was Leif talking about Vinland or Vínland? Because the minuscule notation makes quite a difference. Without the mark it means meadow, grassy land, pastureland; with the mark it means wine country, grapevine country. In other words, how far north or south the Vikings camped might depend on whether Leif spoke of grass or of grapes. The sagas clearly

suggest that Tyrkir was uncommonly exhilarated, and nobody ever has been known to get drunk on crushed grass,
which argues that he was loitering amidst the vín, not the
vin. But things aren't that simple. Perhaps Tyrkir stum-
bled upon wild berries, not grapes, and the Vikings sailed
home to Greenland with a boatload of berries.

Now about the salmon, a cold-water fish. Today it
swims no farther south than New York, which ought to
establish a southern boundary for Vinland, thus eliminat-
ing Virginia and North Carolina where some students of
the problem have placed it. And a warmer ocean 1,000
years ago would have kept the salmon in still higher latitudes, which would eliminate New York.

On the other hand, because of a remark in the sagas
concerning the winter solstice, a German scholar located
the settlement between 27° and 31°—in Florida. A Norwegian, interpreting this same remark differently, concluded that Vinland must have been on Chesapeake Bay.

A Yankee partisan proved that Leif wintered at Ply-
mouth. He determined not only the exact route from
Greenland but the time of year Leif arrived, even the
time of day. His argument covers many pages and could
hardly be more persuasive. That is, until you listen to
somebody else.

A Harvard professor fixed the site in his own neighborhood, less than a mile from campus.

So the squabble persists, point and counterpoint.

In any event, Leif had not been home very long when
one of his brothers, Thorvald, volunteered to inspect Vinland more closely.

"Well, brother," said Leif to Thorvald, "use my ship, if
you like."

Thorvald picked thirty men and reached the encampment with no trouble. They spent that winter comfortably

and the following summer they explored the western coast. They saw no animals or humans, but they did come across a small wooden structure—perhaps the frame of a tepee.

The next summer while exploring the east coast they saw three unusual humps or mounds on the beach, which turned out to be hide-covered boats with three "skraelings" asleep under each boat. Skraeling cannot be precisely translated, but it refers to the native inhabitants of Greenland and North America and is contemptuous, meaning barbarian or screamer or wretch. Whether these skraelings were Eskimos or Indians is not known. Some anthropologists believe they were the now extinct Beothuk or Micmac Indians. The hide-covered boats, however, might have been Eskimo umiaks which are larger than kayaks. Whatever they were, Thorvald's men crept up to these boats and killed eight skraelings. One escaped.

Then, we are told, after returning to the headland from which they had looked down on these boats, the Vikings became drowsy. This seems curious, but the saga does not explain. Next "they were aroused by a voice shouting: 'Awake, Thorvald! Awake with all your men! Hurry to the ship and leave quickly if you would save your lives!' Then came a great fleet of skin-boats to attack them."

During this fight Thorvald was hit by a freak shot: an arrow struck him in the armpit. "I think it will be the death of me," he said.

He asked to be carried to a place not far away where he had planned to build a house. There he was buried, with a cross at his head and another at his feet, so the place was named Krossanes.

Thorvald's men remained at Leif's camp that winter, loading their ship with vines and grapes. In the spring they sailed back to Greenland.

Another of Leif's brothers, Thorstein, offered to bring home Thorvald's body. He outfitted the same ship and took along his wife, Gudrid. The voyage was a disaster. They got lost, either because of storms or fog, and ended up not in Vinland but at a small Viking settlement on the upper coast of Greenland. They were obliged to spend the winter there, and Thorstein died of plague.

Shortly after his death, while Gudrid was seated near the bench on which his body was lying, Thorstein sat up and began to speak. Translations vary in detail, but essentially this is what Thorstein said:

"I wish to tell Gudrid her fate, that she may endure my death more easily, for I am comfortable in this place. Gudrid, listen. You are to be married to an Icelander and will live with him a long time. Many descendants will you have—stalwart, fair, sweet, and good. From Greenland you will go to Norway, thence to Iceland where you will make your home. In Iceland you will live many years with your husband, but you shall outlive him. After his death you will travel south but then return to Iceland where a church will be erected. In this church you will take the vows of a nun and this is where you will die."

Thorstein then lay down again on the bench. Later his body was dressed and carried to the ship. Another crew was formed because many of his men also had died of plague, and with Gudrid aboard they returned to the main settlement.

That summer the Icelander arrived. He was a merchant named Thorfinn Karlsefni of noble lineage: we read on his family register such aristocratic names as Thorvald Backbone, Thord Horsehead, and Ragnar Shaggypants. As prophesied, he fell in love with Gudrid and asked permission to marry her. Eirik consented. Or perhaps old Eirik was now dead and his son Leif gave permission. In either case, we know there was great joy at Brattahlid, with gaming, the telling of sagas, and other diversions.

"There was also much talk of Vinland voyages. . . ."

Karlsefni, urged by Gudrid, organized a large expedition consisting of sixty men, five women including Gudrid herself, and various kinds of livestock. It appears that they hoped to establish a permanent colony.

They settled in Leif's houses and the skraelings began to come around, peacefully. But one of the skraelings tried to steal a knife or an ax, he was killed by a Viking, and another battle took place.

At this point "The Greenlanders' Saga" and "Eirik's Saga" do not agree. The first says nothing about Leif's terrible half sister Freydis being a member of the Karlsefni expedition; yet according to "Eirik's Saga" she was present, and during this fight with the skraelings she did something so odd that it could hardly have been invented.

First, though, the ballistic missile must be mentioned. The skraelings hurled some objects at the Vikings. These could have been Eskimo harpoons tied to bladders which served as floats, or they may have been stones sewn up in leather cases and launched from the poles—which would suggest Indians. Centuries ago the Algonquins are said to have flung leather-bound stones at their enemies, with a hideous face painted on each bundle. Yet there is no reference to Indian arrows. Whatever they were, these blue-black flying objects terrified the Vikings who turned and ran.

Freydis then appeared. As the skraelings rushed toward her she picked up the sword of a dead Viking, pulled out her breasts, and whetted the blade on them. Some translators say she slapped the sword against her breasts, or made as if to cut them off. Anyway, this spectacle frightened the savages worse than the ballista had frightened the Vikings: "They were aghast and fled to the boats. . . ."

Karlsefni's party spent one more winter in the New

World. They liked it and wanted to remain but anticipated further trouble with the natives; so when spring came they returned to Greenland bringing a load of timber, grapes, and furs. With them was a new passenger—Gudrid's baby son, Snorre, born in America almost six centuries before Virginia Dare.

It is said that Karlsefni, his wife Gudrid, and their son, Snorre, eventually went to Iceland where Karlsefni bought a farm at Glaumby. After his death Gudrid and her son managed the farm until Snorre got married. Then Gudrid made a pilgrimage to Rome, became a nun, and lived the rest of her life in accordance with the prophecy.

Next we hear of Helgi and Finnbogi, two Icelandic brothers who may or may not have been planning a trip to Vinland when they were approached by Freydis. She proposed a joint expedition in two ships, sharing equally whatever profit they might make. Each group would consist of thirty men and a few women. The Icelanders agreed to this, so Freydis went to Leif and asked for the houses he had built on Vinland. Leif said he would not give them to her, although she might have the use of them.

The ships sailed together. Helgi and Finnbogi arrived first. Assuming the expedition was to be fully cooperative, they and their men settled in Leif's houses; but when Freydis arrived she ordered them to leave. And now the brothers learned something else about their business partner: she had brought along five extra men.

"We are no match for you in wickedness, we brothers," said Helgi. The Icelanders then moved out and built a shed for themselves some distance away.

During the winter there was more trouble. The two parties began avoiding each other.

Early one morning Freydis got up, put on her husband's cloak, and walked to the shed where the Icelanders lived.

The door was half open. She stood by the door and Finn-bogi, who was awake, saw her. He asked what she wanted.

"I want you to come outside," she said. "I want to talk to you."

Finnbogi came out of the shed and they sat down together on a log.

"How do you like things here?" she asked.

"I like this country," he said, "but I don't like the quarrel that has come between us. I see no reason for it."

"What you say is true," she answered. "I feel the same. But the reason I came to see you is that I would like to exchange ships. Your ship is larger than mine and I would like to get away from here."

"All right," he said, "if that will make you happy."

Freydis then walked home. She had not worn shoes or stockings and when she climbed into bed her cold feet awakened her husband. He asked where she had been. She had gone to visit the brothers, she told him, and offered to buy their ship, which made them so angry that they had beaten her. "But you," she said, "you wretched coward, you won't avenge our shame! Now I know just how far from Greenland I am!"

Her husband called his men and ordered them to get their weapons. They walked to the shed where the Icelanders lay asleep and tied them up. As each man was brought outside Freydis had him killed. At last there were only five women left alive and nobody wanted to kill them.

"Give me an ax," she said.

One of the men lent her an ax and Freydis slew the Icelandic women.

"After this wicked deed," the saga tells us, the Greenlanders went back to their houses, and it was clear that Freydis felt she had handled the matter very well. This is what she said to her companions: "If we get to Greenland I shall be the death of any man who reveals what took place. Our story will be that they stayed here after we left."

Early in the spring they loaded the brothers' ship with as much as it could carry and sailed to Greenland. There, after bribing everybody to ensure silence, Freydis returned to her farm. But Leif heard rumors. He seized three of her men and tortured them until they confessed. When he learned the truth he said, "I do not have the heart to punish my sister Freydis as she deserves. But I prophesy that no good will come to her descendants."

And after that, we are told, "no one thought anything but ill of her and her family."

How many other Norse adventurers and colonists reached the American continent, either on purpose or by accident, is unknown. There must have been quite a few. Among the first was a certain Bjorn Asbrandsson who vanished after leaving Iceland in the year 1000. The chronicles are not clear as to whether he was on his way to Greenland; but about twenty-five years later, according to the "Eyrbyggja Saga," a merchant named Gudleif who set out from Dublin was blown far to the west by a gale and finally anchored in a cove of some unfamiliar land. There he and his crew were captured by a group of dark-featured natives. They were released after an old white man spoke on their behalf. This man identified himself to Gudleif as Bjorn Asbrandsson. He said he had been living with the natives for a long time and had no wish to go back to Iceland.

In 1059 a Celtic or Saxon priest named Jon is said to have undertaken a missionary voyage to Vinland where he was murdered.

In 1120 or 1121 the bishop of Greenland, Eirik Gnupsson—or Upsi—"sailed in search of Vinland." Or he sailed "to visit" that country, depending on how *leitadi* is translated. Nothing more is heard of him, and presumably he did not return because three years later King Sigurd Jorsalfare—*Jorsalfare* meaning a traveler to Jerusalem—King Sigurd gave the bishopric to a cleric named Arnald.

In 1226 the leaders of Greenland's eastern settlement, Eystribyggd, which Eirik the Red had founded, became greatly disturbed by the arrival of Eskimos. They sent an expedition into Davis Strait, which separates Greenland from Canada, with instructions to find out where the Eskimos were coming from and to learn, if possible, what their intentions might be. Cairns and shelters discovered in that region prove that these men traveled through the extreme north at least to Devon Island—about as far west as Chicago.

Farther south, in the Vinland area, Norsemen were active as late as 1347, probably in the lumber trade. Says the *Flateyjarbók:* "Came a ship from Greenland that had been to Markland, eighteen men on board." With a bit more detail this same ship is reported in the *Skálholt* annals: "Also there came a ship from Greenland, smaller than the small Icelandic boats, which put in at the outer Straumfjord and had no anchor. There were seventeen men on board. They had made a voyage to Markland but were afterwards storm-driven here."

Chests found by archaeologists at Herjolfsnes are made of pine, deal, and larch. Some of this wood might have come from Norway, but the larch did not. It may have been driftwood, though this seems unlikely—not with Canada's tremendous forests just below the horizon.

Indeed, there is a possibility that the entire western settlement, or what was left of it—perhaps several hundred people—emigrated to America; because in 1350, plus

or minus a year or two or three, a cleric named Ivar Bárdarsson was chosen "to goe with Ships to the Westland, to
drive away their Enemies the Skerlengers. But hee com-
ming there, found no people neither Christian nor Heathen, but found there many Sheepe running being wilde,
of which Sheepe they took with them as many as they
could carrie, and with them returned to their Houses."

Bárdarsson saw no indication of a struggle with Eskimos, which means the people must have left voluntarily.
Eskimos may or may not have plundered the empty
houses; his report suggests that they did. Yet the presence
of livestock—not only Sheepe but goats, horses, and cattle—implies that Eskimos had not been near the place because they would have slaughtered the animals for food. If
the Vikings did emigrate they must have crossed the strait
to Canada.

A dozen theories have been offered to explain the disap-
pearance of these people; each answers certain questions
but fails to answer others.

The revolving centuries fought against them, says Gwyn
Jones. The climate grew colder, glaciers crept down. And
ahead of the ice came the skraelings. Events in Europe
also weakened the colony: an increasing preference for
English and Dutch cloth rather than Greenland woolens.
African elephant ivory instead of walrus ivory. Commerce
with Russia. In short, business. It became less profitable
for Europeans to trade with those distant colonists. The
immediate causes, though, beyond doubt, were skraeling
attacks and the encroaching ice.

Gisle Oddsson, Bishop of Iceland at about the time of
Ivar Bárdarsson's voyage, thought the colonists had emigrated: "The settlers of Greenland lapsed of their own free
will from the true faith and the Christian religion; having
abandoned all good conduct and true virtues they turned

to the people of America. Some people believe that Greenland lies very near to the westerly countries of the world."

The mystery of this deserted Christian outpost seems to have troubled King Magnus Smek, who directed Poul Knudsson to take a look at that faraway place. Knudsson sailed in 1355: "in honor of God, for the deliverance of our souls, and for those ancestors of ours who brought Christianity to Greenland. . . ."

Nine years later several of Knudsson's men returned to Norway. What news they brought—if any—concerning Vestribyggd, the western settlement, has not been preserved.

In 1379 the small "middle settlement" near Ivigtut was attacked by Eskimos who killed eighteen colonists and carried off two boys.

The last merchant ship to visit the colonies departed in 1383.

A ship bound from Norway to Iceland in 1406 was driven west by gales and made port in Eystribyggd, where it lay at anchor four years. During this time a crewman named Thorstein Olafson married a local girl, Sigrid Bjornsdatter. Their wedding was celebrated in Hvalsey church on September 16, 1408, "on the Sunday after the Exaltation of the Cross." With the newlyweds aboard, this ship sailed to Iceland in 1410, the last European vessel known to have reached either settlement.

A letter dated 1448—which might possibly be spurious—from Pope Nicholas V to the two bishops of Iceland laments the misfortunes of Greenland colonists: "Thirty years ago, from the adjacent coasts of the heathen, the barbarians came with a fleet, attacked the inhabitants of Greenland most cruelly, and so devastated the mother-country and the holy buildings with fire and sword that there remained on that island no more than nine parish churches. . . ."

A few English ships, mostly from Bristol, might have visited Eystribyggd during this century. And perhaps a joint Portuguese-Danish expedition in 1473, because there is a letter dated March 3, 1551, from the burgomaster of Kiel, one Karsten Grip, addressed to Christian III. Burgomaster Grip reports that "two admirals of Your grandfather, His Royal Majesty Christian I, Pining and Pothurst, on the instructions of His Royal Majesty the King of Portugal, etc., were sent with several ships on a voyage to the new islands and the continents in the north. . . ." But we can only surmise the state of the colonies at that time.

A letter written by Pope Alexander VI in 1492 observes that there has been no priest resident in Greenland for eighty years and the people have nothing to remind them of Christianity except one altar cloth. Alexander fears that they have lost sight of the true faith, and he comments on a Benedictine monk named Mathias who is prepared to live and work as a missionary in Greenland.

About fifty years later a German merchant ship was blown by strong winds into a Greenland fjord. Buildings were visible, so the crew went ashore. They saw a dead European lying on the frozen ground. He was dressed in sealskin and frieze—which is a coarse woolen cloth with a shaggy nap. Beside his body lay a dagger, very thin from constant whetting. Evidently this was the corpse of the last Viking in the New World. There being no one left alive to bury him, he lay on the earth rather than in it.

A resident of Bergen, Absalon Pedersson, writes in 1567 that "many of the nobility hold the deeds of estates in Greenland yet of the country and properties they know nothing. . . ."

Martin Frobisher, who landed on Greenland's west

coast in 1578, observed that some of the Eskimos used iron spearheads and bronze buttons and were able to recognize gold, which meant they had dealt with Europeans.

In 1721 a Norwegian missionary, Hans Egede, saw the ruins of a church and the crumbling walls of houses. He asked about them, and described the Christian services, but the Eskimos indicated that they had never heard of such a religion, nor could they tell him anything about the people who built these houses. Despite this rather convincing testimony, as well as the ruins, Egede maintained that Eystribyggd still flourished: "I believe beyond a doubt that it survives and is inhabited by people of pure Norwegian Extraction, which by God's help in due Time and when Occasion offers, may be discovered. . . ."

Hans Egede had a son named Niels who grew up in Greenland and recorded in his diary a curious legend. An Eskimo shaman who camped among the ruins of the lower settlement, "south by the hot baths," told him that in the old days Eskimos and Norwegians had lived together until they were attacked by men who came from the southwest in ships. At first there had been three ships. Then more ships arrived, with much killing and plundering. When these ships came back again the Eskimos fled, taking several Norwegian women and children with them up the fjord. Months later the Eskimos returned, but saw that the houses had been burned and everything taken away. Then they left the settlement forever and the Norwegian women married into the tribe.

The identity of these marauders cannot be established, but German and English pirates often raided Iceland during the fifteenth century. Perhaps they curled westward looking for fresh victims and delivered the coup de grace to a moribund culture.

In our century, following the Great War that would end

all wars, the Danish government dispatched some archaeologists to Greenland. They located the remnants of buildings and of farms—the fields now smothered by weeds and horsehair oats—and many graves.

In the northeast chapel of Gardar cathedral, which was the episcopal seat of Eystribyggd, lay the skeleton of a sturdy middle-aged man who still wore his shoes, though not much else. For some inexplicable reason part of his right foot was gone. He held a crozier made of ash, with an iron ferrule, the upper part carved from a walrus tusk by his wife, Margret, and on the fourth finger of his right hand he wore a bishop's gold ring. This was Jon Smyrill, or Sparrowhawk, who died in 1209.

The grave of a woman named Gudveig was empty, except for a rune rod which served as a proxy. She had died at sea and was buried like a sailor, sewn into sackcloth, a stone at her feet for ballast. A huge stone weighing more than a ton had been placed above the empty grave, either to guard her soul or to keep it from walking abroad.

Ozuur Asbjarnarson died on some island during winter and was buried in unhallowed ground with a wooden stake planted over his chest. Eventually a priest would arrive; then the stake could be withdrawn and consecrated water poured into the hole. That's all we know about Ozuur Asbjarnarson. It seems hardly enough.

The graves of quite a few children were located. Most of them had been buried with their toys.

Herjolfsnes cemetery yielded what was left of fifty-eight adults arranged in neat rows with their heads to the west. When time came for them to sit up on Resurrection Day they would face the rising sun. Each skeleton held a cross with a runic inscription:

GOD THE ALMIGHTY PROTECT GUDLEIF.

THORLEIF MADE THIS CROSS IN PRAISE AND WORSHIP OF GOD ALMIGHTY.

And so forth.

These Herjolfsnes colonists were fashionably dressed in accordance with European styles of the late Middle Ages, although in homespun wool rather than dyed silk or Italian velvet. From this rough material they had cut handsome cloaks and those tall Burgundian caps pictured by Memling, Christus, and other Flemish artists. They had copied the hood with a long tail, called a liripipe—de rigueur for modish gentlemen—which we recognize from descriptions by Dante and Petrarch. And they had imitated the cotte hardie, a man's tight short jacket which fully exposed his legs, except that the Greenland cotte hardie was less revealing. The garment as Europeans wore it must have seemed too bold.

One thing about these cloaked and hooded skeletons is unforgettable: their size. They look like children pretending to be adults. The tallest woman measured just four feet, nine inches. The men were not much bigger.

Half of these people died before the age of thirty, and all of them had been feeble—their bodies deformed. This was not true of the early Greenlanders, Eirik's colonists, nor of their first descendants whose bones indicated that they were healthy enough. But it appears that toward the end, about the time Eystribyggd was raided and plundered, the colonists were suffering from tuberculosis, malnutrition, and rickets.

So it may be argued that the Viking impetus failed. Nothing was born of these people, nothing developed from them.

But that violent westward surge, foaming against the littoral of the New World, has not yet receded from the imagination because even today, a thousand years after Bjarni Herjolfsson was blown off course, we wonder just how far west the Vikings traveled.

This brings up the Kensington runestone, a memorial

tablet approximately the size of a tombstone. Medieval Scandinavian characters on its face tell a grim story:

> [WE ARE] 8 GOTHS AND 22 NORWEGIANS ON
>   EXPLORATION JOURNEY FROM
>   VINELAND THROUGHOUT THE WEST. WE
> HAD CAMP BESIDE 2 SKERRIES ONE
> DAY'S JOURNEY NORTH OF THIS STONE.
> WE WERE OUT FISHING ONE DAY. AFTER
> WE CAME HOME, FOUND 10 MEN RED
> WITH BLOOD AND DEAD. AV[E] M[ARIA]
>   DELIVER [US] FROM EVIL!
>
> HAVE 10 MEN BY THE SEA TO LOOK
> AFTER OUR SHIP, 14 DAYS' JOURNEY
> FROM THIS ISLAND. YEAR 1362.

On July 20, 1909, a Minnesota farmer filed this deposition with the local notary public:

I, Olof Ohman, of the town of Solem, Douglas County, Minnesota, being duly sworn . . . In the month of August, 1898, while accompanied by my son, Edward, I was engaged in grubbing upon a timbered elevation, surrounded by marshes, in the south-east corner of my land, about 500 feet west of my neighbor's, Nils Flaten's, house, and in the full view thereof. Upon removing an asp, measuring about 10 inches in diameter at its base, I discovered a flat stone inscribed with characters, to me unintelligible. The stone lay just beneath the surface of the ground in a slightly slanting position, with one corner almost protruding. The two largest roots of the tree clasped the stone in such a manner that the stone must have been there at least as long as the tree. . . . I immediately called my neighbor's, Nils Flaten's, attention to the discovery, and he came over the same afternoon and inspected the stone and the stump under which it was found.

I kept the stone in my possession for a few days; and then left it in the Bank of Kensington. . . .

Nils Flaten, who accompanied Ohman to the office of the notary, swore to his part in the discovery. This much can be verified, along with a few unimportant details.

Is it a fake, or not?

The runestone's leading advocate was Hjalmar Holand, a Norwegian-born Wisconsin cherry farmer who learned about it in 1907 while he was a student at the University of Wisconsin. He tried to buy it. He offered five dollars, but Ohman wanted ten. Holand could not afford ten. Ohman by this time had put up with a certain amount of ridicule because almost every geologist and philologist who examined the stone had concluded that the carving must be recent, and perhaps because of this he suddenly gave the stone to Holand.

For the next fifty-five years Holand tried to authenticate the grisly tale—which he himself had translated. He even took the stone to Scandinavia for examination. And there have been authorities in one field or another who agreed with him that it could not be a fraud. The American ethnographer Stirling called it one of the most significant finds ever made on American soil. A German geographer, Richard Hennig, said that the stone's authenticity was certain "and consequently the presence of Scandinavians in America a good one hundred and thirty years before Columbus can no longer be doubted." The *Preliminary Report of the Museum Committee of the Historical Society of Minnesota* pronounced it genuine. And so on. Most experts, however, look upon the Kensington stone with distaste, boredom, resignation, and contempt.

The Danish rune specialist Erik Moltke, for instance: "Even the non-specialist will observe that the text, when it is transcribed into Latin, is easy to read. That is not the language of the fourteenth century, but rather of the nineteenth. In the language of the late Middle Ages 'we had' should be written 'wi hafd hum' not 'wi hade'; 'we were' as 'wi varum' not 'wi var'. . . ." Moltke also pointed out that the carver had invented a runic *j*, and had included a modified *ö* which was not introduced into Swedish until the Reformation.

Among Olof Ohman's possessions when he died was a book with this resounding title: *Carl Rosander, Den kunskapsrike Skolmästare eller hufvudegrunderna uti de för ett borgerligt samfundsliv nödigaste vetenskaper.* It contains a chapter on the development of the Swedish language and gives, as one example, a fourteenth-century prayer ending with "fraelse [os] af illu," which is to say, "Deliver [us] from evil." In Ohman's copy the page on which this prayer occurs had been well thumbed.

Birgitta Wallace of the Carnegie Museum speaks for a majority of professionals when she says that the stone was carved by a nineteenth-century immigrant: ". . . someone with an embryonic knowledge of runes, but who lacked familiarity with medieval Scandinavian languages. The carver could have been almost any one of the early Scandinavian settlers in Minnesota, all of whom knew something about runes but who generally had no philological education." The language employed on the stone, she remarks, is a dialect which developed in the Kensington area and is still spoken by a few old-timers, though it is unknown elsewhere. Furthermore, the tool used in making the inscription was a chisel with a standard one-inch bit, a type sold in American hardware stores.

Quite a few bona fide runestones have been found in Scandinavia. They are big, blunt, ugly things that remind you of menhirs or of the weathered teeth of ancient monsters, and their crude messages are seldom dramatic, although real enough:

RAGNHILD, ULV'S SISTER, PLACED THIS STONE—AND THIS BOAT-SHAPED STONE CIRCLE—TO HER HUSBAND GUNULF, AN OUTSPOKEN MAN, SON OF NÆRVE. FEW ARE NOW BORN BETTER THAN HE.

. . . SER PLACED THIS STONE TO HIS BROTHER AS . . . AND [HE] MET HIS DEATH IN GOTLAND [?]. THOR SANCTIFY [THESE] RUNES.

SØLVE ERECTED . . . SPALKLØSE TO [HIS] FATHER SUSER [AND MADE] THIS BRIDGE [TO] HIS BROTHER TROELS. ETERNALLY SHALL THIS INSCRIPTION BE TRUE, WHICH SØLVE HAS MADE.

THORE ERECTED THIS STONE TO HIS FATHER GUNNER.

After you have contemplated the homeliness and innocence of such epitaphs you are even less apt to be persuaded by that wild Minnesota drama. Still, one wants to believe. THORE ERECTED THIS STONE TO HIS FATHER GUNNER. All right, but who cares? A fight between Vikings and Indians does more for the imagination.

Now, along with that Minnesota runestone, and no less celebrated, we have Rhode Island's Newport tower—alleged to have been built by Knudsson's party either before or after they visited the Midwest, or by some earlier Viking expedition. Or it was built by sixteenth-century Portuguese explorers. Or perhaps by the governor of Rhode Island, Benedict Arnold—not *the* Benedict Arnold—shortly before 1677, the date it first appears in historical records. Those who believe in the authenticity of the Kensington runestone almost without exception believe in the Viking origin of the tower. And, naturally, vice versa.

Here is what we know for certain: it is a cylindrical stone structure approximately twenty-five feet high, with eight arches supported by columns. The walls are about two feet thick with traces of stucco coating. Only the shell of the tower remains, the interior wooden components having disintegrated. It became a proper subject for argument in 1839 after a Danish antiquarian said he thought it was a Norse church or baptistery, and that it had been built by Vinlanders of the eleventh or twelfth century.

True believers point to architectural similarities between the tower and medieval Scandinavian structures: segmental arches, double-splayed casement windows, et cetera. They mention a unit of measurement known as the "Rhineland foot" which they say was used in the design of the tower, whereas all Colonial buildings used the English foot.

Skeptics reply that because of the tower's condition the unit of measurement cannot be determined. Besides, the Rhineland foot was still in use as late as the nineteenth century. Then, too, carefully supervised digging around the foundation has brought up such items as a gunflint and a seventeenth-century clay pipe.

"This is fourteenth-century architecture," said a European archaeologist. "There would be no question as to its age if this were in Europe."

So the dispute continues.

Excluding various knickknacks from L'Anse aux Meadows, there is only one batch of indisputably Norse objects to have surfaced on the American continent. This is the Beardmore find, which consists of a broken sword, an axhead, a horse rattle, and three scraps of iron. In the judgment of almost every authority who has studied these relics they date from the latter part of the Viking Age: the sword from the tenth century, the axhead and rattle from the eleventh. They were found, according to one report, while dynamiting on a mining claim near Beardmore, Ontario. But another report says they were retrieved from the basement of a home in Port Arthur and that they were brought to Canada about fifty years ago. Both reports are substantiated by witnesses and by circumstantial evidence. Once again, therefore, you have an option.

All in all there are perhaps 100 objects, a couple of dozen inscriptions, and at least fifty sites which purport to show that Vikings reached America. By far the most engaging souvenirs are some rusty crescent-shaped little axes from the Great Lakes region, home of the embattled Kensington runestone. Because they are too light to be weapons they have been described as ceremonial halberds. But medieval halberds did not look exactly like that. Furthermore, these specimens apparently were manufactured by the American Tobacco Company in the late nineteenth century for use as plug tobacco cutters—the business end of the hatchet being attached to a cutting board by a hinge. They were given away during an advertising campaign to promote the sale of Battle-Axe Plug and quite a few midwestern housewives probably used them to chop cabbage.

Nevertheless, Hjalmar Holand submitted one tobacco cutter and two of the halberds that he thought were medieval Norse to the department of chemical engineering at the University of Wisconsin. Professor R. A. Ragatz, chairman of the department, examined all three and wrote to Holand: "The metal [of the tobacco cutter] is a rather poor quality of gray cast iron, showing the following micro-constituents: graphite plates, ferrite, pearlite, steadite. The structure is totally different from the frames of the two genuine halberds. . . . I can state positively that the two halberds sent me last fall were not of the same origin as the tobacco cutter recently submitted."

Other disputed evidence of Viking tourists includes "mooring holes," found on Cape Cod and quite plentifully around the Minnesota lakes. These holes, about an inch in diameter and six or seven inches deep, have been drilled into boulders on the shores of past or present waterways. They are said to have been used for mooring a boat temporarily, a line from the boat being tied to an iron pin inserted in the hole. A sequence of such holes should indicate the route traveled; and it so happens that they often appear beside northern rivers and lakes that feed the Mississippi. Now, what this suggests is that Vikings may have traveled up the Saint Lawrence to the Great Lakes, or south from Hudson Bay via the Nelson River into the Wisconsin-Minnesota area. From there they could have gone south with almost no trouble, as far as they cared to float, drifting at last into the Gulf of Mexico below New Orleans. And what a dramatic voyage that would be.

Regrettably we must deal with Birgitta Wallace, archenemy of romantics: ". . . the method is unknown in Norse seamanship, medieval or modern." Ms. Wallace goes on to say that other stones with identical drillings in the vicinity of these so-called mooring holes provide a clue as to what they really are: they are blasting holes drilled by early settlers. It seems that during the latter half of the nineteenth century these settlers obtained foundation stones for their houses by blowing boulders apart. Occasionally the dynamite didn't go off, or the prospective home builder changed his mind, or for some other reason all that endured was the hole—somewhat like the smile of the Cheshire cat.

If Birgitta Wallace & Co. are correct we find ourselves

restricted to L'Anse aux Meadows, which is either a grave disappointment or an exciting discovery, depending on your outlook. The name could mean the cove or bay with grass around it, or possibly Meadows is a corruption of Medusa—for the shoals of jellyfish found there during summer. Old sailing charts call it Méduse Bay, Jellyfish Bay. It is on the northernmost tip of Newfoundland, about the latitude of London, within sight of the Canadian mainland, and near this bay are the ruins of a Norse settlement. Carbon 14 tests give a date of approximately A.D. 1000.

Not much is left. There is the ground plan of a big turf-walled house—fifty by seventy feet, with five or six rooms—and the outlines of various smaller structures including a smithy, a bathhouse, five boat sheds, a kiln, and two cooking pits.

Very little handiwork has survived, partly because there is so much acid in the soil. Almost everything made of bone or wood has disintegrated, whatever was not carried off by Eskimos, Indians, and early Newfoundland settlers. There are rusty traces that once were nails, a piece of copper with cross stripings that might have come from a belt, a whetstone, a bone needle, a bit of jasper, a stone lamp of the old Icelandic type, a steatite spindle whorl—meaning there were women in the house—and a bronze ring-headed pin. Pins of this type were used by Vikings to fasten their capes. And in the smithy was a large cracked flat-topped stone—the anvil—together with scraps of bog iron, clumps of slag, and patches of soot.

The great house burned, says Dr. Helge Ingstad, who supervised the excavation, although it is impossible to say whether this happened by accident or design.

L'Anse aux Meadows must have been an agreeable place to live. There were fields of berries and flowers, salmon in the lake, herds of caribou—many more animals and birds than there are now. The sea was alive with cod, seals, and whales, and the weather probably was mild.

Then why was Paradise abandoned? And why is there no sign of other settlements?

The answer seems to be that these people arrived too soon. Europe was not ready to support them, and with only spears, axes, knives, and swords these few colonists could not hold out against the skraelings. Whether they were killed in one overwhelming raid, whether they intermarried with the natives, or perhaps moved farther south, or at last gave up and retreated to Greenland—neither the ruins nor the old vellum manuscripts reveal.

It is certain, though, that they got this far on several occasions, and it would be exceedingly strange if they traveled no farther. Even the most conservative archaeologists admit the possibility of Viking sites on the mainland.

A lump of coal uncovered in a Greenland house strongly implies a voyage to Rhode Island. This house, which stood at the head of Ameralik fjord in the western settlement, may have belonged at one time to Thorfinn Karlsefni and his wife, Gudrid. The coal was found deep in the ruins by Danish archaeologists, and there are two curious things about it. First, there was just one lump, with nothing but wood-ash in the fireplace. Second, it is meta-anthracite, which does not occur in Greenland, nor anyplace along the east coast of North America except in Rhode Island.

And there is an eleventh-century Norse penny, probably struck between the years 1065 and 1080, during the reign of Olaf III, which turned up at an Indian site near Bar Harbor, Maine. It's possible, of course, that the penny was lost by a Colonial American coin collector. Or it might have been brought from Newfoundland by an acquisitive Indian. However, the obvious deduction seems best: eleventh-century Vikings either lived or traded in Maine.

What all of this means is that you are at liberty to follow the mooring holes of imagination as far as you care to. Through the Saint Lawrence waterway, for example, to the Great Lakes and beyond. After all, nobody can prove that a party of Norse adventurers did not reach the Mississippi and follow it to the Gulf, and from there sail west, following the downward coast.

The Mexican Indian legend of Quetzalcoatl says that a bearded white man appeared out of the east on a raft of snakes and later departed in the direction from which he had come, promising to return in 500 years. So you may imagine a Viking ship with a carved serpent head on the prow, with a fair-haired bearded Norwegian in command. And when five centuries had passed a bearded foreigner did arrive, not exactly commanding a raft of snakes, although many people swear he had a complement of snakes aboard. He was, of course, much darker than a Norwegian; and his name, Hernando Cortés, is not unfamiliar.

You will get a chilly reception from anthropologists if you attempt to relate Quetzalcoatl to a Viking, or any other such fabulous theory. But the alternative is to join the conservatives, in which case you will have to be satisfied with a spindle whorl, a bone needle, and some furnace slag.

4

Gustav's Dreadnought

King Gustavus Adolphus was of the opinion that building small ships was a waste of young trees, so when he wanted a new flagship to intimidate his enemies he commissioned a monster. The *Vasa* was 165 feet long, 40 feet wide, 180 feet from the keel to the tip of the mainmast, and weighed 1,400 tons. She carried sixty-four bronze cannons—forty-eight jutting through a double row of gunports on either side, sixteen smaller ones on the top deck—and she was decorated like an opera house. A gigantic golden lion lunged from the prow, a golden lion's head roared from every gunport, and both decks were painted bright red so that the sailors' blood would scarcely be noticed. Above this majestic spectacle floated the orange-yellow and deep indigo colors of seventeenth-century Sweden.

The captain, Söfring Hansson, should have been delighted with such a command, but there were things about the ship that he did not like. He thought the *Vasa* was too long and narrow and the superstructure uncommonly large. He reported as much to the grand admiral of the

Swedish Navy, Klas Fleming, but the admiral did not respond; or, if he did, Captain Hansson was not satisfied.

Consequently, a few weeks before the scheduled launching, Hansson invited Admiral Fleming aboard to witness a test. With the ship tied up at her mooring thirty sailors were told to run across the deck. When they did so the *Vasa* heeled "by the breadth of one plank." Hansson immediately ordered them to rush across the deck in the opposite direction. This time the ship heeled by the breadth of two planks. Hansson sent them across the deck a third time and the ship heeled still farther. At this point, according to testimony given during the court-martial, Admiral Fleming ordered the demonstration stopped.

Because the meaning of Captain Hansson's test was perfectly clear you would assume that preparations for the launching were suspended. After all, it would be insane to continue outfitting a ship for disaster.

But of course the work went right ahead.

The explanation for such a paradox is simple and it will not surprise the good student of human affairs. King Gustav had commissioned this vessel. He had selected the builder and personally had approved the plans. Gustav looked forward to the *Vasa* leading his fleet. Nobody wanted to tell him what was going to happen.

So, about three o'clock one Sunday afternoon in August of 1628, while thousands of Stockholm citizens crowded the wharves to wish her Godspeed, Captain Hansson gave orders to cast off. The *Vasa* had been loaded with 2,000 barrels of food, plenty of beer and cannonballs, 133 sailors, assorted bureaucrats and politicians, and a good many wives and children. There may also have been 300 soldiers aboard; the *Vasa* was to carry them, but perhaps they were ashore. They may have been at Älvsnabben, waiting to get on when the visitors got off.

It is said that a mild breeze was blowing across the harbor that afternoon, yet the *Vasa* listed farther than expected when the first sails were broken out. As she righted herself the chief ordnance officer, Erik Jönsson, ran below to make certain the cannons were lashed in place.

A few minutes later a gust of wind blew around the high cliffs of Söder and the *Vasa* heeled sharply. Again she righted herself, but Captain Hansson ordered the topsails cut loose.

The wind dropped. The ship moved heavily toward Beckholmen.

Then a fresh gust struck the sails and for the second time Jönsson ran below. Water was pouring through the open gunports. He gave orders to untie the cannons on the lower side and to haul them up the slanting deck, but this was impossible. Several cannons broke loose, crushing the sailors who unwisely had tried to push them.

The *Vasa* went down almost at once and came to rest nearly upright on the bottom—her mainmast angling above the surface and Sweden's banner fluttering valiantly in the sunshine. She had traveled less than a mile.

About fifty people drowned. Many more would have been lost except that the giant ship was accompanied by a fleet of pleasure boats which picked up survivors.

Captain Hansson, along with every other officer, was arrested that same afternoon. Also arrested were those involved with the construction—excluding the designer, a Dutchman named Henrik Hybertsson who had died the previous year.

On September 5 a formal inquiry opened. The official record seems to have been destroyed, though we do not know whether this was deliberate or accidental. However, copies of certain parts of it have been found so that the procedure, as well as quite a few names and details, can be

established. We know there were seventeen members of
the court including six councilors of the realm, two naval
captains, and the lord mayor of Stockholm. The president
was Lord High Admiral Carl Gyllenhielm, King Gustav's
half brother.

The court's first purpose was to determine the cause of
the disaster, then to fix the blame. Yet it becomes obvious
that while they did want to know why the ship went down
they were more anxious to learn who was responsible. The
suspects may or may not have been aware of this priority;
if so, they must have felt uncomfortable because seventeenth-century punishment was no pat on the wrist.

For instance, according to Swedish naval articles of
1644, a helmsman who ran his ship aground could be keel-
hauled—which meant being towed underwater from stem
to stern. Or he might be dragged from port to starboard by
way of the keel. The penalty for causing a fire aboard ship
was more direct: the guilty man was promptly thrown
into the flames. Less serious offences, such as whispering
during a lecture, brought fourteen days in irons. Nor does
there seem to have been much plea bargaining.

If records of the *Vasa* inquiry are accurate, the first
crew member of any importance to be narrowly questioned was the ordnance officer, Erik Jönsson. After testi-
fying that the cannons had been secured and could not
have rolled across the deck, causing the *Vasa* to capsize,
Jönsson added that he thought the ship "was heavier over
than under." It would have capsized in any event, he said.

Admiral Gyllenhielm asked why he had not discussed
this with the captain.

Jönsson replied that he was an artilleryman and pretended to be nothing else. The captain, he said, should be
better able to judge whether the ship was properly bal-
lasted.

Gyllenhielm pointed out that the ship's builder had said

that if he had been informed the ship was top-heavy he would have recommended loading her down another foot.

How could that have been done, Jönsson asked, when the gunports already lay but three feet from the surface?

Lieutenant Petter Gierdsson, who had been in charge of rigging, told the court that he, too, considered the ship top-heavy. When asked why he had kept this opinion to himself he replied that ballast was something about which he knew nothing. He did not even know what sort of ballast the *Vasa* carried. He had been concerned only with the rigging.

Jöran Matsson, sailing master, was formally charged with having paid too little attention to the ballast "and other things as his calling and office made incumbent upon him, whereby disaster had befallen His Majesty's ship."

Matsson answered that he had stowed as much ballast as possible. Furthermore, he said, he personally had supervised this work. He had gone down into the bilge with a light to inspect the loading. He felt that he had done whatever was incumbent upon him.

Did he notice that the ship was top-heavy?

Matsson then revealed what everybody in Stockholm except the high officers of the court must have known—that while the *Vasa* was still at her mooring Captain Hansson, in the presence of Admiral Fleming, had ordered a capsizing test. Matsson then repeated a short discussion between himself and the admiral in which the admiral said that the ship rode too low in the water because of so much ballast. To this criticism Matsson had replied: "God grant that she'll stay on an even keel." And to this Admiral Fleming replied: "The builder has built ships before. You need not worry about it."

After questioning several other people the court summoned the builder, Hein Jacobsson. He had not begun the work, but he had completed it after the death of Henrik

Hybertsson. He was asked why he had made the *Vasa* so narrow. He answered that he had not laid the keel, he had only finished what already was begun. Furthermore, King Gustav had approved the plans. There were no blueprints in the seventeenth century, merely a table known as a "sert" which listed the principal dimensions and which was regarded also as a contract to build. Hybertsson had drawn this sert, said Jacobsson, in accordance with the king's wishes.

Arent Hybertsson de Groot, the original builder's brother, was questioned. Why, he was asked, did the *Vasa* have such a large superstructure?

His Majesty had approved it, said de Groot. And all who saw or inspected the ship had agreed that she was irreproachably built.

If that is true, asked the court, why did she capsize?

"God must know," de Groot answered. "His Majesty the King was told by me how long and how broad the ship was, and His Majesty was pleased to approve and wished to have it so."

The court probed this delicate situation. Although the king had approved the sert, should not the builder in good conscience have informed His Majesty as to the correct dimensions?

Neither Jacobsson nor de Groot would argue. Both of them replied: "The King wished it so."

Too many footsteps led toward Gustav's palace. The inquiry ended without establishing a cause and without finding anyone responsible—as far as we know.

If that actually is how the investigation concluded, it's hard to believe. Could everybody be innocent? Fifty people were drowned, either through incompetence or negligence, therefore somebody must be guilty. Yet whom would you convict?

The ordnance officer? Beyond doubt the cannons were

tied down. Even if they were not, they couldn't have been the cause.

The sailing master? Unquestionably he checked the ballast. Furthermore, he had spoken to Admiral Fleming about the ship's instability.

The builder? He didn't plan the *Vasa*, he only completed it.

The designer, Henrik Hybertsson?—because it was he who drew the sert and laid the keel. Would you accuse and convict a dead man?

Or perhaps Captain Hansson? He, more than anyone else, had been worried. He had demonstrated very clearly to Admiral Fleming what might happen.

Would you charge Admiral Fleming? He had no part in constructing the ship, nor in the sailing, though he could have prevented the launching. That is, he might have suggested this to his superior, Lord High Admiral Gyllenhielm.

Did Fleming in fact suggest it? We don't know. Yet even if the records were complete they would not likely settle the question. Powerful men seldom expose themselves, as we have learned these past few years. Their fortunes depend too closely on the fortunes of their associates. That could be why Fleming was not charged with negligence.

Let us suppose he did urge his superior to cancel the launching and Gyllenhielm refused. Would you then charge the presiding officer of the investigative court? How many men in Gyllenhielm's position would take such a risk?—because surely it would earn the king's wrath. Gustav himself had approved the ship. He was most anxious for the *Vasa* to be launched.

Well then, the king. Gustav himself must be at fault. But who would be foolish enough to accuse the king?

What a shame the records are incomplete. How many scenes from this eerily familiar drama were lost? Did the court choose a scapegoat? Perhaps a sailor was flogged to death.

Alas, without the full account we can only speculate, and the vaporous conclusion remains not quite believable—until we reflect that, given a change of centuries and circumstance, we might be reading yesterday's newspaper. Ask yourself what punishment was administered for the crime at My Lai. Consider what happened. More than 100 civilians were shot by American soldiers: a fact as obvious as Old Glory. Yet the American government, in view of an expectant nation and most of the world, could not find anybody guilty. Years after the massacre one lieutenant was restricted to his barracks for a while, that was all. One lieutenant could not go dancing.

And why was nobody guilty? Because everybody was following orders. The king wished it so.

In other words, nothing changes. As the French aphorism tactfully reminds us: "Plus ça change, plus c'est la même chose."

Well, even before the inquiry opened, almost before the *Vasa* touched bottom, scavengers were descending on Stockholm: a Dutch shipwright, a Scottish baron, a "mechanicus" from Riga, somebody named "Classon," "a man from Lübeck," and various others.

First to obtain permission from the privy council was an Englishman, Ian Bulmer, who started to work less than three days after the catastrophe. He strung ropes from the *Vasa*'s masts to shore, hitched up teams of horses, and managed to pull the ship into a vertical position. What he planned to do next is not known, but the scheme failed and he either quit or was replaced.

For a while Admiral Fleming took charge. In July of

1629 he notified King Gustav: "As far as *Vasa* is concerned, we have been working with all industry, trying to raise her, but until now we have accomplished little . . . I have again fixed seventeen stout hawsers and chains with which, this week, if weather permits, we shall try to see what can be done. It is a heavier weight down there than I could have supposed."

Some time after that the Scottish baron, Alexander Forbes, obtained the rights to all salvage operations in Swedish waters for a period of twelve years, though he knew nothing about marine salvage. When he was unable to raise the *Vasa* he leased the rights to a syndicate that included a Swedish colonel named Hans Albrekt von Treileben. Hans must have been a clever fellow; not only did he jiggle Baron Forbes out of the picture, he managed to get control of the salvage rights and then he went after the prize with a diving bell.

This recent invention, which resembled a church bell, was about four feet high and made of lead. The diver wore gloves, two pairs of leather boots, leather pants, a leather jacket lashed around his body to make it waterproof, and a wool cap. He stood on a platform slung beneath the bell and as he descended the water came up to his chest, leaving a pocket of compressed air at the top. He had a pair of pincers, a hooked pole, and some rope.

It seems impossible that a man with these elementary tools, inside a lead bell in frigid muddy water almost up to his neck, could accomplish much; yet the syndicate divers tore apart the *Vasa*'s superstructure and brought up about fifty cannons, most of which were sold abroad. Von Treileben then lost interest and began making plans for a voyage to the West Indies where he hoped to pick the bones of a Spanish galleon.

A man named Liverton, or Liberton, arrived in 1683

with a "special invention." After being granted a license
he recovered one cannon, which he tried unsuccessfully to
sell to the Swedish government. That seems to have been
the last salvage attempt.

It was now fifty-five years since Gustav's monster went
down. The tip of the mast had rotted away, or had been
sawed off, so that nothing broke the surface. The *Vasa* was
a hulk sinking imperceptibly deeper into the mud. And to
the surprise of elderly citizens there were adults who
never had heard of the famous ship.

How could it be forgotten? If you consider her size and
prestige and splendor, as well as that spectacular maiden
voyage—to say nothing of the evasive inconclusive court-
martial which must have been talked about for many
years—how could people forget the *Vasa*?

But of course it's naïve to think like that. A nation is not
anxious to remember its tragic miscalculations. Germany
has been unable to forget Hitler, yet you can be sure that
today's German children do not think of him as their
grandparents do, and by the long measuring rod of history
the Nazi war has just ended. America cannot forget Viet-
nam, but be patient. Several centuries from now—unless
our omniscient Pentagon does something cataclysmically
stupid—you should be able to read American history without once encountering that painful word.

So, as debris stopped floating to the surface and mud
built up against the hulk, and those who knew about
the calamity died, the *Vasa* disappeared. Until at last
there came a pleasant Sunday afternoon when the
wharves were crowded with Stockholm citizens, none of
whom could have told you anything at all about King
Gustav's benighted flagship.

In 1920 a Swedish historian was searching the archives
for information about another seventeenth-century ship—

the *Riksnyckeln,* which had sailed into a cliff one dark September night—when he came across the minutes of the *Vasa* court-martial and a reference to Treileben's diving bell. Being an historian he naturally wrote a paper about it, and a boy named Anders Franzén heard about the *Vasa* because his father happened to read what the historian had written.

Now, the Franzéns usually vacationed on the island of Dalarö and there Anders saw a wooden gun carriage salvaged from the warship *Riksäpplet* which foundered in 1676. Although the gun carriage had been submerged more than two centuries the wood was still solid. This fact did not mean anything to him until 1939 when he took a boat trip with his father through the Göta Canal on Sweden's west coast. There he saw the skeleton of another old ship, but its wood was spongy—eaten by the insatiable shipworm, *Teredo navalis.*

Given two long-submerged pieces of wood, one solid and one soft, most of us would say how curious and move on to something livelier. Young Franzén, however, did not let go. He thought there must be a reason for the discrepancy. The reason turned out to be *Teredo navalis,* which likes the taste of salt water. The Baltic around Stockholm has a salinity of 0.7 percent at most. *Teredo navalis* requires a minimum of 0.9 percent.

Again, after noting this tedious fact, most of us would move along. Not so young Franzén.

The Second World War interrupted his plans, but with that out of the way he began to get organized. He listed fifty ships known to have gone down in the vicinity of Stockholm. From this list he chose twelve: *Sastervik, Resande Man, Vasa, Mars, Schwan of Lübeck, Riksäpplet, Kronan* . . .

He started with the *Riksäpplet* because he knew approximately where to look, and because the ship had foundered in shallow water. He found it without much trouble, but he was too late. Very little remained. For 200 years the hulk had been crushed by drifting ice and waves. However, the few planks that he brought up were as solid as the gun carriage.

Franzén decided to hunt for the *Vasa*. Other ships might be easier to locate but this one sounded important.

He talked to Professor Nils Ahnlund, the historian, and after having learned to read seventeenth-century script he spent as much time as possible—by now he was a petroleum engineer—searching the naval archives. At last he knew the names of the men who had built the ship and those who had sailed it, and he knew quite a lot about the salvage attempts. But what he needed most, which he could not find, was a precise reference to the location of the ship. The *Vasa*, if it still existed, lay somewhere in Stockholm Ström "toward Lustholmen, Blochusudden, near Danuiken."

By 1953, having read enough old documents to fill a closet, he was ready. This meant cruising back and forth across an expanse of Stockholm harbor in a motorboat, week after week, sweeping the bottom with wire drags and grapnels. In plain view of anybody who cared to watch he dredged up a great many lost, stolen, or undesirable artifacts: automobile tires, rusty bicycles, stoves, bedsteads, tangled fishing line, Christmas trees, goggles, boots, dead cats, chains, bottles—jetsam of the city.

This is not a job for a man sensitive to ridicule, especially when it becomes known that the man in the motorboat is hunting for a seventeenth-century battleship.

That winter he read another stack of musty documents, and he found an eighteenth-century map on which a cross had been drawn near Stadsgårdskajen. The cross allegedly marked the position of the *Vasa*, so Franzén spent the following summer cleaning that part of the harbor bottom.

Came winter, back to the library.

Summer, sweeping the harbor.

By this time Stockholm's authentic fishermen must have stopped laughing and merely tapped their heads while Franzén reeled in his latest catch.

During the winter of 1956, once again in the archives sifting flaky old records, he came upon a letter from the Swedish parliament addressed to King Gustav, dated August 12, 1628. Gustav had been leading an army through Poland when the *Vasa* was launched. This letter was parliament's report to the sovereign:

"And on that fateful Sunday, which was the tenth of this month, the *Vasa* set sail. But it happened that she got no further than Beckholmsudden, where she entirely fell on her side and sank to the bottom with cannon and all else, and lies in eighteen fathoms. . . ."

Beckholmsudden was doubly significant because while hauling up rubbish in that area Franzén had encountered a long muddy obstruction. Government engineers had told him it was rock blasted out of the island when a dry dock was built, so he had not investigated the strange hump. Now he went back to it, equipped with an instrument he had devised—a steel cylinder with a hollow punch in the front end. He threw this instrument overboard, waited until it struck bottom, and reeled it up. Inside the cylinder he found a plug of old black close-grained oak.

He dropped the cylinder at intervals along the length of the hump. Each time it brought back a plug of oak. So there could be no doubt that a wooden ship of *Vasa*'s dimensions lay on the bottom, very close to the navy diving school.

Franzén did not attempt to claim the ship for himself. He went to the navy, displayed his oak samples, told them what he suspected was there, and asked them to send a man down.

It is easy to guess what would have happened under these circumstances in the United States. After making an appointment and waiting in an air-conditioned lounge the applicant would have been ushered into the office of a lieutenant who would have listened with somnolent courtesy, looked at the plugs, and thanked the visitor for bringing this matter to his attention. The lieutenant might then dictate a brief report which, in due course, would be forwarded to the executive officer of the base, who might conceivably mention it to the commanding officer; and if the commandant happened to be feeling adventurous he might instruct his executive officer to forward a copy to Washington where it would have dried and curled until it resembled the Dead Sea Scrolls.

The Swedes, after listening to Franzén's story, dispatched their most experienced diver.

Chief Diver Per Edvin Fälting went down and reported that he had landed in mud up to his chest. He could not see anything.

Franzén suggested trying another area.

Just then Fälting said that he had felt what might be a wooden wall. It was a big wall, he said, possibly the side of a ship. Fälting then climbed partway up and discovered a square hole—almost certainly a gunport. Higher on the wall he felt another square hole, which meant that he was clinging to the *Vasa* because no other ship with a double row of gunports had been lost in Stockholm harbor.

Everybody got excited. Here was a relic of the days when Sweden had been a formidable power, when every

nation in Europe listened apprehensively to King Gustavus Adolphus.

A television camera dipped into the water to prove to
the Swedes that what they had been told was there actually was there. And indeed it was. The camera relayed a
blurred, sinister image of the giant warship: upright,
sealed to the waterline in hard clay. The stubs of her masts
thrust violently toward the surface. In the muck that
covered her decks lay the tangled chains and irons of seventeenth-century scavengers.

Millions of kronor later the *Vasa* had been pried from
the mud, lifted a few feet by two gigantic pontoons, and
very cautiously towed like an implausible submarine to
nearby Castle Island where, in shallow water, the deposit
of centuries was scraped off.

And what came to the surface, dragged from the grasp
of The Old One—Den Gamle—was at times unexpected
and beautiful and wondrous: gilded carvings of cherubs,
musicians, caryatids, mermaids, tritons, knights, dragons,
heraldic devices, a bird with an eel in its beak, a man in a
rippling cloak, Hercules with the hellhound Cerberus
chained at his feet, the god Nereus, King David playing a lyre.

But more often what came up was useful and ordinary
and pathetic: mugs, clay pipes, a pocket sundial, a cock-
aded felt hat, ramrods, axes, smashed beer kegs, tankards,
leather boots, pottery, wood bowls, casks of butter, carpenters' tools, muskets, ladles, a slipper, a bronze candlestick, one blue Dutch picture plate showing a bird on a
rock, an apothecary's kit, a gold signet ring from which
the seal was missing, a seaman's ditty box, another little
box holding a lock of hair. Many such personal items Den
Gamle released, after being urged by the suction hose.

On the deck beside Captain Hansson's dining table,

among shards of crockery that must have fallen when the *Vasa* heeled, lay a tightly stoppered flask containing some dense, dark liquid. When Eisenhower visited Sweden in 1962 he was offered a taste. Ike, not a reckless man, observed and sniffed Captain Hansson's schnapps but declined a drink.

And the great lion figurehead—carved from limewood, weighing two tons, springing toward the enemy—this mighty sculpture was raised from the bottom.

Den Gamle also permitted a number of skeletons to be taken from his ship, most of them still attached to their clothing, and scientists learned that there had been at least two ethnic types aboard. The skulls of one man and one woman were short, with conspicuous cheekbones, suggesting that they were Finnish. The other skulls were typically Nordic. One skull held the residue of a brain.

Among the crew members there had been a man in his late twenties or perhaps thirty, judging by the bones. A scientist who worked on the project had this to say about him: "He was dressed in a knit vest of thick wool and knit wool trousers which showed folds above the hips and were apparently fastened below the knees. Over the vest he wore a long-sleeved jacket with pleated coattails. Under the vest he wore a linen shirt. A pair of sandals and sewn linen stockings completed his dress. A sheath and a knife with a bone handle, as well as a leather money bag, were fastened to his belt. A few coins were in his trousers pockets. Altogether he had about twenty öre in copper money."

In 1628 you could buy a chicken for twenty öre. One chicken and maybe a drink of rum. That was what the sailor had in his pocket when the *Vasa* capsized—enough to buy a chicken. A swallow of rum, perhaps, with a chicken for lunch, or a moment in the arms of a pretty girl.

What else is there to say? Given a description of his clothes, given those coppers in his pocket, we could just about summarize a sailor's life to the hour of his death. And we know when that occurred: August 10, 1628, not long after three in the afternoon, while King Gustavus Adolphus marched fearlessly through Poland.

5

The White Lantern

In the seventh century, according to Polynesian tradition, a flotilla of canoes under the leadership of Ui-te-Rangiora sailed to a place where the cold was beyond understanding, where the sea was covered with white powder and great white rocks met the sky. Such a legend might have been invented, but probably it was not; it sounds like a report of something actually seen—just as we know, without a twig for evidence, that some Kiowa Indians who claimed to have visited a land where the trees were filled with little men must have traveled to Mexico.

After Ui-te-Rangiora's colossal adventure nobody sailed that far south for the next millennium, which is not surprising when you realize how inhospitable the place is. Sir Douglas Mawson on the coast of Wilkes Land during the early part of this century recorded an average wind velocity for a period of twenty-four hours—average, mind you—of 90 miles an hour. Gusts reached 200 miles an hour. A violent eddy picked up a tractor as though it were an umbrella and tossed it 50 yards. Mawson and his companions lived in a hut submerged in snow, which caused the atmosphere to become so electrically charged that their fingertips glowed blue with St. Elmo's fire. The noise of the storm made conversation impossible, but they got accustomed to this and during an occasional lull when they managed to exchange a few words they felt uneasy because their voices sounded peculiar, almost threatening.

A young Oxford graduate named Apsley Cherry-Garrard, a member of Scott's expedition, went hunting for penguin eggs on Cape Crozier one brisk morning. This was not his idea. He had signed on as an "adaptable helper"—in fact he had contributed 1,000 English pounds for the privilege—and he was told to help the zoologist. In midwinter they started out: zoologist-artist Edward Wilson, Oxford man Cherry-Garrard, and Lieutenant Henry R. "Birdie" Bowers who had once been a gunboat commander on the Irrawaddy River. They were gone five weeks. Cherry-Garrard later wrote a book titled *The Worst Journey in the World*. This is a brash claim but you don't have to read much of his book to conclude that he may have been right.

They took two sledges so heavily loaded that all three of them were required to drag each sledge, which meant dragging one a certain distance, then going back for the other. And it was cold. Their clothes were always frozen and the canvas harness by which they attached themselves to the sledge was so stiff that a man couldn't get properly harnessed by himself; his companions had to bend the frozen canvas around his body.

As for relatively simple matters such as breathing, in the daytime there was no problem; temperatures far below zero merely coated the lower parts of their faces with ice and soldered the balaclavas to their heads. The trouble began at night. They had to enclose themselves in their sleeping bags like caterpillars because the frigid outside air was impossible to breathe: "All night long our breath froze into the skins, and our respiration became quicker and quicker as the air in our bags got fouler and fouler. . . ."

Seventy below zero is not bad, he tells us, not comparatively bad, if you can see where you are going and where you are stepping, where the sledge straps are, and the cooker, the Primus, the food, and so on. But for twenty of each twenty-four hours they lived in darkness. The rest of the time a dull gleam on the horizon helped them along.

They set a course by the planet Jupiter and retraced their steps to the second sledge by candlelight. Once when the sky grew overcast a brief ray of moonlight was all that saved them from plunging into a crevasse just three steps ahead.

They suffered from optical illusions, hunger, frostbite, and—although this sounds odd—snow blindness. On an average day they progressed a couple of miles, traveling ten miles to do it. For one entire week the thermometer registered sixty below, or worse.

During a blizzard, contrary to what you would expect, the temperature began rising. It climbed fifty degrees to a delightful nine below zero.

Cherry-Garrard insists that one morning when he peeped out of the tent his clothing froze instantly, trapping his head in that position. He claims that for the next several hours he had to pull the sledge with his head screwed around at an angle. Now this is ridiculous. This is the sort of thing you see in a Hollywood cartoon, but our Oxford egg-collector is no humorist. Presumably it happened.

At last they got to the penguin rookery and after zoologist Wilson had completed his research they stole five eggs and started home. En route Cherry-Garrard broke two of these precious eggs. He was carrying them inside his mittens and he explains simply that they "burst." Maybe. Maybe it happened. But eggs seldom break unless they have been rudely handled. Nevertheless, he tells us without further clarification, his eggs "burst." All right, let it go. He emptied one mitten but kept the broken egg in the other because he thought that when they stopped to eat he would pour it into the cooker. For some reason he neglected to do this, "but on the return journey I had my mitts far more easily thawed out . . . and I believe the grease in the egg did them good."

Not long afterward, while they were camped, a hurricane sucked away their tent and they could do nothing except huddle in their sleeping bags.

The loss of the tent was critical; if they had to sleep outside they might not survive.

"Face to face with real death," he writes, "one does not think of the things that torment the bad people in the tracts, and fill the good people with bliss. I might have speculated on my chances of going to Heaven; but candidly I did not care. I could not have wept if I had tried. I had no wish to review the evils of my past. But the past did seem to have been a bit wasted. The road to Hell may be paved with good intentions: but the road to Heaven is paved with lost opportunities. . . . Well has the Persian said that when we come to die we, remembering that God is merciful, will gnaw our elbows with remorse for thinking of the things we have not done for fear of the Day of Judgment."

Two days after the tent vanished the weather improved enough for them to prepare a meal—tea and pemmican flavored with burnt seal blubber, penguin feathers, and hair from the sleeping bags.

Then, miraculously, they found the tent at the base of a slope half a mile distant; and their lives, which had been taken by the wind, were given back.

When they returned to the base the first thing they heard was an astonished voice crying: "Good God! Here's the Crozier party!"

Somebody decided to weigh their sleeping bags. At the start of the trip the bags weighed forty-seven pounds. Now, with the accumulation of snow inside and out, they weighed almost three times that much.

Scott was troubled by the appearance of his men: "They looked more weather-worn than anyone I have yet seen. Their faces were scarred and wrinkled, their eyes dull, their hands whitened and creased with constant exposure." A photograph taken after they got back is even more expressive. At first you think you have seen it before, then suddenly it reminds you of pictures taken at Dachau and Buchenwald.

Three of the five eggs at last reached the Natural History Museum in London where they were accepted and studied with no particular excitement. The value of this trip, therefore, depends on your interpretation. One biographer commented that it had drawn Cherry-Garrard and his companions together in permanent spiritual bondage— which makes it sound almost worthwhile. Another said that few men ever have absorbed so much punishment for the sake of adding such an insignificant brick to the edifice of knowledge. In other words the rookery had as much meaning, or as little, as the Pole itself.

And though this has nothing to do with our story it might be remarked that the bird—the Emperor penguin as distinguished from the smaller Adélie—seems to be not very bright but is uncommonly powerful, an association of traits often found at home. Five crewmen of the whaler

Baleana, intent upon capturing an Emperor, tried to wrestle one to the ice but were disdainfully flung aside. They leaped on the bird again and after a furious struggle managed to get two leather belts strapped around it. The Emperor then took a breath, snapped both belts, and shuffled away.

Now, in regard to harrowing journeys, if Cherry-Garrard's does not sound sufficiently arduous you might go back to Sir Douglas Mawson. He, too, was a scientist—a physicist, geologist, and the first man to use long-distance radio in the Antarctic. He wanted to map some territory east of Wilkes Land, so when the paralyzing storm blew over he emerged from St. Elmo's hut with two companions: a young officer of the Royal Fusiliers, Lieutenant Belgrave Ninnis, known as "Cherub" because of his complexion, and a big Swiss-German ski champion named Xavier Mertz, called "X."

They loaded three sledges, harnessed eighteen dogs, and set out on November 10, 1912.

They crossed two valleys through which glaciers were flowing toward the coast like immense ice tongues and Mawson named them after Ninnis and Mertz. The weather was good. They traveled about 300 miles with no difficulty except that Ninnis suffered from an infected finger, and one sledge which got rather banged up had to be abandoned.

On December 14, a bright clear day, Mertz was skiing ahead, serenading the inconceivable emptiness with Teutonic drinking songs, while Mawson rode on a sledge not far behind him. Ninnis was riding the other sledge.

Mertz abruptly lifted a ski pole: the danger signal.

Mawson stopped to inspect the snow. He could find no indication of a crevasse. Then he looked around. Ninnis was gone. However there was a low ridge that might possibly have obscured him.

The two men hurried back.

On the other side of the ridge they saw an enormous hole. Mawson, a precise man, states that it was eleven feet across. Two sets of sledge tracks led up to the hole, but only Mawson's led away from it.

When they looked down through binoculars they could see a shelf of ice projecting from the shadowy turquoise depths. On this shelf lay a pair of dogs, together with a section of the big tent and a canvas bag holding a ten-day supply of food. One of the dogs appeared to be dead. The other, named Franklin, was moaning; its back seemed to be broken, and very soon it died.

Ninnis' sledge had been pulled by the strongest dogs and was loaded with equipment. In addition to the food and the tent it carried some waterproof clothes that Mertz had not worn because of the mild weather, most of their plates, cups, eating utensils, a number of implements—including a pickax, which might be crucial—and all of the dog food. The most important thing was their own food. On the shelf lay enough to sustain three men for ten days.

To find out how far down it was they tied a theodolite to a 150 foot fishing line and lowered the instrument into the crevasse. The legs of the theodolite just touched Franklin's body.

Mertz wanted to lower himself to the shelf on a rope, but Mawson convinced him that this would be suicidal.

For several hours they remained at the lip of the hole, gazing into it, listening, and occasionally calling Ninnis. Not a sound came from the depths, only a draft of frigid air.

At last Mawson read a burial service and they decided on a course to the base; they could not waste any more time pretending Ninnis might be alive or that his body could be recovered. They were so near the Magnetic Pole that the compass swung back and forth like a pendulum and the sky had grown overcast, which meant they would not have the sun for a guide, but they knew they must start at once. Whether or not they survived would depend on how fast they traveled. They were 300 miles out with no supply depots.

Mawson recorded the location of the crevasse: "It is 35 miles east-southeast of the headland. . . ."

The dogs no longer could be treated decently. In this situation their existence had just one purpose—to contribute toward the survival of their masters. Without food, because there was nothing to feed them, they were mercilessly lashed forward: Haldane, Ginger, Pavlova, Mary, George, and Johnson.

At the site of the abandoned sledge the men inspected the supplies they had discarded a few days earlier. What had seemed useless might now be valuable. The huskies were starving so Mawson sliced up a pair of wolfskin gloves, some worn-out finnesko boots, and a leather strap, divided this into six portions and offered it to them. The dogs gulped down everything and licked the snow. Mawson and Mertz, attempting to conserve their own rations, did not eat anything that night.

Next morning the dog named George could not stand up. Mawson shot the husky and butchered it. The lid of the Nansen cooker became a skillet in which they fried George's hind legs, but there was so little fat on the animal that the meat only scorched. Mertz disliked the taste. Mawson pretended to enjoy it, although he admitted it was somewhat musty and strange and exceedingly tough.

Two days later he was stricken with snow blindness but they could not afford to stop. On they went, Mertz probing the ice for danger, while Mawson—with cocaine and zinc sulfate tablets beneath his eyelids and one eye bandaged—took George's place among the huskies.

Johnson provided the next meal. Mertz shot him through the ear, skinned him, and threw the least appetizing parts to his former friends who instantly crunched his bones, tore his pelt to shreds, and even swallowed his teeth. We are told that Johnson had a strong odor when alive, and after death, although the choicest cuts were sliced into tiny pieces and stewed, he continued to smell.

Mertz and Mawson looked forward to eating the livers of the dogs, not because they were good—in fact they were slimy and stank of fish—but because it seemed to them that the liver must be nourishing. This part of the animal was saturated with a substance which would be isolated eight years later by laboratory technicians and named vitamin A. Twenty years after that discovery the effects of an overdose would be catalogued: nausea, vertigo, loss of hair, cramps, skin fissures, extreme fatigue, dysentery, delirium, and convulsions, often ending in death. Still later it would be learned that eating a Greenland husky's liver was especially dangerous. As Lennard Bickel points out, under the evolutionary pressure of centuries during which these dogs had been fed so much polar bear meat and seal meat the husky's liver had built an abnormal capacity for storing vitamin A. Four ounces of a husky's liver is enough to be considered poisonous. Mawson and Mertz, who ate six livers, swallowed about thirty toxic doses apiece on the assumption that it was good for them.

Haldane and Mary soon disappeared into the pot, then it was Pavlova's turn.

Mawson shot her, smashed her bones with a spade so they could be more easily boiled, and cut off her paws which he added to the soup. This must have been difficult because Pavlova was his favorite. She was named after the great dancer who had come aboard ship in England and talked to him awhile. There on the Thames he had asked if she would be godmother to his ship; so Anna Pavlova poured a little wine on the forestem and reminded God to watch over this voyage. Before going ashore she stopped to pet one of the huskies.

On Christmas Day at the bottom of the world they brightened the stew with a dollop of butter, after which Mawson set up his theodolite to fix their position: "We are some eighteen miles farther south on the glacier than when we were here a month ago. . . ."

Christmas did not end happily. They examined themselves and realized that their bodies were beginning to rot. Patches of skin could be lifted off. Hair was falling out. Teeth were loosening.

The last dog on the menu was Ginger, and because they had thrown away the rifle in order to lighten the sledge it was necessary to kill her with the spade. Mertz could not do it, so Mawson took the spade and broke her neck. Then he cut off her head, which they boiled for an hour and a half. Now, unless you have had some experience it's hard to know when a dog's head is properly cooked. Mawson is not specific, but we must assume that from time to time they uncovered the pot and looked in to see how Ginger was progressing. The idea may seem repugnant, but of course our values fluctuate depending on circumstances.

When they decided she had been cooked enough Mawson drew a line with his knife over the top of the skull, symbolically dividing it, and they took turns eating— gnawing away the lips, jaw muscles, and eyeballs. Their metal spoons had gone down the crevasse with Ninnis, but Mawson had whittled two wooden spoons out of a sledge strut which enabled them to scoop up the brains. In his diary he noted that Ginger's head made a good breakfast.

The death of this animal left them with a sense of loneliness they had not anticipated. They seem to have felt Ginger's absence emotionally as well as physically.

Mertz was beginning to fall apart. He developed stomach cramps and often rested on the sledge while Mawson struggled to pull it. Some days they made no more than a couple of miles.

On January 6 Mawson wrote: "Both our chances are going now." The implication being that if he abandoned Mertz and went on alone he might reach the base. But it is doubtful that he even considered such a thing, though he knew the man was dying.

About ten o'clock the next morning Mertz screamed. Then he thrust one of his fingers into his mouth—the little finger of the left hand, if such details interest you. He thrust this yellow frostbitten little finger into his mouth, chewed it off, and spat it out.

Mawson bandaged the stump and persuaded him to drink some cocoa, which quieted him. After a while he went to sleep, but woke up several hours later and thrashed around so violently that Mawson was obliged to sit on his chest. He complained that his ears ached, he lost control of his bowels, and during the night he died.

Mawson was now alone, at least 100 miles from the base, with very little food: pemmican, raisins, almonds, cocoa, chocolate, dog meat, and a kind of jelly he had made from boiled dog bones.

He began to modify the sledge and camping equipment "to meet fresh requirements," as he puts it. He threw away whatever was not essential and cut the sledge in half, discarding the rear section. He constructed a mast and a spar, and fashioned a sail out of a clothes bag and Mertz's jacket in order to take advantage of any wind. He then dragged the body a short distance from camp, piled blocks of snow around it and raised a cross made from the discarded sledge runners.

"As there is now little chance of my reaching human aid alive," he wrote in his diary, "I greatly regret inability to set down the coastline as surveyed for the 300 miles we traveled. . . ."

When the weather cleared he set out, pulling the front half of the renovated sledge.

En route, aware that his feet seemed numb and rather squelchy, he stopped to inspect them. He had not taken off his socks for quite some time. He remarks that after taking off the third and final pair the sight of his feet gave him a bit of a jolt. The thickened skin of the soles had become entirely detached, forming a separate layer, and the socks were saturated with "an abundant watery fluid." Several of his toes had turned black and the nails were loose. "I began to wonder," says Mawson, "if ever there was to be a day without some special disappointment."

However, one must make the best of a bad situation. He smeared his raw feet with lanolin, tied the soles in place with bandages, put on six pairs of thick wool socks, fur boots, and finally his crampon overshoes. These overshoes, having large stiff soles, spread the weight nicely, he tells us with unmistakable satisfaction, and helped protect his feet from the jagged ice he encountered soon afterward. But it was sticky going. He walked for a while on the outside of his feet, then on the inside, and when he could not endure the pain either way he went down on all fours and crawled—towing his sledge, pausing occasionally to wet his throat with melted snow or nibble at a stick of chocolate.

Presently he got caught in a blizzard.

Then the sledge nearly dropped into a chasm—"a great blue chasm like a quarry" is how he describes it.

And he felt so put upon by these tribulations, one right after another, that he resolved to treat himself to an extra bowl of dog soup.

The next special disappointment occurred the following day when he slipped into a crevasse. Now the predicament in which he found himself is absurd; if it appeared on a movie screen the audience would cackle and hoot. The old Saturday serials used to conclude like this: our hero inextricably, fundamentally, unconditionally, and grievously trapped.

Here is what we have. We have Sir Douglas, harnessed to his sledge for easier pulling, dangling at the end of the rope. Below him the camera reveals a bottomless gorge. Above him the sledge has caught in deep snow but at any instant it may break loose. If that happens Sir Douglas will plunge into frozen eternity.

He is exhausted by his ordeal, having already outlasted two other men. He is dizzy, freezing, poisoned, and half-starved. His feet are not just killing him, they are literally falling apart. He is alone in the Antarctic, the grimmest place on earth, no help within miles. Even if somebody should come looking for him, which nobody will, he could not be rescued because he could not be found. He is out of sight—invisible—not figuratively but actually out of sight, dangling below the surface of the glacier.

So there you have it, a real disappointment. Pauline's perils were nothing. And Sir Douglas certainly thinks he has enjoyed his last bowl of dog-paw soup.

You may wonder how he got out.

Don't miss next week's episode.

"I began to look around," he says in the great tradition of hopelessly mired heroes. Then he goes on to tell us that the crevasse was "somewhat over six feet wide and sheer walled, descending into blue depths below. My clothes, which, with a view to ventilation, had been but loosely secured, were now stuffed with snow broken from the roof, and very chilly it was. Above at the other end of the fourteen-foot rope, was the daylight seen through the hole in the lid."

All right, we have the scene in focus. What next?

"In my weak condition, the prospect of climbing out seemed very poor indeed. . . ."

One would think so. Nevertheless he started up and finally clawed his way to the surface, but all at once was dropped into the abyss a second time when a little more of the crust broke away.

"There, exhausted, weak and chilled, hanging freely in space and slowly turning round as the rope twisted one way and the other, I felt that I had done my utmost and failed, that I had no more strength to try again and that all was over except the passing."

It would be an ignoble, humiliating departure, but what troubled him most was the thought of the food on the sledge that he might have eaten. He had starved himself because there was practically nothing left, now even that little bit was going to be wasted. So, dangling in his harness, looking down and looking up, his palms bleeding, he tried to decide whether he should just wait for the end, or untie the rope and get it over with, or try once more to haul himself out. Then, if you can believe this, he remembered a couple of lines from Robert Service:

> *Just have one more try—it's dead easy to die,*
> *It's the keeping-on-living that's hard.*

You might expect him to think of something by a major poet. Donne, for instance. Or Coleridge or Milton or Blake. No, not at all. He was inspired by Robert Service.

Apparently this wretched poetry saved his life. The incredible man again scrambled to the top. He emerged from the hole feet first, wriggled on his belly to safe ground, collapsed, woke up an hour or two later covered with new snow, and then pitched his tent, figuring he had done enough for the day.

But came morning, on went Mawson, indefatigable, sustained by poetry—this time by Omar Khayyám whom he calls "the Persian philosopher." And if, through some anomaly of nature, he had found his way blocked by a polar bear it seems likely he would have torn the beast apart with his hands, swallowed it, and marched on. Nothing would stop him. If he had dropped into another abyss and plummeted half a mile to the bottom you would expect, after six hours or so, to see him pop out of the ice, resentful of these unwarranted calamities.

One is tempted to exclaim: Oh, come off it, Mawson! And yet, reading the account, one gets the feeling that not only did everything happen just that way, his trial may in fact have been worse than it sounds. He is so anxious not to overstate the case. Very chilly it was, he remarks, describing himself spinning over eternity like a spider on a thread. Very chilly. Yes, no doubt it was.

Somewhat absently he mentions that his toenails continued to fester, numerous boils on his face and body required daily attention, and prolonged starvation abetted by the unwholesomeness of dog meat was affecting him in various ways. Minor inconveniences. And he has thrown away the soles of his feet.

Here is his report of setting up the tent:

"It proved a protracted operation. When the outside was finished off satisfactorily the inside was discovered to be filled with drift snow and had to be dug out. Everything was stuffed with soft damp snow including the sleeping bag, and it took a rare time to put things right."

A couple of nights later the snow-laden tent weighs so heavily upon the sleeping bag that he has trouble moving, and he concludes that if he waits until daylight it may be impossible to dig himself out. Industrious as ever, he sets to work although "the skin was coming off my hands, which were the last parts of my body to peel. A moulting of the hair followed the peeling of the skin. Irregular tufts of beard came out and there was a general shedding of hair from my head, so much so that at each camp thereabouts the snowy floor of the tent was noticeably darkened."

After crossing Mertz Glacier in late January he had thrown away his iron crampons, along with some other equipment. Even the precious diary had been stripped of its cardboard binding. Every ounce mattered. But now he is again crossing wind-polished ice, slipping and falling so often that he worries about breaking a leg—which of course would bring down the final curtain. Obviously a set of cleats would help. He therefore dismantles the mahogany theodolite case and carves a pair of sandals, studding the underside with nails and with the long screws that held the box together.

Having strapped these contraptions to his feet with lampwick Mawson harnessed himself to the sledge and set out again, rather pleased because the ersatz crampons seemed to be working. Imperfectly, to be sure, but he did not slip quite as often.

After a few miles, though, his feet hurt worse than ever. He stopped to find out what had gone wrong. The ice was so hard that it had forced the screws and nails up through the wood—through the socks and bandages—until they were biting into his flesh.

Mawson hammered them down, bound the swollen bloody suppurating lumps that used to be his feet, and went on. He had traveled a fair distance by this time and saw no reason to quit.

Farther up the road his mahogany sandals cracked. He carved a new pair—double-deckers—which carried him a few more miles.

On and on the man goes, day after day, lurching forward, dragging that truncated sledge, now and then with the wind at his back sailing crazily over the ice, leaving an occasional tuft of beard to mark his passage.

Presently he is reduced to twenty chips of boiled dog meat, half a pound of raisins, and several ounces of chocolate. He is still many miles from safety. But Mawson's problems hardly sound alarming anymore, you know he will get through. If the food runs out he will start eating rope. Then he will eat the sledge.

Needless to say, as we say, he got back alive, curiously bald, and somewhat under the weather as he might express it, but he did return. He got back because, first of all, he was Mawson. That's the principal reason. Secondly, he was no amateur. He knew the Antarctic. In 1908 he and the gentlemanly fifty-year-old Professor Edgeworth David had been members of an expedition led by Ernest Shackleton. Shackleton meant to reach the South Pole. Nobody had done this, therefore Shackleton wanted to do it.

He failed. He got within 100 miles before the likelihood of starvation obliged him to turn around. The men had gone as far as they could go, almost too far. They started out with four ponies, three of which they butchered. The other fell into a crevasse. On the way back they were so hungry that they stopped at the place where one of the ponies had been slaughtered and dug into the snow for its congealed blood. However, that's a different story.

While preparations were being made for Shackleton's dash toward the Geographic Pole, Professor David and two associates went off to find the Magnetic Pole. These do not necessarily lie close together. The Magnetic Pole, in fact, drifts across a considerable area because the earth's magnetic field fluctuates—which explains why the first Antarctic explorers could not agree on its location. At present it is not where Professor David and his assistants, Mawson and Dr. A. F. Mackay, found it. But that, too, is a different story.

While they were heading toward it they camped one day on some rather touchy ice. Mawson was in the tent examining photographic plates and Professor David was outside loading the sledge when Mawson heard the professor ask in a strangely resonant voice if he was busy. Yes, Mawson replied through the canvas, he was busy.

A few minutes later Professor David asked the same question. Mawson again answered that he was busy. Then, "with infinite politeness and apology," as Mawson describes it, Professor David said: "I am so sorry to disturb you, Mawson, but I am down a crevasse and I really don't think I can hold on much longer."

Farther up the glacier Mawson himself abruptly dropped from sight, and you get the feeling that these men who trudged around the Antarctic spent half their time rescuing each other.

On top of a high plateau they fixed the position of the Magnetic Pole at 72°25′ S., 155°16′ E. on the sixteenth of January, 1909. Considering that it drifts, you cannot help asking why anybody needed a precise location. Maybe the facts were important in 1909, though today they have about as much value as Cherry-Garrard's penguin eggs.

The good ship *Nimrod* was to meet them at the coast near Professor David's glacier, but they were late for the rendezvous. No ship was in sight, so they camped and waited. Surely somebody would pick them up because, after all, they were the only people on earth who knew where the Magnetic Pole was.

Two days later they heard a cannon shot.

Mawson, Mackay, and Professor David bounded from the tent and there just offshore lay the *Nimrod*. They began running across the ice, Mawson in the lead, when once again he vanished.

Mackay skidded to a stop beside the hole and looked down. Mawson was clinging to a ledge. Mackay asked if he was all right.

"Yes," said Mawson.

He had fallen twenty feet and if he slipped from the ledge he would never be seen again.

I say, Mawson, are you all right?

Yes.

Well, the question was logical and the response was clear, so perhaps one shouldn't wonder at it.

Mackay and the professor lowered a sledge harness into the hole, assuming they could pull him out. Instead, they were almost pulled in. More help would be needed. Mackay, cupping his hands, shouted to the *Nimrod:* "Mawson has fallen down a crevasse and we got to the Magnetic Pole!"

The grand prize, though, was the mystic southern core, the symbolic end of the earth, the Geographic Pole. Shackleton almost made it but stopped ninety-seven miles short. Ninety-seven miles from immortality.

"We have shot our bolt," he writes in his journal. "We hoisted Her Majesty's flag, and the other Union Jack afterward, and took possession of the plateau. . . . While the Union Jack blew out stiffly in the icy gale that cut us to the bone, we looked south with our powerful glasses, but could see nothing but the dead-white snow plain. There was no break in the plateau as it extended toward the Pole. . . ."

Amundsen and Scott are the illustrious names. They got to the Pole within five weeks of each other, which suggests nothing more than good luck and bad luck; but there was such a difference in what happened subsequently that luck cannot explain it. The explanation must be found in the characters of the two men, just as Mawson's trip can be explained only by his outrageous determination.

Roald Amundsen's opinion of luck is terse and revealing:

"Victory awaits those who have everything in order. People call this luck. Defeat awaits those who fail to take the necessary precautions. This is known as bad luck."

There we have it. To be lucky you must know what you are doing.

At the age of fifteen, after reading about Sir John Franklin's disastrous attempt to find a northwest passage, Amundsen began to get ready. He trained his body to endure hardship. He detested football, but forced himself to play it. He went skiing in the mountains whenever possible. He slept with his bedroom windows open all winter. He looked forward to the obligatory term of military service "both because I wanted to be a good citizen and because I felt that military training would be of great benefit to me as further preparation for my life."

When he was twenty-two he persuaded a friend to go with him on a miniature polar passage. West of Oslo is a mile-high plateau extending nearly to the coast. In summer it is used by Lapp herdsmen pasturing reindeer, but when winter arrives the Lapps descend to the valley and the plateau is deserted. There is no record of anyone ever having crossed it during winter. Amundsen resolved to cross it.

In the middle of their third night on the plateau he woke up because of a temperature change. Instead of sleeping on top of the snow he had burrowed into it, hoping to escape the wind, and while he lay snugly in the hole he had been pleased with himself for such a clever idea. He woke up lying on his back, feeling cramped. Without opening his eyes he tried to roll over but was unable to move. The damp snow of early evening had filled the entrance to his burrow, sifted over his sleeping bag, and then had frozen into a solid block of ice. He began struggling and shouting, but he was helpless—absolutely unable to move—and his voice probably was inaudible at the surface. He very soon quit shouting, he says, because it was hard to breathe, and he realized that if he did not keep quiet he would suffocate. Presumably his friend also had burrowed into the snow, which meant he must be trapped in the same way. Unless there should be a quick thaw they both would die in these ice coffins.

Amundsen does not know whether he fell asleep or fainted, but the next time he became conscious he heard the sound of digging. His friend had slept on the surface, too exhausted to do anything else, and was astonished when he woke up to find himself alone. The only trace of Amundsen was a tuft of hair at one corner of his sleeping bag. Another snow flurry would have hidden him until the Lapps returned.

They got back in such poor shape that people who had seen them eight days earlier did not recognize them.

Commenting on this experience years later, Amundsen remarks that an "adventure" is merely an interruption of an explorer's serious work and indicates bad planning.

This trip across the Norwegian plateau seems to have been rigorously educational. What he learned from it, beyond the danger of burrowing, cannot even be estimated; but it is obvious that, like most extraordinary people, he knew how to distinguish the shape of the world from a grain of sand. Again and again he talks about preparation. Planning. Attention to detail.

He chose the site of his South Polar base only after studying every existing description of the Ross Ice Shelf from the day it was discovered in 1841. Each member of his expedition was judiciously selected. Every bit of equipment, right down to the tent pegs and buttons, was inspected for weakness or inadequacy. He ordered the boots ripped apart and rebuilt according to his own ideas of comfort and safety. He insisted that a new dog whip be designed.

Aboard the *Fram*, in addition to nineteen men, were almost 100 huskies. Amundsen was convinced that dogs were essential to success and he had a false deck constructed on the ship to protect them from the tropic sun. He watched their health as closely as he watched the health of his men. He had calculated the day-by-day weight of the sledges that must be hauled to the Pole, and he knew how much weight each animal could pull. As the journey progressed the sledges would become lighter, which meant that fewer dogs would be required. Logistics demanded, therefore, that at a certain point a certain number of dogs be slaughtered. Yet even in death they must contribute. He had calculated that the average dog carried fifty pounds of edible meat. He worked out the precise day on which he intended to kill each dog, and he adhered to this schedule almost exactly.

Amundsen says nothing about the liver, but Arctic Eskimos had known for a long time that you should not eat a husky's liver and he probably was aware of this. He would not have known just why the liver was dangerous, but it would be characteristic of him to credit the Eskimos with some valid reason for their belief.

On the central plateau twenty-four huskies were killed.

"We had agreed to shrink from nothing," he wrote. "The pemmican was cooked remarkably quickly that evening and I was unusually industrious in stirring it. I am not a nervous man, but at the sound of the first shot I found myself trembling. Shot now followed shot in quick succession, echoing uncannily over the great white plain. Each time a trusty servant lost his life."

The Norwegians afterward referred to this campground as the Butcher's Shop.

At first they were reluctant to devour their trusty servants, but the cook Wisting knew his trade. He selected a young animal named Rex.

"I could not take my eyes off his work," says Amundsen.

The delicate little cutlets had an absolutely hypnotizing effect as they were spread out one by one over the snow. They recalled memories of old days, when no doubt a dog cutlet would have been less tempting than now—memories of dishes on which the cutlets were elegantly arranged side by side, with paper frills on the bones, and a neat pile of petits pois in the middle. Ah, my thoughts wandered still farther afield—but that does not concern us now, nor has it anything to do with the South Pole. . . . The meat was excellent, quite excellent, and one cutlet after another disappeared with lightninglike rapidity. I must admit that they would have lost nothing by being a little more tender, but one must not expect too much of a dog. At this first meal I finished five cutlets myself, and looked in vain in the pot for more. Wisting appeared not to have reckoned on such a brisk demand.

About three o'clock on the afternoon of December 14, 1911, Amundsen's men calculated that they had reached the end of the trail.

There were no cheers, no orations. All together the five men grasped a Norwegian flag and thrust it into the snow:

Amundsen, Sverre Hassel, Oskar Wisting, Helmer Hansen, Olav Bjaaland.

"Thus we plant thee, beloved flag, at the South Pole, and give to the plain on which it lies the name of King Haakon VII's plateau."

That brief speech was the only concession to ritual. One gets out of the way of protracted ceremonies in these regions, says Amundsen. The shorter they are, the better.

The Norwegians were in no hurry to leave. The trip had not been difficult, the weather was mild, and they had more than enough food. They stayed several days, taking measurements, circling the area on skis to be sure they truly had encompassed the Pole, and otherwise enjoyed themselves.

They were camped in the middle of a continent almost as large as Australia and Europe combined. The Ross Ice Shelf, over which they had traveled at the beginning, appears to be only a deep indentation on the map of Antarctica, although it is about the size of France. Ice has buried the entire continent—all of its mountains, plains, and valleys, with very few exceptions—in some places to a depth of two miles. Astronauts say that it is the earth's most noticeable feature and that it radiates light from the bottom of the world like a great white lantern.

Once upon a time Antarctica was different. There were pine forests, swamps, and fern jungles. Shackleton's party found a seam of coal eight feet thick near the top of Beardmore Glacier. Scott, following the same route, came across fossilized twigs and leaves:

"The best leaf impressions and the most obvious were in the rotten clumps of weathered coal which split up easily to sheath-knife and hammer. Every layer of these gave abundant vegetable remains. Most of the bigger leaves were like beech leaves in shape and venation, in size a little smaller than British beech."

On the Palmer Peninsula are traces of fig leaves, sequoia, and an evergreen called araucaria that reached a height of 150 feet and still grows in South America. At Mount Weaver, close to the Pole, is a petrified log eighteen inches in diameter; it dates from the Jurassic period, the age of dinosaurs. What reptiles, animals, and birds lived in prehistoric Antarctica is not known—except for some ancestral families of the penguin, one of which grew as tall as a man.

Nor does anybody know what changed the climate. There are theories, but not much agreement.

At present more than a million people live within a radius of 2,000 miles of the North Pole, yet within that radius of the South Pole—excluding the men at weather stations—there is no human life. There are no land animals or birds, only the indestructible aquatic penguin. There is not a single living tree. There are lichens clinging to exposed rocks, a little moss, some coarse grass, a few spiders and flies. The spiders do not spin webs because of the wind and the flies have no wings. These tiny creatures, as obstinate as Sir Douglas Mawson, spend most of their lives frozen stiff, but thaw out several days a year and hurriedly go about their business in order to maintain the species. Such is life today in Antarctica, which may explain why King Haakon's real estate has never been developed.

Before starting the return journey Amundsen lashed a small Norwegian flag to a tent pole. Inside the tent he left a bag containing a letter to the king, just in case they should not make it back to their ship. He discarded some items: reindeerskin foot bags, mitts, a sextant, a hypsometer case—which is an instrument for measuring heights above sea level. And he addressed a letter to Scott.

"He will be here sooner or later," Amundsen told a member of the party. "I hope for his sake it will be sooner."

What Amundsen meant was that the weather could only get worse.

Their trip home sounds idyllic. They had marked the route, and the wind and sun were at their backs. They planned to travel eighteen miles a day, which they did without effort in less than five hours. There was so much food that sometimes they threw away biscuits and pemmican, and fed chocolate to the dogs. The dogs had such an easy time pulling the sledges that they began to get fat.

"We were in high spirits and bowled along at a cracking pace. . . ."

They reached their base on January 25, the date Amundsen had selected two years earlier in Norway. A week later the *Fram* sailed with all aboard in perfect health.

Scott at this time was hundreds of miles away, writing in his diary: "February 2. Three out of five of us injured. We shall be lucky if we get through. . . ."

On March 18 he wrote: "Ill fortune presses. . . ."

March 19: "The weather doesn't give us a chance. . . ."

Earlier he had told a Melbourne journalist: "We may get through, we may not. We may lose our lives. We may be wiped out. It is all a matter of providence and luck."

Shortly after that while en route to the Antarctic: ". . . fortune has determined to put every difficulty in our path."

Again, the following week: "I begin to wonder if fortune will ever turn her wheel."

At the start of the final journey: "The future is in the lap of the gods. . . ."

While struggling up Beardmore Glacier, unaware that Amundsen had just reached the Pole: "Our luck is very bad."

Eight days later: "I trust this may prove the turning point in our fortunes. . . ."

Near the end of March as he lay dying he wrote to the mother of one of his dead companions: "The ways of Providence are inscrutable. . . ."

And in his *Message to the Public*, found beside his body, he begins: "The causes of the disaster are not due to faulty organisation, but to misfortune. . . ."

Perhaps. Perhaps he was right. Maybe all things rest in the lap of the gods. Maybe "faulty organisation" was not the cause, though it is hard to forget something he had said ten years before:

"To my mind no journey ever made with dogs can approach the height of the fine conception which is realized when a party of men go forth to face hardships, dangers, and difficulties with their own unaided efforts, and by days and weeks of hard physical labour succeed in solving some problem of the great unknown. Surely in this case the conquest is more nobly and splendidly won."

It's arguable, of course, whether one should extract particular phrases from a man's life to offer as proof of anything. On the subject of luck, for example, Amundsen himself occasionally referred to it without disdain, in a rather idle fashion, as something to be hoped for.

Still, there's a difference. And the difference becomes more significant when you learn what others thought about Scott. As a child he was so lethargic and preoccupied that he was called "Old Moony." He seems to have been the storybook sissy: emotional, horrified at the sight of blood, physically weak, pampered by his mother and an older sister. A doctor who examined him before he joined the navy advised him to choose a different career.

Scott himself recognized his languid disposition and tried to do something about it; and considering how rapidly he was promoted in the navy he must have changed. Yet in every photograph he looks bemused, tentative, almost doubtful. His stance, his expression—he lives far

away from the frigid brutal world of Roald Amundsen.
Biographer Peter Brent speaks of a brooding, melancholy
air. "His mouth, with its full rounded lips, suggests a leaning toward sensuality and pleasure. . . ."

Scott's resemblance to his romantic kinsman, Sir Walter
Scott, is startling; they look like brothers. And his written
"impressions" of the Antarctic are what you might expect
from a mystic poet, not an explorer:

> The small green tent and the great white road.
> The drift snow like finest flour penetrating every hole
> and corner—flickering up beneath one's head covering,
> pricking sharply as a sand blast.
> The sun with blurred image peeping shyly through
> the wreathing drift giving pale shadowless light.
> The eternal silence of the great white desert. Cloudy
> columns of snow drift advancing from the south, pale
> yellow wraiths, heralding the coming storm, blotting
> out one by one the sharp-cut lines of the land.

Given such a temperament, why was he chosen to lead
an expedition? The answer seems to be that as a midship-
man he won a whaleboat race. This sounds like a petty
triumph, but among the excited spectators was Sir Clem-
ents Markham, president of the Royal Geographical Society. He invited Scott to supper and later commented: "I
was much struck with his intelligence, information, and
the charm of his manner."

Because of Markham's patronage, when a British ex-
ploratory party sailed for the Antarctic in 1901 its commander was Scott. Even then he admits he is out of place:
"I may as well confess that I have no predilection for
polar exploration. . . ."

Subsequently he married an actress, Kathleen Bruce,

and began to associate with actors, authors, painters, and musicians—a doubtful lot. How much these people unsettled him can only be imagined. Once he wrote to Kathleen: "I seem to hold in reserve something that makes for success and yet to see no worthy field for it and so there is this consciousness of a truly deep unrest."

Now listen to Roald Amundsen on the same subject: "Success is a woman who has to be won, not courted. You've got to seize her and carry her off, not stand under her window with a mandolin."

In 1910 when the South Polar expedition departed Scott once more was put in charge. And it is a little strange—or perhaps not—that the London *Evening Standard* should remark: "We may never see them again."

Scott's wife also had premonitions, confiding to her diary:

"I had rather a horrid day today. I woke up having a bad dream about you, and then Peter came very close to me and said emphatically, 'Daddy won't come back,' as though in answer to my silly thoughts."

"I was very taken up with you all evening. I wonder if anything special is happening to you. Something odd happened to the clocks and watches between nine and ten p.m."

"I was still rather taken up by you and a wee bit depressed. As you ought about now to be returning to ship I see no reason for depression. I wonder."

Ernest Shackleton wrote to a New Zealand friend: "I suppose that we shall soon hear of Scott. I am inclined to think that we will hear from Amundsen first."

Today, from this distance, as one reads about the expedition, a feeling of doom soars overhead like an albatross. Aboard ship—even before they reach Antarctica—things do not go well. Icebergs appear farther north than expected. Then a storm threatens the *Terra Nova* and ten precious bags of coal which had not been lashed down must be jettisoned. At four in the morning the pumps become choked, water rises in the engine room, the men start bailing with buckets. A dog drowns. Two ponies die.

Upon reaching Antarctica they were unable to establish winter quarters on Cape Crozier as they had planned. Three motor sledges were brought along for heavy work but one sledge broke through the ice and sank, so that in order to get the ponies' fodder ashore the men harnessed themselves to bales of hay. And the expedition's photographer, standing quite literally on thin ice, was almost knocked into the water by a scheming killer whale.

About this time they got news of Amundsen, who had set up camp on an indentation sixty miles nearer the Pole. Scott wrote in his diary: "I never thought he could have got so many dogs safely to the ice. His plan for running them seems excellent. . . ."

Three more ponies died while the first depot was being stocked. Two more drowned when the ice disintegrated beneath them. And Scott writes: "I could not rid myself of the fear that misfortune was in the air. . . ."

Despite every problem he scrupulously kept his journal.

January 15: "We left our depot today with nine days' provisions, so that it ought to be a certain thing now, and the only appalling possibility the sight of the Norwegian flag forestalling ours."

January 16: "The worst has happened. . . . Bowers's sharp eyes detected what he thought was a cairn; he was uneasy about it, but argued that it might be sastrugus. Half an hour later he detected a black speck ahead. Soon we knew that this could not be a natural snow feature. We marched on, found that it was a black flag tied to a sledge bearer; nearby the remains of a camp; sledge tracks and ski tracks coming and going and the clear trace of dogs' paws—many dogs."

Next day Scott reached the Pole: "Great God! this is an awful place. . . ."

Inside the tent was Amundsen's message.

> Poleheim
> 15 December 1911
>
> Dear Captain Scott:
>
> As you are probably the first to reach this area after us, I will ask you kindly to forward this letter to King Haakon VII. If you can use any of the articles left in this tent, please do not hesitate to do so. The sledge left outside may be of use to you. With best regards, I wish you a safe return.
>
> Roald Amundsen

The British party stayed just long enough to verify the location. By their measurements, Amundsen's tent was only a few hundred yards from the geographical center.

It is hard to understand why they loitered on the way back. They did not have much food, the weather was savage, and they had 900 miles to go. But here is Scott's journal entry on February 8: "I decided to camp and spend the rest of the day geologising. It has been extremely interesting. We found ourselves under perpendicular cliffs of Beacon sandstone, weathering rapidly and carrying veritable coal seams. From the last Wilson, with his sharp eyes, has picked several plant impressions, the last a piece of coal with beautifully traced leaves in layers, also some excellently preserved impressions of thick stems, showing cellular structure. In one place we saw the cast of small waves in the sand."

Why did they do this? Two explanations have been proposed. If they could bring back some scientific information that the Norwegians had overlooked their defeat would not be total. Certainly they knew that. The other explanation, which seeps through Scott's journal like a stain, is that they sensed they could never make it. By now they were crippled and suffering from the cold. Wilson had pulled a tendon in his leg. Evans' hands were so badly frozen that his fingernails had begun to drop off. Oates' feet were turning black. Scott had injured his shoulder. Bowers seems to be the only one in good shape.

Yet the next day they again stopped to collect geological specimens. Scott remarks on "the delight of setting foot on rock after 14 weeks of snow and ice."

A few days later Evans died.

Temperatures dropped so low that in the mornings it took them an hour to put on their footgear. The cooking oil was almost gone. Food rations were cut. Scott meditates: "I wonder what is in store for us. . . ."

On the fifteenth of March while they waited in the tent for a blizzard to let up Oates said, "I am just going outside and may be some time." His feet had become so painful that he could hardly walk, and he did not want to delay the other men.

The bodies of Scott, Bowers, and Wilson were discovered eleven miles from a food depot. Their tent was almost buried by snow. The men lay in their sleeping bags, Wilson with his hands folded on his chest. Bowers also appeared to have died without anguish. Between them lay Scott, the flaps of his sleeping bag open. His diaries were in a green wallet underneath the bag, the last letters on a groundsheet beside him. His left arm was extended, his hand resting on Wilson's shoulder. The interior of the tent had been kept neat. There was an improvised lamp, a bag of tea, a bag of tobacco, and their scientific notes.

Outside stood the sledge. Along with the necessities, it carried thirty-five pounds of rock.

Scott's wife was aboard ship en route to New Zealand to meet him when she learned of his death—five days after the captain got the news by radio. The captain had been so distressed that he could not approach her. She reports in her diary that his hands trembled when he finally showed her the message. After reading it she said to him: "Oh, well, never mind! I expected that. Thanks very much. I will go and think about it."

Then, as she usually did each morning on the ship, she took a Spanish lesson. Then she ate lunch and discussed American politics and in the afternoon spent a while reading about the *Titanic,* determined to avoid thinking of her husband's death until she was sure she could control herself.

She mentions that because it was too hot to go to her cabin she stayed on deck the whole day. Immediately after this commonplace statement, and without a pause, as though it were the most natural sequence in the world, she writes the following passage: "My god is godly. I need not touch him to know that. Let me maintain a high, adoring exaltation, and not let the sorrow of contamination touch me. Within I shall be exultant. My god is glorious and could never become less so. Loneliness is a fear that I have never known. Had he died before I had known his gloriousness, or before he had been the father of my son, I might have felt a loss. Now I have felt none for myself. Won't anybody understand that?—probably nobody. So I must go on and on with the tedious business of discretion. Must even the greatest visions of the heart be blurred by discretions?"

That last line, once you have memorized it, cannot ever

be forgotten, although when analyzed it doesn't make much sense. It suggests some deep communication with her husband, nothing more. But that's all right, many of Shakespeare's indelible lines don't make sense.

What is curious and moving about this passage is the radiance emanating from Scott through the adoration of his wife. To arouse such transcendent feelings in a woman, he must have been extraordinary. And that such a man should have been misplaced seems all the more pathetic.

Just as curious—perhaps more so—is the fact that Amundsen, the victor, is not as renowned as the loser. Quite a few people think Scott was the first man to reach the South Pole. There is no logical explanation for this belief, though his dramatic death may account for it, together with the fact that he and his companions are still there—frozen like insects or splinters on the side of the great white lantern. However, they won't stay there indefinitely. Calculations by scientists at McMurdo Sound indicate that the bodies now lie fifty feet beneath the surface and fifteen miles closer to the edge of the ice shelf. What this means is that sometime in the future Scott and his companions will be carried out to sea on an iceberg.

As for Roald Amundsen, who knows what became of him? Almost no one. He died on a gallant but useless errand, searching for General Umberto Nobile whose dirigible crash-landed in the Arctic. Amundsen's plane may have developed engine trouble; pieces of it were found off the Norwegian coast. The plane had been lent by the French government, which had at that time two modern seaplanes: one with a water-cooled engine, the other with an air-cooled engine. The French, exhibiting that singular wisdom we have come to associate with all federal government, provided Amundsen with the water-cooled engine for his long flight through subzero temperatures.

A Swedish pilot later rescued the Italian general.

Scott is now remembered and honored throughout the English-speaking world while Amundsen is not. One might say this is folly, because Amundsen has more to teach us. But in the end, of course, they are equally instructive.

6

Syllables Here and There

Those of us who are not overly familiar with the nuances of Ugaritic, Luvian, Hittite, Mesopotamian cuneiform, Palaic, or Creto-Mycenaean Linear B, do know a little something, nevertheless, about the Rosetta stone. Ah yes!—the Rosetta stone! Of course, of course. Haven't thought about that in years. Let's see now, they dug it up someplace. The thing was covered with hieroglyphics. Yes indeed, the old Rosetta stone.

More specifically—just where and when it was found, who deciphered it, what the message was—on these points we grow a bit hesitant. And soon the subject becomes tiresome. After all, the translation of dead pronouncements scarcely relates to our daily round. Still, some people consecrate their lives to such matters. For example, George Smith.

That name sounds almost as fictitious as John Doe, but our George Smith was a particular individual—a nineteenth-century London banknote engraver employed by Messrs. Bradbury and Evans of Bouverie Street. Forsaking this career with its many benefits, Smith advanced to the

British Museum where he was taken on first as a restorer, then as assistant keeper of Oriental antiquities. Day after day he spent gluing together and reading shattered clay tablets excavated at Nineveh. We are told that the job fascinated him; his only complaint was the London fog which obliged him to study the tablets by lamplight.

Soon he had become not only an expert on Akkadian cuneiform but had partly deciphered the Cypriot syllabary, which sounds just as exciting. However this was nothing compared to the day in 1872 when, bending over some newly delivered tablets, George Smith understood that he was reading a story. Those little wedges, like so many chicken tracks, spelled out not just one more Assyrian memorial inscription but the adventures of the hero Gilgamesh, one-third human and two-thirds divine, who built the walls and temples of the ancient city of Uruk. Then came the hairy antagonist Enkidu, an account of his fight with Gilgamesh, and their subsequent exploits together.

On the chance that you might care to know what a hairy antagonist looks like, there is in the Louvre a miniature gold pendant from Mesopotamia, almost 5,000 years old and about the size of your thumb, which shows Enkidu flanked by two bison standing on their hind legs. The bison appear to be embracing him, and for some reason—perhaps their tiny gold ringlets and smooth gleaming haunches—they bring to mind a couple of preposterously costumed chorus girls. Enkidu himself gives rather that same impression. He has a bison rump complete with tail, and bison legs right down to the hooves, although his torso belongs to a natural man and he is not wearing horns. What he and his precocious friends might be up to, I have no idea. Anyway, there stands Enkidu as a Mesopotamian goldsmith imagined him, but if you plan to inspect him you should take along a magnifying glass.

Now back to George Smith and those baked clay tablets.

The tablets revealed how Gilgamesh and Enkidu over-powered Khumbaba, Lord of the Cedar Forest, and cut off his head, and how they overcame a fierce bull sent by the goddess Ishtar. At last, searching for eternal life, Gilga-mesh sought the advice of his ancestor Ut-Napishtim, the one survivor of the Deluge.

It is said that Smith continued reading "feverishly" be-cause Gilgamesh certainly would ask his ancestor about the Deluge, although to hear Smith tell it you might think he had only deciphered a Mesopotamian recipe for bouil-labaisse. Listen to this phlegmatic recital:

"On looking down the third column, my eye caught the statement that the ship rested on the mountains of Nizir, followed by the account of the sending forth of the dove, and its finding no resting-place and returning. I saw at once that I had here discovered a portion at least of the Chaldean account. . . ."

He was unable to find the piece he wanted—a dialogue between Gilgamesh and Ut-Napishtim about the Flood—possibly because his collection of shards was incomplete; but what he already had learned was important enough, and on December 3, 1872, he informed the members of the Society of Biblical Archaeology.

The London *Daily Telegraph* then offered 1,000 guineas to finance an expedition to search for the missing text, on condition that the search be directed by Smith. His em-ployers, in a surprising display of logic, gave their ace philologist a six-month leave of absence and off went George Smith to Nineveh.

Now it must be understood that he was looking for some dirty bits of clay almost indistinguishable from thousands and thousands of other bits scattered across the ruins, which measured eight miles in circumference. Smith might just as well have shuffled through the woods in autumn looking for half-a-dozen specific leaves, yet he picked up the pieces in a week. Considering the amount of rubble, how did he do it? Nobody knows. You couldn't get away with this in a novel or a movie because the odds against such a thing happening are outrageous.

Was Mr. Smith himself amazed? Not much.

"On the 14th of May . . . I sat down to examine the store of fragments of cuneiform inscriptions from the day's digging, taking out and brushing off the earth from the fragments to read their contents. On cleaning one of them I found to my surprise and gratification that it contained the greater portion of seventeen lines . . . fitting into the only place where there was a serious blank in the story."

He brought back 384 scraps from Nineveh, which almost completed the epic:

What I had loaded thereon, the whole harvest of life
I caused to embark within the vessel; all my family
*   and my relations,*
The beasts of the field, the cattle of the field,
*   the craftsmen, I made them all embark.*
I entered the vessel and closed the door. . . .

For six days and nights
Wind and flood marched on, the hurricane
*   subdued the land.*
When the seventh day dawned, the hurricane
*   was abated, the flood*
Which had waged war like an army;
The sea was stilled, the ill wind was calmed,
*   the flood ceased.*
I beheld the sea, its voice was silent. . . .

When the seventh day came,
I sent forth a dove, I released it;
It went, the dove, it came back,
As there was no place, it came back.
I sent forth a swallow, I released it;
It went, the swallow, it came back,
As there was no place, it came back.
I sent forth a crow, I released it;
It went, the crow, and beheld the substance
  of the waters;
It eats, it splashes about, it caws,
  it comes not back.

The tablets were from the library of King Ashurbanipal, circa 650 B.C. But the story is older, much older, older than Abraham.

In 1929 Sir Leonard Woolley uncovered its origin. Mucking about in Mesopotamia beneath remnants of the 5,000-year-old Erech dynasty, he probed an eleven-foot layer of silt brought down from the upper Euphrates valley—the residue of a gigantic flood—and saw traces of reed huts. According to Genesis the water was fifteen cubits deep, about twenty-six feet. Woolley calculated that the depth of the Mesopotamian flood must have been at least twenty-five feet, which would have inundated everything for 300 miles.

So there we are. A few reed hut dwellers guessed what was coming; they leapt into their boats and escaped and never stopped talking about it.

Woolley seems to have been a man of rare equanimity. You would assume that anybody who had just put his finger on the source of a great Christian legend would display some excitement. Not Sir Leonard.

"I was convinced of what it meant," says he, "but I

wanted to see whether others would arrive at the same conclusion. I brought up two of my staff and, after pointing out the facts, asked for their conclusions."

If his staff members were disconcerted, Mrs. Woolley was not. As cool as Sir Leonard, she remarked, "Well, of course, it's the Flood."

Whereupon everybody went back to work.

George Smith was more unpredictable: one moment jubilant, then altogether self-possessed when a little exuberance might be expected—or at least tolerated. For instance, during the Gilgamesh affair he sounds calm enough, methodical and scholarly; but on another occasion he looked up from a cuneiform cylinder and startled his associates by exclaiming in a loud voice that he was the first person to have read it in 2,000 years.

Now, among professionals such ebullience is thought rather gross. But the disorderly scene was not over. George Smith then stood up and went striding back and forth "in a high state of excitement."

And then he began taking off his clothes.

This occurred, mind you, on an upper floor of the British Museum, in the room directly above the office of the Royal Asiatic Society's secretary.

What happened next, we don't know. In other words, after having removed his laboratory smock, his necktie, his shirt, and possibly his trousers, did he—as we say—come to his senses?

Meanwhile, what were his fellow archaeologists doing? One would suppose they frowned. At the very least they must have frowned. But did any of them protest? Did they ask each other what was going on? Or, having lifted their eyebrows in order to register disapproval, did they consider it prudent to mind their own business?

Several years ago in Los Angeles during the evening

rush I was driving along Wilshire when a naked woman appeared on the sidewalk. She was about forty years old, plump, an average sort, neither beautiful nor homely. She wore ballet slippers, that was all, and she was scowling when she marched past me with immense resolution toward—toward what? I can't guess. Toward an inconceivable destiny. But the way that sea of Los Angeles citizens rolled apart, she could have been Madame Moses. Nobody stared. Very few looked at her twice. Obviously, unquestionably, undeniably the woman was mad, and we cannot endure much contact with those who are mad. We cannot even estimate what such a person might say or do, which means that we avoid the encounter. Instinctively we give way, submitting to the incomprehensible strength of madness.

Not only did every man avoid this mad naked creature, so did every woman. She dominated the street, no question about it. She may have realized this, but if so she was indifferent. Or perhaps not. Perhaps that was her purpose. All I can be sure of is that nobody—not one person in that vast polluted city of savages—would have been reckless enough to touch her.

Now about our man in the museum. Was he, also, cautiously ignored? Did his colleagues pretend to find nothing odd about his behavior? Did they go right on reading their baked clay tablets? Or did some fearless staff member speak up?

"I say, George old chap, aren't you carrying things a bit far?"

We don't know because whoever kept the records in those days didn't think it was important. It was, though. Such details, like fine plums, ought to be plucked and tenderly boxed.

So much for George Smith.

The young genius who unraveled Egyptian hieroglyphics, Jean-François Champollion, is altogether as engaging and neurotic as our British exhibitionist. One appealing thing about him, which has been nearly overlooked because of his success with hieroglyphics, is the title of his first scholarly paper, written when he was twelve: "A History of Famous Dogs." Information of this sort should be preserved.

Anyway, glyph by glyph, year after year, Jean-François had been working on the puzzle but with no significant results until September 14, 1822. That morning he either received or began to study a consignment of drawings from the architect Huyot, who was traveling through Egypt and Nubia.

On the first page of Huyot's drawings from Abu Simbel he saw a cartouche beginning with the circular sun-symbol: *Ra*. Beside it was a sign he could not translate. Then came the sign representing folded cloth: *os*. And the *os* was repeated. In hieroglyphic writing, as everybody knows, the Egyptians dropped their vowels, so that what Champollion had within the boundaries of this cartouche was the ancient equivalent of *R-ss*.

Could it be the pharaoh Ramses?

On the second page of Huyot's drawings he saw a cartouche beginning with the ibis, a bird sacred to the god Thoth. Beside the ibis stood the unknown symbol from the first cartouche. Next to this was the folded cloth: *os*.

There could no longer be any doubt. If the unknown symbol represented *m*, which it must, here were two great names: Ramses and Thotmes.

The lock would not open easily, but Champollion had the key. In time it would be possible to read hieroglyphics, and Egypt's enormous history—lost for 1,500 years—would never be lost again. Provided, of course, that the symbol did represent *m*.

He was certain it did because the identification of two

famous names could hardly be coincidence. Still, one does not like to make a fool of one's self. He therefore spent the entire morning bent over Huyot's sketches looking for additional proof. At last he was convinced. Gathering up the papers he rushed to the Institut de Paris where his elder brother Jacques-Joseph worked. It is said that he burst into the library of the Institut and threw the papers on Jacques-Joseph's desk:

"Je tiens l'affaire!" he cried in a hoarse voice.

Then he fell over in a dead faint and spent the next five days in bed.

Champollion's excitement seems appropriate, in contrast to George Smith's vulgar display, although of course the important thing is not a linguist's personality but his accomplishment. And because of Champollion's detective work the Rosetta stone, which had baffled everybody for twenty-three years, would not be an enigma much longer.

The fact that the stone was not translated for twenty-three years surprises people. Since its message was trilingual—given twice in unknown languages and once in Greek—why couldn't the unknown scripts be quickly correlated with the Greek? Because not until Champollion identified Ramses and Thotmes had anybody realized that the hieroglyphic system was partly phonetic, partly symbolic.

As to where the stone was found, and how this came about, we are indebted to Napoleon. At least, if there had not been a Napoleon it is unlikely that the stone would have turned up. Whether one justifies the other is not a bad question, but outside the limit of this discussion.

Napoleon invaded Egypt in 1798, which displeased the Turks whose domain it was, as well as the British who had become uneasy about their expansive neighbor. So a bombardment was undertaken, and in the course of this a

French captain named Bouchard ordered his men to dig in at Rashīd, or Rosetta, close to the mouth of the Nile.

Now, while they were digging trenches an Arab soldier's pick clanged against something inexpressibly hard: a slab of black basalt covered with unintelligible writing. Bouchard, smarter than most captains, thought this object might be important.

The stone was carted off to the Institut d'Égypte in Cairo, which Napoleon had founded, where copies were made of the text and sent at once to France—almost as if everyone had a presentiment that something unfortunate was about to happen. In Paris, Professor Du Thiel translated the Greek. The stone was a memorial, dated fourth Xandikos, equivalent to the eighteenth Meshir of the year 9, equivalent to March 27, 196 B.C. What it said, in brief, was that the priests of Memphis wished to express their gratitude to Ptolemy V Epiphanes. Ptolemy had evidently crossed various palms with silver, a most ancient custom, and the priests declared that because of his virtue this endorsement should be posted in all Egyptian temples of the first, second, and third class.

Meanwhile the stone had been shipped to the house occupied by General de Menou in Alexandria, where presumably it would be safe.

Then the British landed.

"I shall defend myself to the last extremity within the walls of Alexandria," wrote Menou to Napoleon. "I know how to die, but not how to capitulate."

This is a noble sentiment, the utterance of a proud and valiant soldier. Just the same, under certain conditions it may be advantageous to restate one's views, and after a good many poilus had been rudely deprived of their existence General Menou exercised his prerogative to suggest the possibility of negotiation. As a diplomat he succeeded triumphantly, obtaining terms identical to those obtained by other French generals who surrendered. Now it happens that Menou himself had been offered these terms somewhat earlier and had scornfully rejected them, insisting upon peace with honor—which may remind you of events elsewhere. But of course one does not expect high logic on the battlefield or at the conference table.

So it came about that the Rosetta stone journeyed to the British Museum, though not before some stiff words between Generals Menou and Hutchinson:

The stone, Menou declared, was his private property.

Article XVI of the treaty of capitulation, replied the British general, specifies that such objects, as well as everything else collected by French scientists in Egypt, must be surrendered.

"I have just been informed," Menou wrote to Hutchinson a few days later, "that several among our collection-makers wish to follow their seeds, minerals, birds, butterflies, or reptiles wherever you choose to ship their crates. I do not know if they wish to have themselves stuffed for this purpose, but I can assure you that if the idea should appeal to them, I shall not prevent them. I have authorized them to address themselves to you."

Hutchinson either did not want a cargo of butterflies and crocodiles detracting from the glory of his return to England, or he was moved by the loyalty of the French scientists to their pickled specimens. Whatever the reason, he told them to keep their crates. But he insisted upon having the stone.

Menou responded: "You want it, Monsieur le général? You can have it, since you are the stronger of us two. . . . You may pick it up whenever you please."

Even so, the mills of God grind exceeding small; it was

not to be an Englishman but the neurasthenic Jean-François Champollion whose name would be associated forever with that big black slab of basalt.

Grotefend and Rawlinson are names as redoubtable in their field—Old Persian—as are the names of Smith and Champollion. Grotefend was a Göttingen schoolteacher, Rawlinson an employee of the East India Company. Although their lives overlapped by some thirty years it is doubtful if they met.

Grotefend first. The son of a cobbler, born in a small town, never a professional Orientalist, he is your basic Outsider. According to some scholars, he undertook the job of deciphering Persian cuneiform as the result of a bet made while he was drunk. Others say a librarian persuaded him to try it. What we know for certain is that he liked puzzles. An evening packed with acrostics, rebuses, palindromes, wordplay of any sort—that was young Grotefend's idea of a jolly time.

Quite a few schoolteachers, along with a great many less bookish people, share this odd passion, so the question comes up as to why, or how, one undistinguished crossword puzzle fan did something important enough to get his name in the encyclopedia. The answer is that we don't know. The computer cannot be built that will tell us why one brain may seize and interpret in a fresh way the data accessible to all. Therefore we use the term *genius*, a word sucked dry through misapplication. Now it may be extravagant to call Grotefend a genius. However, Karl Marek has this to say: "Among many other things, genius implies the ability to reduce the complicated to the simple, and to recognize inclusive structural principles. Grotefend's inspiration was astoundingly simple."

Whatever guided or motivated him, he broke the spine of the Persian riddle. Not altogether by himself—which

never happens, or very seldom. Linguists as well as inquisitive tourists had studied the crisp little marks chis-
eled here and there across Iran and had tried without
success to make sense of them. Only once in a while a clue
would be noted.

Near the end of the tenth century a traveler named ibn-
Haukul visited the colossal bas-relief at Behistun. This
huge and almost unapproachable sculpture high on a rust-
colored cliff illustrates the victory of Darius the Great
over some rebellious princes; but ibn-Haukul, after contemplating the figures, stated that in his opinion they represented a schoolmaster chastising a group of disobedient
pupils.

Two centuries later the Arab geographer Yaqut thought
it represented the Sassanian hero Khusru Parviz astride his
stallion Shabdiz, accompanied by Queen Shirin. Yaqut
must have been smoking something because it is hard to
visualize a lady in the tableau, and certainly there is no
horse.

A nineteenth-century French traveler to Behistun
thought he saw twelve apostles beneath a crucifix.

An Englishman, Sir Robert Ker Porter, saw the conquest of Israel by Shalmaneser: the ten little victims fac-
ing Darius being members of the ten tribes. This must be
so, Ker Porter said, because the pointed bonnet worn by
the last rebellious prince was undoubtedly the miter of a
Levite priest.

All of which should remind us that what we see, wherever we go, is usually what we expect to see.

The Spanish ambassador to Persia, Don García de Silva
Figueroa, after examining "a remarkable inscription
carved on black jaspar," provided one of the first authentic clues. These letters, he said, "are neither Chaldean, nor
Hebrew, nor Greeke, nor Aribike, nor of any other Nation

which was ever found of old, or at this day to be extant."

A wealthy young Roman named Pietro della Valle, touring the East to regain his equilibrium after a disastrous love affair, met and married a bewitching maiden in Baghdad—which sounds implausible because a foreigner, even a wealthy young Roman, is not apt to meet a Baghdad maiden. Nevertheless he did; and with his bride, Sitti Maani, Pietro resumed traveling. At the ruins of Persepolis he copied some announcements which he brought back to Italy, the first examples of Persian cuneiform to reach European scholars.

Then came Sir Thomas Herbert who saw and studied "lynes of strange characters . . . so mysticall, so odly framed . . . consisting of Figures, obelisk, triangular and pyramidall, yet in such Simmetry and order as cannot well be called barbarous." They might, he thought, "conceale some excellent matter, though to this day wrapt up in the dim leaves of envious obscuritie."

A wandering jewel-trader, Jean Chardin, correctly guessed that the odly framed lynes should be read from left to right and noted that they often occurred in groups of three, though he did not suspect that three languages were involved.

Next came Engelbert Kämpfer and Samuel Flower and Cornelius van Bruyn and Carsten Niebuhr, experienced and dedicated philologists even if they do sound like suspects in a British murder mystery.

Kämpfer spent three days at Persepolis: "To copy the sculpture and inscriptions of all these buildings with the measurements, decorations, and all that is worthy of being noticed would take more than two months. I shall communicate faithfully all I have been able to acquire. . . ."

Neibuhr assiduously copied several tablets and was the first to delineate an Old Persian alphabet. He insisted that he could recognize forty-two letters among the chicken tracks, and in fact he did identify thirty-two.

Then there was Abraham Hyacinthe Anquetil du Perron, a theological student in Paris who became obsessed by the idea that he must read the sacred literature of the Parsees, the *Zend Avesta*. He obtained a grant from the French government and sailed to Pondicherry, at that time a French outpost, where he set about learning modern Persian. Having accomplished this, he ventured north in search of Parsee fire-worshipers. He found some, which was not difficult, though it was dangerous. He made friends with the dasturs, the priests, and seven years later returned to Europe with a copy of the *Zend Avesta* written in the ancient script. Nobody could read it—not even the dasturs—but until then no European had so much as seen the book.

Thus, from here and there, came bits and pieces that occasionally fitted together, but most often did not, until one day Grotefend perceived an underlying pattern.

You would suppose that the academic world—at least the philologists—would rush to congratulate the young schoolteacher. Especially after they had read an excerpt from his stimulating article "Praevia de cuneatis quas vocant inscriptionibus Persepolitanis legendis et explicandis relatio" which appeared in the *Göttinger Gelehrten Anzeigen*.

Not so. Well, you may ask, why not?

Alas, the reply is familiar. Its author lacked credentials. He was not a recognized Orientalist. For this reason the journal's editors refused to print the complete essay. The full text did not appear until 1893, forty years after his death.

And while Grotefend's manuscript began to acquire the fine patina of age, Henry Creswicke Rawlinson was born.

Grotefend, the puzzle-master, lived indoors; Rawlinson, a vigorous athletic man, wanted some action. At sixteen he joined the East India Company which shipped him to Bombay. There he worked as paymaster of the first grenadiers, but languages came easily to him—Arabic, Persian, Hindustani—and before long he was regimental interpreter.

When the Afghan Wars seemed about to erupt he was dispatched to Kermānshāh because of his linguistic skill. Here he learned of Behistun, twenty miles away. He rode over to take a look.

His first view was from the Khurasan road, a caravan route that had been in use for at least 5,000 years, and he returned many times. Should you wish to locate Behistun, where so many early tourists had seen whatever they wished to see, it is about 200 miles northeast of Baghdad. And when discussing this with a professional you must say Bīsitūn, not Behistun, the latter being a popular corruption. Professionals care about these things.

An experienced armchair traveler can seldom be startled, but the cliff at Behistun appears quite astonishing from any angle. The bas-relief commemorating Darius' great victory is perhaps 150 feet long and 100 feet high, and the bottom of the carving is at least 300 feet above the ground. Invincible Darius, twice the size of his defeated adversaries, stands nonchalantly with one foot on the stomach of a supine captive and seems to be addressing nine unhappy princes who are roped together by the neck, each with his hands tied behind his back. Darius gestures in a rather benevolent way, which no doubt is misleading; he must be signifying displeasure, or else he is acknowledging the salute of a winged deity who hovers nearby. One gets the impression that Darius and the deity are on familiar terms.

Rawlinson, having admired the giant memorial through a telescope, decided to copy the part he considered most important. This meant, first, a dangerous climb up the rock face.

Here is what he has to say about the situation:

"On reaching the recess which contains the Persian text of the record, ladders are indispensable in order to examine the upper portion of the tablet; and even with ladders there is considerable risk . . . the upper inscriptions can only be copied by standing on the topmost step of the ladder, with no other support than steadying the body against the rock with the left arm, while the left hand holds the notebook, and the right hand is employed with the pencil."

In brief, Rawlinson was high above the Khurasan road without a net, with absolutely nothing for protection except nerve and his sense of balance. You can, if you are imaginative enough, get a touch of vertigo just thinking about it.

Visualizing him at the top of a rickety ladder propped on a rock ledge 300 feet above the ground, with a notebook in one hand, meticulously copying some little wedge-shaped marks—seeing him in that position one is reminded of other nineteenth-century English men and women: Mawson and Shackleton at the South Pole, Franklin in the Arctic, Fanny Bullock Workman in the Himalayas, "Chinese Gordon" in Egypt, Mary Kingsley having tea with cannibals, Lady Hester Stanhope costumed as a Bedouin riding in triumph through the ruined streets of Palmyra. Faced with such people, one can't help thinking that the nineteenth-century English must have been utterly bonkers.

Now back to Rawlinson on his ladder:

"To reach the recess which contains the Scythic translation of the record of Darius is a matter of far greater difficulty."

Why? Well, there was a split in the cliff and the only way to get across was to bridge this gap with a ladder. Rawlinson calls his first attempt "unfortunate." Because of the narrowness of the ledge he was obliged to turn his ladder on its side. That is, with the rungs in a vertical position. He planned to walk across the underside while holding on to the upper side.

All right, here we go:

"If the ladder had been a compact article, this mode of crossing, although far from comfortable, would have been at any rate practicable; but the Persians merely fit in the bars of their ladders without pretending to clench them outside, and I had hardly accordingly begun to cross over when the vertical pressure forced the bars out of their sockets, and the lower and unsupported side of the ladder thus parted company with the upper, and went crashing down over the precipice."

Rawlinson now is dangling by his hands from a broken ladder that may snap at any moment. Below him, empty space. Nor can anybody help him. Good luck, Henry.

Hand over hand he went. You may remember this tingling sensation from childhood—nothingness underneath as you worked your way out a tree limb with the ground at least ten feet below. Rawlinson was a bit higher. From the Khurasan road he must have been about the size of a bug.

Somehow he scrambled back up the Persian side of the cliff. The Scythic translation would have to wait awhile.

A third account of Darius' victory, written in Babylonian, was more difficult to approach than either the Persian, where one need only stand on the topmost rung of a ladder, or the Scythic, where one must cross a chasm.

After studying this new challenge Rawlinson decided it was too dangerous. Peasants who lived nearby and who were accustomed to tracking mountain goats across the face of the mountain told him that the Babylonian legend could not be reached.

While he was wondering how to obtain this text "a wild Kurdish boy" volunteered to try. Rawlinson promised him a fat reward so the boy started up. Using ropes, driving wood pegs into the cliff, hanging by fingers and toes, he crossed a twenty-foot sheet of perpendicular rock "in a manner which to a looker-on appeared quite miraculous." From this point it was easy.

"He had brought a rope with him attached to the first peg, and now, driving in a second, he was enabled to swing himself right over the projecting mass of rock. Here with a short ladder he formed a swinging seat, like a painter's cradle, and, fixed upon this seat, he took under my direction the paper cast of the Babylonian translation of the records of Darius."

The question that remains, though, is this: If an agile Kurdish boy, risking his life, could just manage to reach the text, how was it carved? Unless you believe in levitation the answer seems to be that a fantastic scaffold was attached to the cliff in 516 B.C.

Rawlinson says no more about the Kurdish daredevil. Presumably the boy got down, collected his reward, lived more or less happily ever after, and bored his grandchildren with the details of his famous climb. Concerning the mad Englishman, we do know that he lived happily ever after, more or less, wrote learned papers which were read to the Royal Asiatic Society in London, and sometimes was pointed out on the street—although today you would have a hard time finding anybody who recognized his name. But of course if you should mention Darius the

Great these days everybody would think you were talking about a wrestler.

And if—at a cocktail party, let's say—you should mention Michael Ventris or Sir Arthur Evans you probably would get an uncomprehending stare. Evans might possibly draw a response. He excavated the palace at Knossos and there are people who remember that, just as they remember the Rosetta stone.

Knossos! Ah yes, let me think. It was on Crete or Mykonos, one of those islands, and there were murals showing acrobats somersaulting over bulls. Also, some kind of labyrinth. Yes indeed, the old palace of Knossos! King Minos lived there, I believe. Or was that Theseus? Or Croesus? Or did Knossos have something to do with the sword of Damocles? Those Greek names all sound alike.

Mykonos, no. Crete, yes. Damocles and Croesus, no. Minos, yes. Theseus, not quite; he found the apartments exciting but it cost an arm and a leg to live there.

Now back to Michael and Sir Arthur.

In 1889 the Ashmolean Museum at Oxford received a collection of artifacts, the bequest of a wealthy traveler. The museum's steward was Arthur Evans, an extremely nearsighted little man who always felt his way around with a cane, and while examining this bequest he was puzzled by a carnelian seal with oval sides bearing unfamiliar hieroglyphs. It was said to have come from Sparta.

Four years later Evans himself visited Sparta where he noticed several of these curious objects. He was told they came from Crete.

The following year he visited Crete and saw quite a few village girls wearing them as amulets, calling them *galópetrais*, milkstones. It was important to wear a milkstone while pregnant.

He bought as many as he could, traded modern cameo brooches for others, and managed to copy the hieroglyphs on most of those whose owners would not give them up. Occasionally he saw one with linear characters suggesting an alphabet. This, in turn, suggested the possibility of not one but two unknown systems of writing.

The next step, logically, would be to excavate. The site of Knossos seemed a good place, but Turkey controlled the island and there was difficulty with Turkish bureaucrats. Schliemann had run afoul of them years earlier. Evans was balked until 1899 when the Turks left Crete. Then he got a permit. He dug into King Minos' palace, cemented it together, and painted it as he imagined it must have looked in 1500 B.C. His re-creation was not very convincing; a number of archaeologists are upset, and today even the tourists look suspiciously at those ponderous brown Victorian colonnades. However, the job seems to have satisfied Evans. Anyway he was less concerned with architectural niceties than with the people who used to live there.

In the ruins he found almost 3,000 baked clay tablets and after studying them he concluded that the linear inscriptions were of two sorts.

"Much study and comparison will be necessary for the elucidation of these materials," he wrote in March, 1901, for *The Monthly Review*.

If, as may well be the case, the language in which they were written was some primitive form of Greek we need not despair of the final decipherment of these Knossian archives, and the bounds of history may eventually be so enlarged as to take in the "heroic age" of Greece. In any case the weighty question, which years before I had set myself to solve on Cretan soil, has found, so far at least, an answer. That great early civilisation was not dumb, and the written records of the Hellenic world are carried back some seven centuries beyond the date of the first known historic writings. But what, perhaps, is even more remarkable than this is that, when we examine in detail the linear script of these Mycenaean documents, it is impossible not to recognize that we have here a system of writing, syllabic and perhaps partly alphabetic, which stands on a distinctly higher level of development than the hieroglyphs of Egypt or the cuneiform script of contemporary Syria and Babylonia. It is not till some five centuries later that we find the first dated examples of Phoenician writing.

In 1909 he published a handsome volume entitled *Scripta Minoa I* which had to do mostly with the hieroglyphs. Subsequent volumes, he announced, would focus on scripts A and B.

Up to this point, excepting the doubtful reconstruction of Minos' palace, Arthur Evans was highly esteemed by his colleagues and celebrated by the public. But now he insisted on keeping the tablets to himself. He would not permit other specialists to examine them, and because he himself could not translate them the ancient Cretan language, or languages, remained a mystery. Situations like this are always surprising: one never expects an intelligent, brilliantly educated humanist to play dog-in-the-manger. But because of Evans' recalcitrance the second volume of *Scripta* was not published until 1952, eleven years after his death.

Michael Ventris and his associate Chadwick, who share credit for the decipherment of Linear B, would later say, "Two generations of scholars were thus deprived of the possibility of doing any constructive work on the problem."

Yet it was Evans, despite himself, and without realizing it, who encouraged Ventris.

In 1936 Evans gave a lecture at Burlington House in London where one member of the audience was young Michael, fourteen years old. He did not attend by chance, nor because his parents wanted to hear the elderly scholar discuss Minoan riddles; he was there because he enjoyed linguistic challenges. At the age of six, for example, while other children were struggling with English, he taught himself Polish. "He had not only a remarkable visual memory," says Chadwick, "but, what is rarely combined with it, the ability to learn a language by ear."

Ventris would go on to become an architect specializing in prefabricated schoolhouses; at the same time, though, he followed the progress of linguistics as closely as a flower tracks the sun. How much Evans influenced him can only be guessed, but when he was just eighteen he published an *Introduction to Minoan Writing*—based on the tablets Sir Arthur did not have locked up in his closet and whatever else was available. Ventris thought the language might be Etruscan, an opinion he maintained for several years.

During the Second World War he served as a navigator in the RAF and later with the British Army of Occupation in Germany, but no matter where he went he managed to take along some copies of Minoan documents. After the war, between prefabricated schoolhouses, he continued chipping away at the problem.

This kind of thing: "certain words of the same type afforded in their endings variants which could be considered as flexional endings of declensions, whereas other words of the same type showed notable modifications . . ."

and so on. The point is that Ventris, an amateur, was making more progress than the professionals, and some of his notes were handed along to a young Cambridge philologist, John Chadwick.

Chadwick was busy but he took a look at what Ventris had done. Then he looked again. Later he would write: "Those four days were the most exciting of my life. . . ." He had recently been married, so it would be instructive to know what his wife thought of that statement.

Ventris and Chadwick began corresponding and a time would come when they chose to address each other in Mycenaean Linear B—which surely establishes a record for snobbery. Although it should be mentioned that Champollion occasionally talked to himself in Coptic.

With Chadwick's help, Ventris proved that the language was an early form of Greek. This surprised philologists, who thought the Greeks of that era had not known how to read and write. Even those hoplites who later besieged Troy were assumed to be illiterate. However, there could be no doubt about the age of the Minos tablets because a style of pottery found with them also turned up in the Nile valley among ushabtis and mummies from the Eighteenth Dynasty: 1580 to 1350 B.C.

So we have learned when Linear B was in use, and it must have developed from Linear A, thus pushing back the literary frontier several more centuries. And because Linear A probably evolved from the hieroglyphs it seems quite possible that Aegean children started going to school 5,000 years ago. But the first day of class is less interesting than the fact that some tablets discovered on the mainland refer to Achilles and Theseus as well as to unlucky Hector and his comrades.

Achilles, Hector, Priam, Ajax—such names would lead anybody to expect a bloody confirmation of Homer's best-seller. Unfortunately, what the tablets have preserved almost without exception are common lists—invoices—of people or things. References to carpenters, masons, bath attendants, weavers, gods, goddesses. List upon list of commodities. Figs. Olives. Tunics. Spices. Lamps. Helmets. Cauldrons. War chariots. Goats.

"Most of the phrases are quite short," said Ventris. "The longest sentence I can find has eleven words and occurs on a tablet from Pylos which seems to be an assessment of tithes, somewhat as follows: 'The priestess holds the following acres of productive land on a lease from the property-owners, and undertakes to maintain them in the future.'" How tedious. Nothing about Europa aboard her white bull, not even Icarus plunging into the Aegean from 30,000 feet. Nothing but inventories and leases.

Not only is it disappointing that the Cretans bequeathed us such mundane information, it is also rather odd. You would expect them to hand along the big news, as Darius the Great did on his tremendous Behistun panel, or Hammurabi on his black diorite legal stela, or the various pharaohs who celebrated on sandstone their immortal triumphs. The explanation is thought to be this: important Cretan records were written on some sort of expensive paper, whereas the inventories were scratched on clay which could be discarded or broken up to be used again. But the terrible fire that swept Knossos and destroyed Cretan civilization burned all the paper and baked these inconsequential clay tablets for posterity.

That there was such a fire, and that it devastated King Minos' palace, seems undeniable. If you visit the ruins you will see, despite Sir Arthur's handiwork, many dark and sinister tongues of soot; you can even tell which direction the wind blew on that calamitous day 3,500 years ago— from the south, which means that the palace burned in late April or early May, because that is the season when a south wind blows across Crete. Whether the palace was burned by invaders or by some natural catastrophe, perhaps the eruption of Thera, will usually get you an argument in academic circles.

Evans himself suspected a militant invasion: "Under the closely compacted pavement . . . there were built in, between solid piles of masonry, double tiers of stone cists lined with lead. Only a few were opened and they proved to be empty, but there can be little doubt that they were constructed for the deposit of treasure. Whoever destroyed and plundered the Palace had failed to discover these receptacles. . . ."

Whatever happened, the wrath of the gods broke over Knossos. Nobody argues that.

One further catastrophe, very small by comparison, must be inscribed on the Cretan record. We cannot yet read Linear A or the primitive hieroglyphs. Ventris would have gone to work on them, of course, but time ran out. In 1956 at the age of thirty-four he was killed in the ugliest way: a car accident.

Chadwick, himself an ex-serviceman, carefully avoided taking credit for deciphering Linear B: "I have always endeavoured to make it clear that all the merits of the discovery are due to Ventris; my role was that of the first infantry division sent in to widen the breach. . . ."

It's a sad conclusion. Working together, they might have solved Linear A and then the hieroglyphs. Maybe. Maybe not. We'll never know. As it stands, the first Aegean stories wait. Eventually, we assume—because we dislike the assumption of defeat—eventually a new cryptographic prodigy will appear, entranced by linguistic puzzles. Then we may look forward to some laundry lists, to the names of forgotten kings, perhaps to a new epic which begins:

It was a dark and stormy night . . .

If we do not know much about the earliest language of
Crete, we know practically nothing about that of India—
except what it looked like. Hundreds of amulets and
incised seals made of copper or soapstone have been collected from the ruins of Harappa and Mohenjo-Daro in
the Indus valley. They date from the second or third millennium B.C. and, like Cretan milkstones, they bear a variety of symbolic signs together with representations of
monkeys, tigers, parrots, doves, humped cattle, squirrels,
crocodiles, et cetera.

As yet these curious objects have not met their Champollion, nor does he seem to be waiting just offstage; almost no progress has been made toward understanding the
symbols or the exquisite little pictures. Ordinarily the
script should be read from left to right, but sometimes the
opposite is true. Sometimes it should be read as the ox
plows, one way and then the other—a method called
boustrophedonic. We do not even know how many separate signs there are. One scholar claims to have distinguished 900, although 250 is a more commonly accepted
number, the rest being variants.

The script is a stiff, precise mélange of stylized images
and "alphabetic" symbols unrelated to any other language
except, perhaps, that of Easter Island—and we will come
back to Easter Island in a moment. It cannot be linked to
the oldest comprehensible language of India, a precursor
of Sanskrit, because Sanskrit-speaking people did not enter the Indus valley until about 1500 B.C. The *Rig-Veda*, in
fact, refers to these first citizens as *dasyus* or *dāsas:* a
swarthy, pug-nosed race of infidels who spoke gibberish.

Harappa and Mohenjo-Daro—which means Mound of
the Dead—seem to have been their great cities, but the
ruins of many others have been located, and it is thought
that the Indus culture extended from the Simla hills to the

Arabian Sea, a distance of 1,000 miles. The area covered by all of their dead cities is twice the size of the old Egyptian empire.

Harappa and Mohenjo are twins, so much alike that archaeologists believe they could have been built by the same ruler, despite the fact that they are 400 miles apart. They may have been twin capitals. They did not grow by chance, as most cities do; they were planned as deliberately as Brasília or Salt Lake City and are just as predictable. Everything was arranged. The mechanical, conservative, windowless, unchanging architecture—block after block after block—implies a totalitarian attitude. These are barracks, not apartments. There is a terrible efficiency about this culture, observes Stuart Piggott, which recalls the worst of Rome, and with it "a stagnation hard to parallel in any known civilization of the Old World." And he goes on brusquely: "There is something in the Harappa civilization that I find repellent."

Where did such people come from? Because the earliest inhabitants of the valley lived in ragged, disorderly villages. But then, 2,500 years before Christ, out of the dust and mist came these unimaginative, dark, flat-nosed builders who knew exactly what a city should look like. And they lived in their geometrical barracks for ten centuries without changing a thing. The style of building never changed. The language did not change. The first carved amulets are the same as the last.

The longest inscription contains seventeen characters. Most contain five or six. They may be invocations to a god, or laundry lists. No Harappan poems have been found— unless they are as brief as haiku. Obviously there are no historical records. This means that even if the script could be deciphered we wouldn't learn much. What it does tell us, though, is something about the monotony of their life.

Egypt was conservative, yet over the centuries its language changed. So did Mesopotamian. So do all languages, or almost all. At Harappa and Mohenjo-Daro nothing changed.

They were, it must be said, a clean race of people. Mother India today is less than that, but the ancient mounds have disclosed bathhouses and sanitation systems. In fact these people used the seat toilet: a channel through the wall connecting with a pottery receptacle or a brick drain outside. The drains were engineered as skillfully as those at Knossos; they empty into a central drainage system beneath the street.

Very little else can be deduced about the Indus people. They traded with Mesopotamia, that much has been established. Sumerian cylinder seals were discovered at Harappa, and Harappan seals have turned up in the Tigris-Euphrates ruins. And cuneiform tablets from the Near East speak of a marvelous land where the sun rises, called Dilmun or Telmun, whose ships bring pearls and cosmetics and stone beads and much copper and silver and ivory combs. Dilmun might refer to Bahrein in the Persian Gulf, a port of call, or it might mean the source of this wealth, the great Indus civilization.

Just how far the commercial interchange extended, and when it declined and ultimately stopped, is uncertain. One Harappan bead—dated about 1600 B.C.—was found on the island of Crete. Trade with Persia might have lasted another century.

Then came the Sanskrit invaders.

Harappa and Mohenjo-Daro fell quickly. Their civilization may already have been disintegrating, which usually is the case when a nation succumbs to an invader. There is evidence of this in the cheap construction of later buildings, in subdivisions, and so forth—things we ourselves are familiar with.

But the end was abrupt. Thirteen skeletons were uncovered in a room at Mohenjo: all showed signs of violent
death. One skull had been split by an ax or a sword. In a
different arrondissement nine skeletons huddled together—five of them children. Nearby lay two elephant
tusks. The adults may have been ivory workers who had
planned to escape with the valuable tusks.

If these people chose not to write about themselves, and
apparently they did not, we might expect them to describe their lives some other way. After all, we find nothing so consistently absorbing as our own unprecedented
existence. But again, they left practically nothing. No
Pompeiian mural, no crushed golden harp, not even a bas-
ketball court. As for sculpture—tiny fragments. Fragments
of tiny people, goggle-eyed ceramic caricatures, as though
they considered themselves too insignificant to be remembered. There are not more than half a dozen genuinely
revealing figures. One is an insolent dancing girl loosely
modeled in bronze, with lanky arms and legs, extremely
sure of herself, nude except for a necklace and bracelets,
with her long hair twisted into a rope, one hand cocked on
her hip, and a look of hard experience. Another is a carved
stone figure—an important, bearded ruler with slit eyes
and thick lips, coldly arrogant. They do go well together,
this antipathetic couple, the dancing girl—who might
have been a slave—and the merciless middle-aged man:
they seem to represent two persistent types. Or you could
say they symbolize life and death.

One more thing. In the rubble of a little city called
Chanhu-Daro an archaeologist noticed a brick with the
print of a cat's paw slightly overlapped by the paw of a
dog. These were not symbolic designs but actual prints
left by the animals as they raced across a wet brick. And it
was clear from the impress of the pads that both had been
going full speed, the dog chasing the cat.

There you have the Indus testament. Beads. Copper and stone seals. Pots with brief legends. A few rings. Bracelets. Clay caricatures. Crumbling skeletons. Elephant tusks. Millions of bricks. Two sculpted individuals altogether different, equally expressive.

At present this is one of the most desolate regions on earth—hot, windy, colorless, salty, and dry. The trees are twisted and small. Bushes are gray, cloaked with dust. No civilization could have developed here unless the land at one time had been fertile. As indeed it was. Excavators found dikes, which means that the valley often was flooded. Nor are the bricks sun-dried, they are kiln-baked. If the Indus never had much rain there would be no reason to bake bricks; only in wet weather do you need durable building blocks. So there must have been plenty of drizzly days once upon a time in that blistering valley.

As to why the climate changed, we must guess. It may have been a natural sequence; or the people, not realizing what they were doing, may have altered the climate. An immense supply of wood was needed to fire the kilns to bake those millions of bricks, but as they chopped down the trees they reduced the amount of water vapor provided by the forest, and water vapor returns to the earth as rain. Thus the kilns were fueled, bricks plopped off the assembly line while the forest shrank, and one day the rain stopped.

The Indus valley civilization vanished like the trees and the rain. The people are gone, their language a mystery. In a sense, of course, they have become an eternal part of India; but as a race or a nation with an intricate history of kings, or a politburo, and holy days and public events and famous ball players and dignitaries—they are gone.

Now about Easter Island, that isolated South Pacific rock halfway around the world from the Indus valley.

Nothing connects these two. They could hardly be farther apart, chronologically there is a 3,000-year gap, and no language pertaining either to the Indus script or to the Easter Island "talking boards" has been found anywhere else. Yet the languages appear to be related. It is not a matter of occasional similarity but of a great many similarities. This must be coincidence because all knowledge of the Indus language was lost soon after the Aryan invasion about 1500 B.C., whereas the Easter Island script is recent; it was understood well into the nineteenth century A.D. and seems to have developed only a few centuries before that.

Kohau-rongo-rongo, the talking boards, may be less spectacular than the monstrous stone heads but to a philologist they are more exciting. The island must have been studded with them in 1722 when Admiral Jaakob Roggeveen landed on Easter Sunday, but after the arrival of Belgian and French missionaries, who did not like the look of such devilish lettering, the boards started to disappear. Only twenty-one have survived. Or nineteen, because two of them might be fakes.

A certain Father Zumbohm, more inquisitive and less bigoted than his brothers, asked some natives for an explanation. The sight of a tablet pleased them, he reports, and one immediately began to read the text by singing. "But others shouted 'No it is not like that!' The disagreement among my teachers was so great that, in spite of my effort, I was not much more informed after their lesson than beforehand."

About 1870 a few of the boards reached Bishop Jaussen in Tahiti. Rather than start a fire, as clerics are apt to do when confronted by mysterious objects, Jaussen tried to find somebody who could interpret them. A former citizen of Easter Island, Metoro Tauara, was at that time working on a nearby plantation and the bishop asked him to read a board. Metoro was happy to oblige. He chanted a line, then he turned the board upside down in order to chant the following line. This, most scholars agree, is correct. Every other line of Easter Island script is inverted. Nobody knows why.

The first scientist to study these boards was a British anthropologist, Mrs. Katherine Routledge. In 1914 she interviewed the last surviving native who had been trained to read them; but the old man, dying of leprosy, did not say very much.

Then, in 1954, a German ethnologist named Barthel came upon a bilingual document in the Roman archives of the order to which Bishop Jaussen had belonged: Metoro's Polynesian along with the bishop's French translation.

This should have been a great help. It wasn't. Metoro, anxious to please, had given the impression that he understood what the boards were talking about, when in fact he understood very little. Even so, Barthel managed to obtain a few fixes, enough to determine that there were approximately 500 signs and that the language was based upon what specialists call the phonetic rebus. For example, the Polynesian word *pure* means shell but it can also mean prayer. Now, if you know most of the words or syllables in a sentence and come to *pure* you could probably interpret it correctly; but if most of the words were unknown—and so far very little of the Easter Island script has been deciphered—you would be forced to guess. And, of course, one mistake encourages another.

Nevertheless, Barthel kept at it and came up with a sensational line: "Then they addressed their prayers to the god of Rangitea."

Rangitea means "bright field." It is the name of one of the Tonga or Friendly Islands close to Fiji, about 1,500 miles west of Easter Island. If Barthel's translation is correct he has provided a clue to the origin of the Easter Islanders—something which has caused squabbles among ethnologists, historians, and archaeologists.

Metoro's reading, however inadequate, was the best that could be obtained. Other natives gave totally different translations of the same text.

If or when the language is resolved we might learn about a connection with the Indus valley. It's at least very curious that present-day Islanders speak a form of Munda, a language once spoken in India.

Professor Piggott, an authority on the Indus civilization, does not think they are related and he is displeased by such conjecture: "One can only say that, apart from attempts to connect it with the nineteenth-century 'script' of the natives of Easter Island in the Pacific, the Harappa script has perhaps suffered less from lunatics than the Minoan. But perhaps it is only the shortness of the available Harappa inscriptions that has deprived us of such entertaining fantasies as the transliteration of the Phaistos Disc into Basque hexameters."

Professor Hans Jensen, with appalling erudition, has summarized the argument in his thick study of practically everything ever written anywhere, *Die Schrift in Vergangenheit und Gegenwart:*

> Hevesy believes the Easter Island script to be very old; in addition, he is convinced of the reliability of the native tradition that Polynesian immigrants brought sixty-seven inscribed wooden tablets with them some 900 years ago. Now he puts forward the hypothesis that the Easter Island script and the Indus script go back to a common primordial form. . . . The close correspondence between the strange stone monuments on the is-

land of Guam and ones just like them on Easter Island seems to him to indicate the route the script followed in its migration from south-east India. Even the oldest Chinese picture-script, he believes, in agreement with the views of Heine-Geldern, Rottauscher and Shiro-gorov, must be regarded as closely related. . . .

In short, you'll have to wait awhile.

When it comes to Old Mayan we have another kettle of glyphs and a new scenario. The locale is neither an island in the South Pacific, Homer's wine-dark sea, nor a sun-blasted Asiatic valley, but the breathless green jungle of Yucatán, and this time the principal actor is villainous. It was churlish of Sir Arthur Evans to lock up his Minoan tablets, but for authentic wickedness in the department of linguistics you must look to Diego de Landa; although it should be pointed out that he did only what he thought was proper—an impenetrable defense—and there are those who do not consider him malevolent. Dr. Michael Coe, for instance, whose Mayan credentials should not be doubted, refers to "the great Bishop Landa."

However he is to be judged, this is what happened.

A shipment of Franciscan monks arrived at Mérida in 1549, among them Diego de Landa, twenty-five years old and abristle with Christian energy. He wasted no time. Scarcely had he unpacked his bags when native shrines began dropping like tenpins, their idols smashed, and young Diego definitely became a monk for the Indians to remember.

Then, on July 12, 1562, he staged an auto-da-fé that still—after four centuries—brings down curses upon his tonsured head. Into the fire on this occasion went several thousand examples of Mayan sculpture, as many painted books as Diego and his associates were able to find, and a number of distressed Yucatecans who lifted incomprehensible prayers to the Great Spirit.

We will say nothing more about the people, who would be gone by now in any case. Their art work and their books, though, would still be around.

Serious charges require scrupulous attention, so it must be pointed out that Diego de Landa was not the first vandal cleric; the deliberate destruction of Mayan culture was under way when he arrived. It must also be mentioned that his pious orgy shocked many Spaniards. The bishop of Yucatán, Francisco Toral, had been in Mexico City when de Landa supervised the auto-da-fé, and upon his return to Mérida he was so outraged that he ordered an investigation. He wrote angrily to King Philip II that the monks responsible for this act were men of little knowledge and even less charity, and he submitted the case to the Council of the Indies. Because of Bishop Toral's protest, de Landa was recalled to Spain.

In Spain, preparing to defend himself against charges that he had usurped the bishop's authority and that his attempt to crush idolatry had been unnecessarily harsh, de Landa wrote his famous account of life among the New World barbarians: *Relación de las cosas de Yukatán.*

It is in this account that we meet the terrible yet familiar justification for book-burning:

"These people use definite signs or letters to record in their books their early history and their lore. By means of those letters, as well as by drawings and figures, they can understand their own story and make others understand and learn from it. We found a great number of books, and since there was nothing in them but superstitions and lies of the devil, we burned them all, to the great woe and lamentation of the people."

In 1573, after having been censured for excessive zeal,

Diego de Landa was promoted and returned to the New World as Bishop of Yucatán, a fact which may or may not surprise you.

And because of his *Relación*—the most important document concerning sixteenth-century Mayans—we are left to muse upon this paradox: a man who did everything possible to annihilate their civilization is the man who preserved what little we know about it.

The painted books that he incinerated were, to those with an eye for such things, almost unbearably beautiful. They were made from hammered plant fibers sized with lime, they unfolded like a Chinese screen and were exquisitely illustrated in various colors: orange, blue, red, black, yellow, white, blue-green. Many of them were bound in wood or leather inlaid with semiprecious stones, so that they resembled those sumptuous European books from the Middle Ages. Our friend and future bishop Diego burned all but three, which somehow escaped his dragnet.

One is in Dresden. It is known to be a copy of an earlier manuscript dating from the peak of Mayan artistic activity, the so-called Classic Period, which ended around A.D. 900. Of the three, this codex—eight inches high and twelve feet long, consisting of seventy-eight pages—is the most exotic; and though Mayan writing has been only partly deciphered, enough has been learned to know that this book contains mathematical and astronomical tables.

The priests of Copán, incidentally, understood our planetary system better than did the ancient astronomers of the Near East; they were calculating on a scale of hundreds of millions of years at a time when sophisticated Europeans thought the earth was 5,000 years old; and they measured the length of a solar year more accurately than does our modern calendar. Yet, says Leo Deuel, for these people the concern with time did not imply a tyranny of time. The past and the future might merge. "This world would come to an end, but it would have a new beginning."

The Codex Tro-Cortesianos in Madrid is the longest, and its cumbersome label needs to be explained. Part of this codex turned up in 1865, the property of a Madrid paleographer named Tro y Ortolano, after whom it was called the Troano. Fifteen years later another manuscript was found in Estremadura, called the Cortés because this famous conquistador might have owned it. Then a French scholar realized that these were not independent codices; they belonged together. But somehow, somewhere, for some reason, the book had been cut almost in half.

Like the Dresden codex, the Tro-Cortesianos is a replica of a Classic Period manuscript. It seems to consist of ceremonial directions that relate to hunting, rainmaking, and planting, together with the dates of religious festivals. Most authorities believe it was copied just for the information, without regard to aesthetics, by somebody who was not an artist—maybe a priest. If that assumption is true the Mayans must have been supernaturally talented because the artistic level of the Madrid codex is beyond the reach of an untrained person today.

You can see this book at the Museo de América, and despite the faded colors and half-obliterated drawing it is not an exhibit you overlook. The halves are displayed separately. The "Fragmento Cortesiano" is perhaps ten feet long, the "Fragmento Troano" a bit longer. Each of the 56 sheets—112 pages because they are painted on both sides— each is about the size of a modern book page, but there all similarity ends. The information that unfolds is singularly unfamiliar.

For instance, among the birds, beasts, and glyphs you will come upon a sequence of sixteen little panels in which an animal, possibly a dog or a deer, has been tied to a tree—either a tree or a hat rack—by its right foreleg. In several panels the rope has been looped around the creature's neck and it is grimacing as though it were being strangled. Now, the pragmatic observer will say this clearly depicts game caught in a snare. Myself, I have doubts. After studying the remorseless scene for a few minutes it is easy to persuade yourself that what you are looking at is a parable of man's existence.

These two fragments of a single codex just might not have been painted by the same hand. The Troano is in slightly better shape—the black, blue, and reddish brown colors less faded; but what is significant is that the drawing appears sharper, more precise, more accomplished. It is unmistakably more satisfying than the Cortesiano. If indeed these halves were painted by different men that fact might almost explain the mysterious separation.

The Codex Peresianus, in the Paris Bibliothèque Nationale, contains various prophecies and is thought to have been painted during the tenth or eleventh century. It was found beneath some waste paper in the basement of the library, the name *Pérez* scrawled on its wrapping. So tell me, if you can, how it got there. How could anybody handle such a thing—an extremely old, richly illustrated book in a totally unintelligible language—how could anybody pick it up and toss it aside?

Only these three codices escaped the fanatic Franciscan, although there is in Mexico City a fourth whose authenticity has been questioned. Thus we can study three books for clues to the Mayan civilization. As Coe remarks, it is as if future historians of the English-speaking world were obliged to evaluate us on the basis of two prayer books and *Pilgrim's Progress*.

But there are rumors of a fifth book, owned by an individual—somebody in Mexico—who would be willing to sell it if the price is right; if he, or she, could do so without being prosecuted. The Mexican government would seize this book, of course, if it could be located. If it exists.

And de Landa tells us that priests sometimes were buried with their books. Scraps of paper flecked with color occasionally have been found in Mayan graves, which seems to verify his statement, so another Dead Sea treasure might turn up, though that would be miraculous.

Then there are glyphs on the gloriously decorated bowls you see in galleries, museums, private collections, and textbook reproductions, in addition to glyphs carved or painted on temple walls at archaeological sites. So there does remain quite a lot to work with, but not enough, not nearly enough. Except for Diego de Landa we probably would understand Mayan as well as Egyptian.

Still, we are indebted to this violent priest. If it weren't for his curiosity about Mayan picture writing we would have no Mu. The line of descent may appear circuitous, but in fact it is easily traced.

Young Diego, while smashing idols and baptizing converts, decided to find out what these un-Christian symbols meant. He therefore attempted to reduce them to an alphabet, more or less as Bishop Jaussen did—or tried to do—with the Easter Island symbols. He went through the letters of the European alphabet as they are pronounced in Spanish and he asked a Mayan prince, Nachi Cocon, to draw for each letter the appropriate glyph. If Prince Nachi had been subjected to this exercise by an English-speaking inquisitor the result, obviously, would have been different. There was no Englishman present to amplify the confusion, but what de Landa got by himself deserves some kind of a prize:

Como se escribe a?

The Spanish *a*, as everybody knows, does not sound like the English *a*. To Nachi it sounded like the Mayan word for turtle. He drew a stylized picture of a turtle's head.

Como se escribe b?

Nachi drew an oval which he divided into three sections by means of two horizontal lines, and in the center section he drew an irregular oval accompanied by three dots. *B*, or *bay*, sounded like the Mayan word signifying a path or a journey; he therefore had drawn parallel lines to indicate the borders of a path and he had placed a foot between them. The irregular oval represented the sole, the dots indicated toes. It was logical, perfectly clear, and it had the charming incoherence of language spoken in a dream.

Como se escribe c?

And so on until *zed*.

De Landa presumably was satisfied with this Alice-in-Wonderland equation, and if one considers the witless auto-da-fé for which he was responsible there is something fine and just about his accomplishment.

Nachi, one might suppose, was handsomely rewarded for his part in the translation. Well, we are told that some time after his death his body was exhumed and his bones were scattered by order of the bishop of Yucatán, Diego de Landa. Why? It seems that de Landa grew suspicious. He feared that Nachi Cocon's apparent conversion to Christianity might not have been genuine; the Mayan prince might secretly have clung to the idolatrous faith of his fathers.

In any event, the alphabet which these two had created was lost and forgotten until 1863 when *Relación de las cosas de Yukatán* turned up in the Madrid archives. And the man who found it, the remarkable French abbé Charles Étienne Brasseur de Bourbourg, soon crowned the bishop's peculiar achievement with fantasy. Out of de Landa's alphabet he concocted Mu.

Mu has not become as famous as Atlantis, but of course Plato's story has been on the market quite a bit longer. Mu is doing all right, and if you don't think so you have not looked in the pseudo-science department of any large paperback bookstore. There you will see *The Lost Continent of Mu, The Sacred Symbols of Mu, Cosmic Forces as They Were Taught in Mu,* ad infinitum. The French abbé did not write any of these; he was far too intelligent, and the fact that he was intelligent makes him all the more preposterous.

He is described as a tall, courtly man, a savant who could speak twelve languages and read twenty. He traveled a lot and seems to have spent relatively little time at his trade. "I am an abbé in the Church," he told an American acquaintance in Rome, "but my ecclesiastical duties have always rested very lightly on me."

He was fascinated by the pre-Hispanic cultures of America, a predilection growing out of the books he read as a child, especially an account of the ruins of Palenque in Yucatán, and he resolved to become an archaeologist. However, without a wealthy father or an indulgent government, he was obliged to earn a living.

This he did in Paris by laboring as a journalist for *Le Monde* and *Le Temps,* meanwhile writing novels with such splendid titles as *l'Exil de Tadmor* and *Sélim ou le Pacha de Salonique.*

Five years of the literary life seems to have left him exhausted or depressed: he enrolled in a seminary at Ghent. And from there, after wandering about Switzerland, he settled in Rome to complete his theological education.

Upon being ordained he got himself shipped to the Sacred College of the Propaganda in Quebec—farther north than he wished, but at least it was the right continent.

Soon he popped up in Mexico City where he studied Nahuatl, the Aztec language, and wrote a little book on antiquities. He then went back to Rome where he spent a while searching the archives for material on early explorations in America. His position with the Church must have been somewhat ambiguous because he took time off to fabricate several more dreamy novels which he described as works of "lesser importance," meaning that he hoped they would make money. Apparently they did not because on his next trip to America he sold his portable missionary chapel. This may sound shocking, but of course when you are in the grip of an obsession you have no choice.

So, back and forth he went from continent to continent, studying, producing potboilers as well as erudite papers, making a name for himself. Then, among stacks of musty documents at the Academy of History in Madrid, he saw de Landa's *Relación,* which had been ignored for almost 300 years.

Greatly excited, thinking he would now be able to translate Mayan, Brasseur went to work on a section of the Codex Tro-Cortesianos.

Nobody has been able to explain what went wrong. That is, we know what happened but we cannot account for it. Here was Abbé Brasseur, a man of high intelligence, a bona fide scholar—a man who had spent years in Mexico and Central America studying the Indians—who actually spoke several native languages. In other words, he was thoroughly qualified. Yet he failed to perceive that the story unfolding from the Madrid codex was a very odd story indeed. Intuition ought to have told him that something somewhere was dreadfully wrong. Nevertheless he went right on translating.

Professor Robert Brunhouse, who has richly summarized this baroque era, observes with neat academic restraint: "Why his fertile imagination got the better of him is not clear."

Others have suggested that perhaps he was overwhelmed by the mass of information he had accumulated, or that the complex Indian mythology affected his judgment. Whatever happened, the abbé's translation of the Tro-Cortesianos—inscribed with a turkey-quill pen and a bottle of homemade reddish brown ink—commences thus:

"The master of the upheaved earth, the master of the calabash, the earth upheaved of the tawny beast . . ."

Halfway through this epic he encountered two symbols more or less resembling the *m* and *u* of de Landa's wondrous alphabet, and he concluded—by what logic, unfortunately, we do not know—that the name of the upheaved real estate was Mu.

This brings us to Dr. Augustus Le Plongeon—"Dr." because at some point in his serpentine career he decided that he was a physician and should be addressed as such. Quite a few peculiar individuals have gone poking through the Mexican jungle, but it is likely that Augustus Le Plongeon with his patriarchal white beard, gleaming blue eyes, great round bald head, and "beautiful brick-dust complexion" was the most unconventional.

He was born in 1826 on the island of Jersey, his father a commodore in the French navy, his mother the daughter of the governor of Mont-Saint-Michel. He went to military school, later attended the Polytechnic Institute of Paris, and one fine day embarked for California on a yacht which foundered off the coast of Chile. Only two men survived. What became of Augustus' companion has not been recorded, but he himself washed ashore at Valparaiso where he learned Spanish and taught school while his clothes dried out. Then he made another attempt to reach California. Again he met foul weather—"the ship was reduced to a pitiable condition"—and for the second time Augustus Le Plongeon nearly ended his career some fathoms down.

Arriving in San Francisco too late for the gold rush, he got a job as county surveyor but this was a bore so he moved along. Hawaii. Tahiti. Australia. Back to San Francisco. Then to Peru where he wrote a book about the Incas, which nobody would publish, though he did break into print with a treatise on earthquakes. And he may have invented a seismograph.

He showed up in New York with three valuable paintings—two by Murillo, one by Juan del Castillo—which he claimed to have discovered in a Peruvian church. He wanted to sell them. He could not find a buyer but he did find Miss Alice Dixon of Brooklyn. Augustus at this time was forty-seven, Alice was twenty-two. They got married and went to Mexico.

For several years they explored deserted cities on the Yucatán peninsula. An 1875 photograph shows them at work in their field headquarters. Augustus, his imperial dome handsomely sun-browned, is seated on a box and appears to be reading aloud. Alice, dressed in white, as immaculate as a Hollywood heroine, listens pensively. Propped against the wall are two perfect symbols of a nineteenth-century marriage: his shotgun and her guitar.

In the spring of 1877 they are on the island of Cozumel. Le Plongeon writes a thirty-page letter to the Honorable John W. Foster, United States Minister to Mexico, announcing a definite similarity between Mayan and Greek: ". . . Who brought the dialect of Homer to America? Or who took to Greece that of the Mayas? Greek is the offspring of Sanscrit. Is Maya? or are they coeval? A clue for ethnologists to follow the migrations of the human family on this old continent. Did the bearded man whose portraits are carved on the massive pillars of the fortress of Chichen-Itza belong to the Mayan Nations? The Maya language is not devoid of words from the Assyrian. . . ."

One day at Chichén something occurred which recalls Schliemann's intuitive feeling for Troy. A party of tourists from Mérida came across him meditating among the ruins. They saw him jump up, rush to the top of a little mound, stamp on it, and order his workmen to dig. Very soon they unearthed a carved tiger with a human face. Le Plongeon ordered them to dig deeper. Twenty-three feet down they uncovered the famous statue of Chacmool that you see in Mexican travel brochures.

Decoding glyphs was as easy as divining the location of buried statues. After all, he explained, the inhabitants of Yucatán were Mayans who still spoke the language of their ancestors even if they could not read the hieroglyphs. And there was de Landa's instructive alphabet.

So, to prove that he knew what he was talking about, he wrote a history of the Mayan people, basing it on Brasseur's fantastic translation of the Madrid codex. His version makes the abbé's account of an upheaved land sound like a neighborhood mud slide. He gave the story dimension and structure. A doomed country with a brilliant civilization, a beautiful queen, a fearless king, intrigue, love, hate, war. Two princes named Coh and Aac in love with their sister, Queen Kinich Kakmo, sometimes called Móo. Coh murdered by Aac, who fled to Uxmal, and so forth. At last the gods speak up:

"In the year 6 Kan, on the 11th Muluc in the month of Zac, occurred terrible earthquakes . . . ten countries were torn asunder and scattered. Unable to stand the force of the convulsion, they sank with their sixty-four million inhabitants. . . ."

Queen Móo escaped to Egypt where, under the name

Isis, she founded Egyptian civilization. A few other refugees populated Central America.

In 1885 Dr. and Mrs. Le Plongeon returned to New York where he published an unusual study of the Mayan alphabet. The language spoken by Jesus, he said, was not Aramaic but Mayan. "Eli, Eli, lama sabachthani!" did not mean what everybody thought it meant. Instead, the outcry was pure Mayan—"Helo, helo, lamah, xabac ta hi!"— and should be translated: "Now, now, I am fainting; darkness covers my face!"

Eleven years later he published his masterpiece, *Queen Móo and the Egyptian Sphinx.*

After that Augustus himself began receding into the darkness. Not Alice, his second self. She went on writing. *Queen Móo's Talisman* appeared in 1902—500 rhymed couplets embellished with songs and pictures. Here is a sample:

> *Loved by the Will Supreme to be reborn,—*
> *In high estate a soul sought earthly mourn;*
> *Life stirred within a beauteous Maya queen*
> *Of noble deeds, of gracious words and mien.*

It did better than you might suspect. The songs were scored for harp, piano, and violin, and the assemblage was produced as "a tragic drama of ancient America, in five acts and ten scenes."

Augustus died not long afterward. There does not seem to be a connection between his death and his wife's drama. Probably he died of heart failure and disappointment. His reputation had evaporated; he was ridiculed and his work ignored. Several times he threatened to destroy his Mayan papers. Instead, he lent them to an ex–Bengal Lancer named James Churchward who was living in Mount Vernon, New York, and who liked to be addressed as "Colonel."

Augustus Le Plongeon and Charles Étienne Brasseur and Bishop Diego de Landa are names that very few people recognize, but you can drop Colonel Churchward's name with some expectation of a response. He is a famous author. His earliest work, quite possibly his most important, was *A Big Game and Fishing Guide to North-Eastern Maine*, but his reputation depends on Mu.

He claimed to have learned about it while serving in India. A friendly temple priest allowed him to see, and later helped him to interpret, the Naacal tablets—seen by nobody else before or since—which revealed to him that Mu had occupied an area of the central Pacific. It was a flat, lush territory, supported by belts of gas—however improbable that may sound. Some 12,000 years ago the gas escaped, hence the deluge.

Your basic commercial hack might squeeze a book out of this which would earn enough to pay the rent for six months, but Churchward knew a really good item when he saw it. Utilizing the ectoplasmic Naacal tablets and several kilos of information supplied by Augustus Le Plongeon—who depended on Abbé Brasseur's upheaved land—derived from Diego de Landa's surrealistic alphabet—Churchward was able to crank out one best-seller after another detailing the life, times, sacred symbols, and cosmic forces of the fabulous continent. Those are the paperbacks you still see in print after fifty years.

Mu does sound like an ideal vacation spot:

Over the cool river, gaudy-winged butterflies hovered in the shade of trees, rising and falling in fairy-like movement, as if better to view their painted beauty in nature's mirror. Darting hither and thither from flower to flower, hummingbirds made their short flights, glistening like living jewels in the rays of the sun. Feathered songsters in bush and tree vied with each other in their sweet lays. . . . On cool evenings might be seen pleasure ships, filled with gorgeously dressed, jewel-bedecked men and women. The long sweeps with which these ships were supplied gave a musical rhythm to the song and laughter of the happy passengers. . . .

For all of which, let the record show, we are indebted to a sixteenth-century Spanish priest. Had Diego de Landa not incinerated the classic Mayan books, nearly obliterating the written language, we could not enjoy this Muvian idyll.

Of course there are other ways of looking at it, such as the fact that even now, after four centuries, despite the work of many scholars, only about half of the Mayan glyphs can be understood: names, dates, relationships—shards of a painted bowl that once was lovely and complete.

You can get some idea of the Mayan world as it used to be if you visit Palenque. Every morning there is a bus from Villahermosa to the village of Santo Domingo de Palenque, and on down the road a few miles you come across a silent, mildewed, ivory city in the jungle. No matter when you go it will be hot. The sun dangles above your head all day like a burning spider.

What this place was called by the Mayans who lived there, we don't know. Palenque, meaning Palisade, is Spanish, but the site had been deserted for almost 1,000 years when Spaniards learned about it. Pottery crushed beneath some of the structures prove that the area was inhabited several centuries before the time of Christ.

From the seventh to the ninth centuries A.D. the Mayan

culture bloomed at Palenque, but archaeologists noticed Totonac votive axes—meaning that enemies from the Gulf Coast may have invaded the city, killed its leaders, and destroyed in a matter of days what had taken many generations to create. This sounds plausible because it sounds familiar.

Other explanations have been offered for Palenque's collapse: earthquakes, hurricanes, disease, depletion of the soil. Or maybe the people just got fed up and revolted against a complacent aristocracy. Whatever happened a millennium ago, the center failed to hold. Peasants subsequently used the vacant buildings for shelter—crude grinding stones have been found in the rubble—and during this period the jungle, which had been slashed and held at a distance by the sophisticated Maya, again crept forward. The city's last inhabitants were parrots, lizards, jaguars, and butterflies.

Cortés rode past Palenque, but it was then so thickly overgrown that he saw nothing. Even the natives who lived nearby, descendants of the founders, were unaware that each tree-covered mound concealed a temple.

John Lloyd Stephens, who visited the place in 1840, wanted to buy it. The ground was reasonably flat, the coast lay not far distant, and he thought he would not have much difficulty shipping the best monuments to New York. Today, of course, Stephens' excellent logic sounds outrageous, but at that time the state of Chiapas was anxious to sell the land: 6,000 acres, ruins included, for $1,500. There was one catch. Mexican law stipulated that no foreigner could buy land unless married to a *hija del país*, a daughter of the country.

Stephens, reflecting upon this, considers it a brilliant stroke, designed to seduce men from their natural allegiance, "for, when wandering in strange countries, alone and friendless, buffeted and battered, with no one to care for him, there are moments when a lovely woman might root the stranger to any spot on earth. On principle I have always resisted such tendencies, but I never before found it to my interest to give way. The ruined city of Palenque was a most desirable piece of property."

However, the situation became embarrassing and complicated. The girl he fancied was already married. Otherwise, there were two middle-aged *hijas del país,* "equally interesting and equally interested," and a fourteen-year-old. For some reason he let these three opportunities pass, so the abandoned city lay unmolested a few years longer.

It was a religious sanctuary, a necropolis, a political seat, an artistic and scientific rendezvous, an unconquered fortress on a lush viridian slope, impregnable until the Totonacs arrived. How large it is—even today nobody knows because much of Palenque remains hidden: symmetrical hills lavishly camouflaged by foliage. In the moist oppressive heat an endless net grows sensuously, almost perceptibly, above Palenque's buried temples.

Those that have been excavated seem to be arranged in groups.

The so-called palace is the largest, constructed on an artificial platform 300 feet long and 240 feet wide: an imperial complex of chambers, galleries, stairways, and gloomy little passages that may have been used by priests who wanted to move from one room to another without being seen. Traces of murals and fantastic stucco masks cling almost everywhere to the lime-streaked walls. Even the damp shadowy passageways have been incised with glyphs—now veiled by moss and calcium deposits, occasionally hidden behind clusters of stalactites that resemble opaque greenish icicles. Bright yellow flowers splatter the rocky slope outside, but within the palace you meet only death, moisture, and indifferent emptiness.

Three murky white buildings blackened by tropical growth and freckled with orange lichen—abstract art at its best—stand on terraces behind the palace: Temples of the Sun, of the Cross, and of the Foliated Cross.

The first was a four-story pyramid. Inside on the back wall is a handsome carved panel. Two priests, one obviously more important because of his size, have offered something to the sun, which is symbolically represented by a round shield and a pair of crossed lances. Enough glyphs have been deciphered to provide a Christian date: A.D. 642.

The Temple of the Cross, matted with vines, rises from a high pyramidal structure that has not yet been excavated. A crumbling black honeycomb on the roof gives it the look of a Dresden apartment fire-bombed during the Second World War. Much of it has collapsed, but another religious scene can be distinguished on carved slabs flanking the door to the sanctuary. Again we have two priests, one accompanied by a panel of glyphs. The other, who wears an elaborate tigerskin headdress, is smoking a cigar. They are worshiping a cross. Here also we find the date A.D. 642. Why that year was significant is not known.

The Temple of the Foliated Cross was built against a hillside which helps to sustain it. Parts of the building have slipped down the hill, but the panel for which it is named still can be seen—the cross ornamented with maize leaves and human heads. The heads are not those of sacrificial victims; they represent ears of corn. Masks of the sun god and rain god surmount the cross, and among several dates registered in the glyphs the most important seems to be A.D. 692.

There is a curious, very human thing about this temple. Carved slabs embellish the stairway leading up to it and on one of these slabs a Mayan sculptor cut the wrong date.

It sounds presumptuous for present-day investigators—especially when they can read only a few glyphs—to announce that somebody 1,300 years ago did not know what he was doing. Nevertheless, Alberto Ruz states flatly that in the Secondary Series the number of the *Uinal*, or twenty-day months, should be ten instead of eleven. The obvious question is: How many citizens of Palenque noticed the botched *Uinal?* Did any of them complain? If so, what happened to the sculptor?

The Temple of Inscriptions, close by the palace, stands on top of a large pyramid so that it rises above everything else. From the doors of this temple you can look twenty or thirty miles—though there's not much to see except a flat green bowl of jungle, and now the railroad station.

Inside are a great many carved panels with some sort of chronology embedded in the text. Several dates have been identified and here again we find A.D. 692. What happened that year?

The stone floor consists of broad slabs carefully joined. Ruz, who directed the exploration from 1949 to 1958, noticed that one slab had a double row of holes plugged with stoppers. Nor did the walls end at floor level, which indicated that there might be a room underneath. The perforated slab was lifted, revealing a staircase deliberately choked with rubbish. Almost a year was required to clean it out.

These steps led deep into the pyramid and apparently ended at a plastered wall—an obvious fake. Excavators broke through and saw the bones of five or six young men. Beyond this macabre display the passage did come to an end. But on the left side of the sacrificial compartment a triangular stone had been set in the wall, and when the triangle was removed they were able to look into a royal crypt.

This funerary chamber at the bottom of the staircase is eighty feet beneath the temple floor and below the level of the plaza outside. It is thirty feet long, thirteen feet wide. The vaulted ceiling, reinforced by girders of yellow-veined stone, is twenty-three feet high. The walls have been decorated with stucco reliefs of nine priests who probably represent the Bolón-ti-kú, Lords of the Night and of the Nether Worlds. Although they might be ancestors of the man who was buried here. If we could read the text, we would know.

Most of the crypt is occupied by a monolithic sarcophagus, the largest ever encountered in North or South America. The elegantly sculpted lid shows a man with a plumed headdress who is either falling or reclining at the base of a cruciform tree of life. According to some scholars he has been portrayed at the instant of death, falling into the jaws of a subterranean monster. A ceremonial belt—three miniature masks and several flat stones in the shape of axes—had been left on top of the sarcophagus. On the floor stood a number of clay bowls that probably held food and something to drink.

After the lid—weighing almost five tons—was jacked up, archaeologists could see that the monolith had been hollowed out in a peculiar, sinuous form. A beautifully polished stone cover exactly fitted this strange, undulant pattern.

Within the cavity, which had been reddened with cinnabar—color of the east where the sun is born and reborn, lay the skeleton of a man who, by Mayan standards, was huge. He had been loaded with jade: necklaces, bracelets, earspools of jade and mother-of-pearl, a breastplate made from concentric rings of tubular jade beads, a jade ring for each finger. Two impressive jades rested among the bones of his hands. Another had been placed in his mouth. A mosaic jade mask, with inlaid shells for eyes and obsidian discs to symbolize the iris, concealed his face. He was buried in a red winding-sheet which long ago disintegrated, but traces of red pigment clung to the jewels and to his skeleton.

The glyphs tell us that his name was pa-ca-la, or Pacal, meaning Shield. He married his sister, Lady Ahpo Hel, and he reigned over Palenque for sixty-eight years, from A.D. 615 to 683. Sixty-eight years! He lived into his fifth *katun*, which is to say that when he died he was at least eighty and possibly one hundred. How long the average citizen lived in those days, we have no idea; but it should be a fair guess that only a few watched the sunrise half as many times as Pacal.

If we take into account how much longer people live today and how much larger they are—considering these factors, if we cast Pacal in the present we might be talking about a king seven feet tall who reigned for a century. It's inconceivable. The Western world has never seen such a man. The nearest thing to him might be Charlemagne, who is alleged to have been of great stature and who reigned forty-six years—two-thirds the length of Pacal's reign.

Could the glyphs be exaggerating? Not likely. Beneath that pyramid rests the skeleton of a king so much taller than his subjects that they should not even be compared.

This astonishing man must have radiated an aura of supernatural wisdom and strength, no doubt the glyphs proclaim his greatness and his achievements. Had he lived in England or France every schoolchild would recognize his name.

One thing more. When Alberto Ruz first peered through that triangular hole into the crypt he saw an immense snake fashioned of mortar crawling from the sarcophagus. It crawled across the stones to the entrance, at which point it became a hollow molding that flowed up the steps all the way to the perforated slab in the temple floor, in this way establishing a magic connection between the dead regent and the priests above. Through them Lord Pacal might hear and speak, and thus look after his subjects forever, interceding with the deities on their behalf to protect them from hunger, invasion, and disease.

So he did, for a few centuries. At least we assume everything went well for Palenque until the Totonac armies approached. One need not read Old Mayan to know what happened then. The story seldom changes.

Peasants moved in when things calmed down, never mind if the floors and walls were smeared with blood. Soon the jungle returned. Lichen mottled the neat white surfaces and discolored the murals. Vines obscured the entrances.

Now you may drive to the ruins in your air-conditioned Cadillac, or take the leisurely Villahermosa bus, and climb the majestic outside staircase to the Temple of Inscriptions. Here, by shading your eyes, you can squint across the forest and think hieroglyphic thoughts until sundown. Below you on the uneven plaza there will be puddles of water so greenly poisonous you can almost count the bacteria; unquestionably there will be a dog because there is always a dog—asleep or scratching, several turkeys, an occasional gringo tourist, perhaps some laborers in a rusty truck.

Nobody will pay the slightest attention to you. One visitor more or less means nothing, no more than the new day. Palenque is too old to care. People lived and worked and died here long before the classic Mayan age, at a time when pharaohs ruled Egypt. And because of this it might occur to you, standing in the shade of the temple with

a lime-stained frieze of priests at your back, high above
Pacal's red bones, that Ikhnaton's "Hymn to the Sun"
could be invoked as appropriately here as at Tell al-
Amarna on the Nile:

Thy light rises in the mountains to the East,
And thou fillest the country with thy beauty.
Thou art beautiful and great, lucent and sublime
    over every land.
Thy rays burn them to the end of what thou hast
    created.

Thou hast subjected them to thy beloved son.
Thou art remote, but thy rays shine upon the earth.
Thou dost illuminate mankind but none sees thy path.

Lord, how great and numerous are thy works,
Hidden from the face of men.

7

Abracadastra

Isaac Newton said that if he saw farther than most men it was because he stood on the shoulders of giants. Such words from a bona fide giant sound agreeably modest, even self-effacing; but the remark happens to be true because scientists—more so than butchers, bakers, and candlestick makers—benefit from the cumulative wisdom of their predecessors.

We are indebted to various Babylonians and Egyptians for the beginning of our celestial inheritance, though we have no idea who they were; not until pre-Christian Greece do we meet any individuals. Thales of Miletus, 2,600 years ago, seems to have been the first astronomer. His conclusions are now meaningless and therefore boring, but he is remembered because in 585 B.C. he predicted an eclipse. He is known to have been a traveler and was thought to have learned the mysterious art in Egypt, but modern scholars say the Egyptians themselves could not predict eclipses. It's possible, of course, that he divined the event. After all, Jonathan Swift located the moons of Mars 150 years before they were discovered.

What Thales did do, beyond doubt, was to earn a pile of drachmas by some astute weather forecasting based on his knowledge of meteorology and local tradition. One winter, after having deduced that next summer would be favorable for olives, he bought options on all the presses. Came summer the countryside grew thick with olives waiting to be pressed, whereupon Thales applied the screws to his neighbors. We remember him also as the first absentminded professor. One starry night, enraptured by the twinkling spectacle overhead, he neglected to watch where he put his feet and stepped into a well.

With the Pythagorean school and a certain Parmenides of Elea we approach astronomical reality: the moon illuminates the earth through borrowed light, and the earth revolves around a central fire. Strangely, though, this central fire was not the sun. How obvious the truth seems to us, yet some contour of the Greek mind determined that the sun merely reflected heat and light. The actual source was invisible, forever hidden behind a "counter-earth"—a counter-earth being required for the sake of harmony.

Old Pythagoras himself never could accept the idea developed by his students of an earth spinning around a fire; he maintained that the earth was motionless. And it was he who generally is credited with being the first to distinguish between odd and even numbers—an article of wisdom you would think must be within the grasp of an average child.

So we progress, possibly by mutation.

Anaxagoras in the fifth century B.C. stated that the moon consisted of soil and the sun was a red-hot rock, and he understood eclipses. A lunar eclipse would occur "when the earth, and sometimes the bodies below the moon, are in line between the moon and the sun. The sun will be eclipsed when the moon, at the dark phase, is between the sun and the earth."

About this time Democritus of Abdera speculated that innumerable stars too small for us to see might account for that hazy white ribbon overhead, a fact not confirmed until 2,000 years later when Galileo looked through a telescope. Democritus also proposed the existence of other worlds.

Next we come to a pair of cautious geometers, Aristarchus and Eratosthenes, who flourished three centuries before Christ.

Little is known about the first, not even where he worked, but he understood that all of the planets, earth included, revolve around the sun. He argued that the stars were fixed; their apparent movement must result from the earth turning on its axis.

Nothing developed from these brilliant insights, perhaps because he could offer no observational proof or because the age could not absorb such original ideas. Plato, Eudoxus, Aristotle, and other accredited philosophers had contrived a model of the universe made up of fifty-six crystalline spheres which—however awkward and false— did explain the apparent motions of the sun, the moon, and the planets. One could, therefore, accept this carefully reasoned theory or one could bet on a wild hypothesis. Given a parallel choice today, the response would be no different. Aristarchus' explanation was regarded as charming and curious, but not something an intelligent man would take seriously.

Eratosthenes, a director of the great Alexandrian library, sits in the hall of fame because he measured the circumference of the earth. He was not the first to do this, but his figures are surprisingly accurate, and his procedure was so simple that quite a few Alexandrians probably went around muttering that anybody could have done it.

Below Alexandria lay the town of Syene, the modern Aswan. At noon on the longest day of the year the sun's

rays illuminated a deep well at Syene, meaning that the
sun must be vertically overhead; yet at the same time the
sun cast a shadow at Alexandria. The angle of the rays at
Alexandria was a little over 7°, which made it one-fiftieth
of a circle. Ergo: if you multiply the distance from Syene
to Alexandria by fifty you have the approximate circumference.

Aswan is not precisely south of Alexandria, nor directly
on the Tropic of Cancer, nor was the measured distance
strictly accurate; but just by luck these mistakes canceled
one another so that Eratosthenes' figure of 24,647 miles is
less than 250 miles off, which is rather good for a backyard
operation.

At this point we come to the Antikýthēra device, recovered in 1900 from the wreck of a Greek ship that sank
near the island of Antikýthēra in the first century B.C. It is
a deeply corroded chunk of bronze with toothed gears and
graduated circles. Nothing comparable has ever been
found, and no ancient writing describes or refers to such
an object, which allows the gods-from-other-worlds huck-
sters to hint that it must be from outer space. There is,
however, some writing on its surface, mostly illegible,
which indicates that the machine correlated celestial
movements; and researchers have traced this inscription
back to an astronomical calendar used on Rhodes.

Careful cleaning has shown the device to be fairly complex. Some of it is missing, and what remains is not altogether understood, but the gears were driven by an axle,
enabling an astronomer to take a reading from three dials.
The large dial contains zodiacal signs and almost certainly
marked the annual course of the sun. The small dials announced the rising and setting of the moon and gave the
motions of five planets.

On one dial was a ring that established a date in accordance with the Egyptian calendar. The Egyptians counted

exactly 365 days a year, ignoring those troublesome hours that create leap year, but the remarkable Greek machine could make allowances for this. The ring had last been adjusted to a date corresponding to 80 B.C., quite possibly the year the ship sank.

Where the ship came from and where it was bound, we have no idea. It was loaded with bronze and marble sculpture—some of which is now in the Athens museum—causing scholars to suspect that it may have been one of the tyrant Sulla's treasure ships.

And although this is irrelevant, we are indebted to the Antikýthēra device for proof that those celebrated Greeks did not spend all their time debating, philosophizing, hurling the discus, and carving alabaster nymphs; once in a while they designed rococo little instruments to astound and mystify the future, which speaks well of them.

The earliest post-Christian astronomer was an Alexandrian Greek named Claudius Ptolemy, or Ptolemaeus, whose contribution to scientific knowledge was that he popularized the epicycle, and so great was his reputation that the epicycle became sanctified. Now an epicycle is not something to be ridden; it is merely a small circle moving around the circumference of a larger circle, and Ptolemy employed a clutch of them to illustrate the mechanics of the universe. Epicycles were necessary because he insisted upon a false premise—that the earth hung suspended and motionless in the middle of things.

Ptolemy's system of interlocking wheels, his Ferris wheel universe, lasted longer than you might think—about fourteen centuries—because it confirmed what we wish to believe: that the system has been arranged for our benefit.

Thus, with Claudius Ptolemy, who was not Cleopatra's uncle, Greek astronomical science ends, not with a revelation but an absurdity. You see the same thing happening in late Greek art, in those graceful Tanagra statuettes where the nude elegance of the Periclean age degenerates into costumery.

Next came the interregnum, the Dark Ages. During these centuries very little was learned, at least not much that now seems valuable, while much that already had been learned was forgotten. Spores of Greek knowledge floated through the Middle East, reentering Europe by way of Arabic Sicily and Spain, but whatever failed to coincide with medieval dogma got a miserable reception. When the erudite Byzantine statesman Georgios Akropolites explained an eclipse to the empress she laughed at him.

Here and there, nevertheless, intelligent men persisted.

Some forgotten genius at the Norwegian court wrote in the *Konnungsskuggsja* for the edification of his lord: "You should understand that the earth is spherical and not equally close to the sun at all points. Its curved orbit . . ."

Pope Pius II declared that in the judgment of educated people the earth was round.

Bishop Nicole Oresme asked if the apparent rotation of the heavens might not be an illusion caused by the rotation of the earth.

Cardinal Nicholas of Cusa insisted that not only was the earth a globe, but the stars were other worlds. "We know already," he said, "that our earth moves, even though this motion is not visible. . . . Only God, who constitutes the center of the universe, may be motionless."

At the beginning of the seventeenth century, during a less tolerant period, Giordano Bruno would be roasted alive on the Square of Flowers in Rome for endorsing such ideas:

Justice done on an impenitent heretic. . . . Hence, at the sixth hour of the night, the Comforters and the

chaplain assembled at S. Ursula and went to the prison
in the Tower of Nona, entered the chapel, and offered
up the prayers. To them was consigned the man Giordano Bruno, son of Gni. Bruno, an apostate friar of Nola
in the Kingdom, an impenitent. He was exhorted by our
brothers in all love, and two Fathers of the Order of St.
Dominic, two of the Order of Jesus, two of the new
Church and one of St. Jerome were called in. These
with all loving zeal and much learning, showed him his
error, yet he stood firm throughout and to the end in his
accursed obstinacy, setting his brain and mind to a
thousand errors and vaingloryings; and he continued
steadfastly stubborn while conducted by the Servants
of the Justices to the Campo di Fiori, and there being stripped and bound to a stake, was burned alive.
Throughout, our Brotherhood sang litanies and the
Consolers exhorted him to the very last to overcome his
obstinacy. But thus ended his agony and his wretched
life.

After all this time it would be impossible to catalog
Bruno's thousand errors, yet that unctuous justification of
torture and murder still revolts us—despite the Nazis,
Hiroshima, and as many more twentieth-century aberra-
tions as you choose to name. We know that he did speak
his mind. He spoke defiantly, imaginatively: "In space
there are countless constellations, suns, and planets. We
see only the suns because they give light; the planets remain invisible, for they are small and dark. There are also
numberless earths circling around their suns, no worse and
no less inhabited than this globe of ours. . . ."
So it's a bit surprising that Copernicus, Niklas Koppernigk, who plucked the earth from the heart of the Christian scheme, was not excommunicated and flogged by an

ever watchful Church. Had he been born a few years later, or if he had lived in southern Europe, he might have been torn apart by wild horses. Liszinski was decapitated, his body burnt, and the ashes blown out of a cannon for teaching that Man created God instead of vice versa.

Church authorities were disturbed and puzzled by Copernicus, but indecisive. People in the street ridiculed him. It is said that during a carnival procession two fools danced side by side: one gave away indulgences for whoredom while the other whirled a pig's bladder on a string and screeched, "I am the sun! See how the earth flies around me!"

Evidently he was protected—perhaps without his knowledge—by a Lutheran clergyman named Andreas Osiander, which is curious because the astronomer himself was Catholic.

Young Niklas grew up steeped in Catholicism. His father died when he was ten so an uncle, Bishop Lucas Watzelrode, became his guardian. Off went Niklas to study theology at the University of Cracow. Four years later Uncle Lucas sent him to Bologna where he studied ecclesiastic law, but he also studied medicine, astronomy, and mathematics.

He seems to have been best known as a physician, which sounds odd, considering that most of his adult life was spent as canon of Frauenburg Cathedral. However, life was less stratified in those days; a poet might also be a king. Indeed, King Sigismund thought of Copernicus as an economist and asked his help in reforming the monetary system. Accordingly, he went to work on the problem, because it is seldom advisable to refuse a king, and being altogether logical he started with a definition: "Muncze wyrdt genennet geczeichennt Goldt, adir Sylber." Obviously, coin is the name given to stamped gold or silver.

And during his examination of the troubled currency he recognized a process which now is called Gresham's Law—bad money forcing good money out of circulation. Bishop Oresme had commented on this phenomenon two centuries earlier, but no matter.

He was also an artist. A self-portrait in the Dürer style shows a bony-featured young man with a book. His right hand, which rests on his left forearm, looks unconvincing, probably because he faked it, being obliged to hold the burin in that hand while glancing at himself in a mirror. Otherwise the picture is forceful and competent, not the work of an amateur. An engraving from the collection of the British Royal Society, clearly by a different artist, again reveals this bony face, the sensual underlip, and a slight—very slight—trace of amusement. In 1509 he published a Latin translation of some "ribald letters" by a minor Greek poet, one Theophylactus Simocatta, and dedicated the volume to Uncle Lucas—which just might account for that suspicion of humor. In neither portrait, though, do we see the face of an affable, jocular man; Niklas Koppernigk is not anybody you would find at the neighborhood tavern.

However adept he may have been at portraiture, fiscal policies, hemorrhoids, or the neat distinctions of canon law, his mind focused insistently on the night sky. And after a while he realized that he mistrusted epicycles.

Of course he was not the first to arrange our local system in its proper order. Various Greeks had understood the situation pretty well—a fact he noted in his iconoclastic book, *De Revolutionibus orbium coelestium.* That he should frankly credit the Greeks would seem to reflect a nature as modest as Isaac Newton's, but this is misleading; his purpose, almost certainly, was to reassure the Church. Resurrected theories are seldom threatening. As canon of

Frauenburg Cathedral and nephew of a bishop his credentials were good, but here and there the Church was
stretching, mashing, twisting, strangling, and incinerating
people who thought they had original ideas. Under such
circumstances one should not be adventurous.

To insure himself further he pointed out that, since
churchmen had been asked to help reform the calendar,
this heliocentric theory might be of some assistance.

Then he took out another policy by addressing the work
to Pope Paul III:

> I can certainly well believe, most holy Father, that,
> while mayhap a few will accept this my book which I
> have written concerning the revolutions of the spheres
> of the world, ascribing certain motions to the sphere of
> the earth, people will clamor that I ought to be cast out
> at once for such an opinion. . . . Thus when I considered
> with myself what an absurd fairy-tale people brought
> up in the opinion, sanctioned by many ages, that the
> earth is motionless in the midst of the heaven, as if it
> were the center of it, would think it if I were to assert
> on the contrary that the earth is moved; I hesitated
> long whether I should give the light to my com-
> mentaries. . . .

Still he dawdled, and finally said the book should not be
published until after his death. But a young mathematician named von Lauchen, who chose to call himself
Rhaeticus, at last persuaded the anxious astronomer to go
ahead with publication.

Some Copernican scholars, though, don't see it that
way. The English astronomer and astrophysicist Herbert
Dingle, for one, finds no evidence that Copernicus worried
about publishing "unless a shrinking from the ridicule

of the unlearned may be so classed. The popular idea that he kept his thoughts secret from fear of persecution is entirely baseless. What he did shrink from was the laughter. . . ."

In any case, we will now ride an epicycle.

Von Lauchen changed his name because he had been born in the Austrian Tyrol, which used to be called Rhaetia. The logic is this: Gutenberg's printing press disclosed the classical Greek and Roman authors to a great many European readers for the first time and northern intellectuals responded by attempting to Latinize themselves. Johann Müller, born in Königsberg, called himself Regiomontanus after that regal summit. Philipp Schwarzert exchanged his black Germanic name for a black Greek pseudonym, Melanchthon. Christopher Schlüssel, whose surname means key, would become Father Christopher Clavius. The physician-alchemist whose family name was Hohenheim would call himself Paracelsus after the first-century Roman encyclopedist and doctor, Celsus. Koppernigk became Copernicus. Et al.

Our epicycle is now complete.

De Revolutionibus was delivered to a Nuremberg printer; and here, at Nuremberg, we meet the Lutheran priest Andreas Osiander.

Copernicus wrote to him, asking what sort of reception the book might expect.

Osiander replied that, first of all, the motions of planets as they appear to us may be explained by any of several theories, and ecclesiastic authorities perceived no harm in such speculation—provided the originator of a system in conflict with Church doctrine did not insist that his proposal was more than speculative. Therefore it might be wise to introduce the heliocentric theory in some such light.

Osiander wrote also to Rhaeticus: "The peripatetics and theologians will be readily placated if they hear that there can be different hypotheses. . . ."

But the astronomer, having resolved to publish, now became obdurate. He would neither disguise nor modify his position: the earth wheeled around the sun, there could be no question about it.

His book appeared with an anonymous preface implying that what followed should be treated as mere supposition.

This preface had been carefully drafted by Osiander, who refrained from signing it in order to give the impression that its author was Copernicus—thereby protecting Copernicus from a charge of heresy.

It is said that the first copy of *De Revolutionibus* was handed to the astronomer on his deathbed; he was then only half-conscious, unable to read his work, and died without knowing about the Judas preface. It is also said that he did read this preface and the shock hastened his death. Either account might be true, but there is a third possibility, supported by a letter from the Nuremberg printer which says in part: "Rhaeticus used to assert . . . that this Preface of Osiander's was clearly displeasing to Copernicus, and that he was more than a little irritated by it. . . ."

Hermann Kesten states that in May of 1542, a year before Copernicus died, he saw galley proofs of the first two pages and was not altogether pleased: "When he saw Osiander's arrogant forgery he fell into the most violent rage; his grief and fury may have aggravated his illness, for he had a hemorrhage followed by a paralysis of the right side and remained unconscious for several days."

In other words, although Copernicus knew exactly what Osiander had written he agreed to it. This would have been the wise thing to do—if wisdom and prudence are at times synonymous. Most of us in that situation would do as the astronomer did. Still, one would like to think he died without knowing.

Osiander had reason for concern; rumors were reproducing like fungus. In 1533, ten years before the book was printed, Pope Clement VII had asked his secretary to explain the ideas of Copernicus. And in 1539 the arch-Protestant Martin Luther said during one of his Table Talks: "Mention has been made of some new astrologer who wants to teach that the Earth moves around, not the firmament or heavens. . . . This fool seeks to overturn the whole art of astronomy."

The blistering remark sounds more emphatic in German: *"Der Narr will die gantze Kunst Astronomiae umkehren."*

Luther's friend and collaborator, Melanchthon, also addressed a few words to the upstart Pole: "Our eyes bear witness against Copernicus, sensual perception speaks against him, the authority of the Bible speaks against him, and the one-thousand-year consensus of learned men. Therefore he is absurd."

John Calvin resorted to the ninety-third Psalm, which assures us that the Lord reigneth and is clothed with majesty. The Lord is clothed with strength wherewith He hath girded Himself. And the world also is established, that it cannot be moved. Calvin then asked—expecting no answer—who would venture to place the authority of Copernicus above that of the Holy Spirit.

Osiander seems to have feared the Catholic response more than that of his own Protestants, whom he understood somewhat better. Indeed there is a jovial undertone to Luther's remarks which suggests that he did not really care what Copernicus had in mind.

And perhaps because of Osiander's disarming preface the Catholics paid little attention. Cardinal Baronius remarked, with an undeniable trace of levity: "The Holy Spirit intended to teach us how to go to Heaven, not how the Heavens go."

But the insubordinate, disagreeable book survived mockery as well as neglect; it refused to wither, it refused to evaporate. And seventy-three years after publication *De Revolutionibus* was placed on the *Index librorum prohibitorum*. There it stood, if you like to keep track of such matters, until 1835.

What is odd, though, is that the preface, which was meant only to shield Copernicus, turned out to be a valid criticism of his theory. He did situate the sun instead of the earth at the center of things, but in other respects his mechanism was false. The planets, as we now know, do not orbit the sun in perfect circles. Copernicus assumed they did, which obliged him to manufacture forty-eight epicycles—eight more than Ptolemy needed. Not until Johannes Kepler went to work on the Copernican system did it become the truth. Only then, as Thomas Digges wrote, would this be recognized: "The sun like a king in the middest of all raigneth and geeveth lawes of motion to ye rest."

Digges, who was English, deserves a moment because in 1576 he published a translation of Copernicus, together with a diagram of the heliocentric system which he himself had drawn. Now, around this circular diagram occurs an astonishing inscription, and if you loosen the knots of Digges' sixteenth-century prose you will see why, because he soars beyond Copernicus, beyond the idea of a closed universe: "THIS ORBE OF STARRES FIXED INFINITELY UP EX-TENDETH HIT SELF IN ALTITUDE SPHERICALLYE, AND THERE-FORE IMMOVABLE THE PALLACE OF FOELITICTYE GARNISHED

WITH PERPETUALL SHININGE GLORIOUS LIGHTES INNUMERA-
BLE. FARR EXCELLINGE OUR SONNE BOTH IN QUANTITYE AND
QUALITYE THE VERY COURT OF COELESTIALL ANGELLES. DE-
VOID OF GREEFE AND REPLENISHED WITH PERFITE ENDLESSE
IOYE THE HABITACLE FOR THE ELECT." And on his diagram
Thomas Digges drew stars outside the outermost circle so
that his meaning could not be mistaken.

Incidentally, *De Revolutionibus* was not a best-seller.
Being so controversial, how could it fail? Yet, commer-
cially speaking, it flopped. The first edition of 1,000 copies
never sold out, though you would have to mortgage a
hotel to buy one of those copies today. The most popular
astronomy book was by a certain Johannes de Sacrobosco,
or John Holywood, which sounds more appropriate; Holywood's smash hit raced through fifty-nine editions.

But if that is true—if very few people read Copernicus—
how did his obscure and faulty book transform the world?
Nobody knows. Arthur Koestler suggests that ideas powerful enough to influence human thought do not act only on
the conscious mind, but seep through to underlying strata
which are indifferent to logical contradictions. Or, let us
say, truly promising thoughts may not develop in the usual
ground, but need different nourishment, like those tiny
Japanese paper flowers that require a bowl of water in
which to unfold and bloom.

If neither of those images suits you, my friend, go ahead
and explain the paradox yourself.

Now, why some people should be celebrated beyond
their worth and profit accordingly, such as John Holywood, while others obtain less credit than they deserve is
another riddle. Ask passersby in the street what they know
about Johannes Kepler. Nothing. Substitute Galileo or
Newton or Copernicus and the name, at least, will be
recognized. Which is not to suggest that these men are

undeservedly famous; it is only that there have been a few, like Kepler, whose contributions have been of equivalent magnitude yet who remain unknown. And how displeasing, if you stop to think about it, that before we see one of history's supreme astronomers on a United States postage stamp we undoubtedly will see the face of a mendacious California politician—which could be interpreted as another instance of Gresham's Law.

Kepler's great stroke may not have been dramatic but it was necessary in order to comprehend the solar system. He demolished a belief held since the time of Pythagoras; he understood what his predecessor Copernicus had not, that the planets in spite of their serene and steady light behave erratically. This may seem no more consequential than a swallow in a barn, but it is deceptive.

Kepler probably was not the first to notice the erratic course of planets. An Arab who studied the sky above Toledo during the eleventh century suspected it, but he was ignored. Arzachel was the man's name. Or if you want to be pedantic: ibn-al-Zarqâla. And if you think Kepler is unknown in the street try ibn-al-Zarqâla. As to why his brilliant hypothesis was overlooked, we can't be sure. The times may have been out of joint. The Queen had a headache. A Christian horde was yowling at the gate. There's always a reason. Still, one feels dissatisfied and puzzled. Arzachel should get some credit.

Anyway, here is the first of three laws conceived for the Western world by Johannes Kepler:

"Planets move in elliptical orbits with the sun at one focal point."

His next two laws are equally soporific:

"The radius vector sweeps over equal areas in equal times."

"The square of a planet's period is proportional to the cube of the semimajor axis."

These laws just might be the reason nobody recognizes Kepler's name; they reek of the textbook, of airless classrooms in April, of theorems, conjugations, participles, and forgotten treaties, of blackboards, chalk, and musty teachers. Yet without them we still would be illustrating the solar system with a Rube Goldberg agglutination of epicycles.

Furthermore, that dreary second law about the sweep of the radius vector indicates that he had found his way to the edge of one of the greatest discoveries of all. Had he pushed ahead one more step he would be at least as famous as Isaac Newton. What Kepler's second law means is that a planet traveling an elliptical path around the sun travels faster as it approaches the sun. Yet why should it? Nobody, including Kepler, could explain this. He guessed that the sun must be responsible; somehow the sun controlled planetary motion: "What else is it but a magnetic emanation of the sun? But what is it that makes the planets excentric with regard to the sun, that compels them to come close to it and move away from it? Nothing else but a magnetic emanation from the planets themselves. . . ."

How very close that is, almost a century before Newton, to the concept of gravity.

And the implications, if reduced from the cosmic to the personal, are enough to make anybody restless. In other words, how often have I myself stopped an instant too soon?

Well, by Kepler's time—about ninety years after Copernicus—the Church was feeling less tolerant. His electric imagination, therefore, did not win many friends among the clergy. He was a devout Lutheran, yet certain aspects of Calvinism and Catholicism attracted him: "It hurts my heart that the three factions have miserably torn the truth to pieces between them, that I must collect the bits wherever I can find them, and put them together again. . . . My attitude, so help me God, is a Christian one; theirs, I know not what."

Naturally he was excommunicated. And in 1630, when he lay dying, the Protestants and Catholics both refused him Communion.

He was buried in the cemetery of Saint Peter outside Regensburg. His grave must have been marked, but three years later—after Swedish, German, and Bavarian troops employed the churchyard as a battlefield—it could not be located. At that hour, no doubt, the battle seemed important. Perhaps it was. Only now it seems less so than the grave of an individual who deduced how the planets turn and who dreamt of celestial music.

This last observation might be clarified. Like other scientists, Kepler at times grew wondrously unscientific. He convinced himself that the planets evoke melodies unheard by human ears—this indescribable concert being played for the benefit of a sublime entity whose soul inhabits the sun.

Then there were the multiplying moons. When he learned that Galileo had seen four moons orbiting Jupiter he decided that Mars would have two. Why two? Because it would be mathematically harmonious. Departing from the sun we find that Venus has no moon, but Earth has one. Therefore Mars, next in line, should have two, because Jupiter, which is next, has four. Obviously then, Saturn would have eight, Uranus sixteen, Neptune thirty-two, Pluto sixty-four, and so on for whatever bodies might be sweeping the latitudes beyond. Regrettably, it doesn't work out. At last count Jupiter had twelve, Uranus five, Neptune two, and we are uncertain about Pluto. Besides, Kepler ignored Mercury whose orbit swings closest to the sun.

He happened to be right about Mars, but that was coincidence.

With Jonathan Swift, though, we might be nearer clair-voyance than coincidence. Gulliver in the course of his fabulous travels visits an aerial island called Laputa whose astronomers have observed two Martian moons. Laputian scientists compute the orbit of the inner moon at ten hours, that of the outer moon at twenty-one hours and thirty minutes. They also calculate the distances of these moons from the planet: 12,600 miles and 21,000 miles.

Swift must have gotten his idea from Kepler, or possibly from a later book by a Capuchin monk, but neither the monk nor Kepler provided much detail. And nobody on earth was able to see those moons until an ex-carpenter named Asaph Hall found them in 1877 with a big refract-ing telescope at the Naval Observatory outside Wash-ington, D.C. Hall measured the periods of rotation: seven hours and thirty-nine minutes for the inner moon, thirty hours and eighteen minutes for the outer. He calculated that they were 5,820 miles and 14,615 miles from the planet.

How, then, with all the time and space in the universe to choose from, did Swift predict the rotational periods and distances so accurately? The average error in dis-tance—over 6,000 miles—at first seems rather large, but not if you are talking about two tiny satellites of a planet fifty million miles from the earth. And these "moons" are mere particles—pinpricks of light in Hall's telescope—fly-ing chunks of rock with estimated diameters of five and ten miles.

In Gulliver's day these satellites had not been dis-covered, yet Swift established their periods of rotation within a few hours and their distances within a few thou-sand miles. How? Various theories have been offered, but these are the most common:

He got hold of a telescope more powerful than any known to exist during the eighteenth century.

He was informed by ESP or some such process.

He was a Martian.

If you like none of these answers you are reduced to saying it was luck. Very well, call it a lucky guess. In any event, Jonathan Swift and the Martian moons is another epicycle; suppose we return to the central gears and wheels.

Kepler's baroque ideas—multiplying satellites, heavenly music and so forth—may have sprung from his personal afflictions. The man was a seventeenth-century Job. In childhood he endured boils, mange, smallpox, hemorrhoids, constant stomach trouble, and such bad eyesight that he occasionally saw his world doubled or quadrupled. Things did not improve as he grew up: "I suffered continually from skin ailments, often severe sores, often from the scabs of chronic putrid wounds in my feet which healed badly and kept breaking out again. On the middle finger of my right hand I had a worm, on the left a huge sore. . . . At Cupinga's I was offered union with a virgin; on New Year's Eve I achieved this with the greatest possible difficulty, experiencing the most acute pains of the bladder. . . ."

But instead of succumbing to these tribulations Kepler somehow utilized them to charge himself with furious energy; he grew fanatical in his pursuit of the winking mysteries overhead. And despite his natural ugliness the hopeless frog almost turned into a prince—darkly Mephistophelian with wiry linear features and a geometrically sculpted little beard.

Even so, life was difficult: "In me Saturn and the Sun work together in their sextile aspect; therefore my body is small, dry, knobby, my soul suspicious and timid; I reject honors, crouch over books, know no pleasures of life aside from science. All this corresponds to my preference for bitter and sharp tastes, for gnawing bones and hard bread. . . ."

He seems to have been impatient, sarcastic, cowardly, and stingy, and he almost never bathed. His disorderliness was alleged to be very great; his good qualities, if any, remarkably few. He married a miller's daughter named Barbara, already twice-widowed, a Chaucerian pilgrim "simple of mind and fat of body." The wedding took place April 27, 1597, "under a calamitous sky," and nine months later Frau Kepler's first child arrived, a boy with seriously deformed genitals. The astronomer, regarding his son, speaks of "a boiled turtle in its shell."

And there never was money enough. "My hungry stomach looks up like a little dog to its master who used to feed it."

Kepler's purgatory does not end. His wife despised him because he did not earn as much as her father. His brother was epileptic. And he himself, in addition to the authentic complaints, was a hypochondriac: "You ask me about my illness. It was a lingering fever which came from the gall and returned four times because I often committed dietary indiscretions. On May 29, my wife ruthlessly compelled me at last to wash my body; she thinks baths are dangerous. She plunged me in a basin full of very warm water; the warmth did not agree with me and gave me cramps in my bowels. . . . I think I am one of those whose gall bladder has an opening into the stomach; such people are usually shortlived."

Then, too, an age of witchcraft was bearing down and his mother Katharina stood accused. She is described as a hunchbacked little crone, swarthy, quarrelsome, and malicious, the archetypal hag. Ominous things happened while she was present. The twelve-year-old daughter of Jeorg Haller, a workman, was carrying bricks to the kiln when she felt a needlelike pain in one arm just as old Frau Kepler hobbled by. The schoolmaster Beutelspacher grew lame after chatting with her. The tailor Schmid's twin babies died after she rocked their cradle. Everyone knew she could glide through locked doors. And she had begged the sexton of Eltingen churchyard for her father's skull, saying she wished to have it silver-plated so that her son might use his grandfather's skull as a drinking goblet.

On August 7, 1620, the seventy-four-year-old woman—who had been living with her daughter—was seized, thrust into a linen chest, and carried from the house late at night. The weird abduction sounds familiar, reminding us of the Gestapo and of the fact that such men are always among us.

Kepler at this time was living in Austria, but when he heard from his sister that their mother had been imprisoned as a witch he hurried back to defend her. He found her locked in a stone cell, dressed in chains. She was about to be tortured. Kepler hired an attorney, Christoph Besold, and also worked on the case himself—searching out natural explanations for the apparently supernatural occurrences. He submitted a 128-page argument on her behalf, much of it written in his own hand, which just saved her from the stake.

So it becomes a little less absurd, considering his private calamities and the fetid atmosphere in which he worked, that he imagined celestial music.

The astronomer with whom Kepler is associated—Tycho or Tyge Brahe—was equally cracked, though of course there was a reason. There always is. He lost his nose. Not all of it, but quite a piece of it, enough to influence everything he said or did from then on; and we will return to Tycho Brahe's missing nose in a moment.

Brahe is linked to Kepler because they worked together

for about a year at Benatky Castle near Prague. Kepler then packed his bag and left, very much displeased that Brahe treated him like an apprentice instead of a colleague.

"I found everything insecure," he wrote to a friend. "Tycho is a man with whom no one can live without exposing himself to the greatest indignities."

Brahe seems to have been puzzled by Kepler's dissatisfaction. He was twenty-five years older and he was famous as the Emperor Rudolph's personal astrologer-astronomer-mathematician. Apart from this, he had invited Kepler to stay at the castle. He therefore considered it natural that Kepler should be subordinate.

The quarrel may not have been Brahe's fault because Kepler subsequently apologized, but throughout his life Tycho Brahe was difficult company. When he was a student at Rostock University he got into an argument with one Manderup Parsbjerg about which of them was the better mathematician. The argument resumed several days or weeks later and was not decisively settled until a third confrontation when they whipped out their swords.

Just where this third encounter took place is disputed. Historians tend to be vague when they aren't sure. It occurred "out of doors," "in total darkness," or, romantically, "at midnight in a vacant house." But there's no doubt about the result: Manderup proved himself the superior mathematician by slicing away the bridge of Tycho's nose.

There is some question about the nature of the replacement, which was thought to be silver, or an alloy of gold and silver. It may have been painted. If indeed it was painted we would assume that Tycho selected an inconspicuous flesh tone. And one might, if one wishes, imagine him embellishing it with little blue and gold stars.

Admittedly this sounds odd, though certainly no more so than a lady with a tattooed rump or a gentleman wearing a diamond in his teeth. But let it pass.

An etching dated 1586, when he was forty, shows Tycho dressed up like an Elizabethan sea dog in a lace ruff and lace cuffs and a huge cloak and a velvet hat, with a sommelier's chain around his neck and an ostentatious ring on his index finger. He is portly, almost puffy, with a Vandyke beard, and his nose looks unreal, as well it should. He must have kept the bridge in place with glue because he carried around a tiny box filled with some sort of gelatinous ointment, and in no portrait of him is there any sign of a strap.

You might think very few people would care about Tycho's nose after three centuries, but in 1901 the citizens of Prague were so nagged by curiosity that they dug him up. Lo and behold!—the metallic bridge had vanished.

Now, if we assume that somebody—let's say the mortician—pocketed this curious item, we are entitled to ask what became of it. Presumably it was melted. After all, that's not the kind of souvenir you want around the house. Although I once knew a man in Chicago who had an impressive collection of walrus and whale penises, which proves that just about anything will appeal to somebody. But let us assume that Tycho's baroque appendage was cast into negotiable form. Then who can say what coins were minted from it?—perhaps that old gold florin your grandmother was given on her wedding day.

There is another possibility. In 1901 a greenish stain typical of oxidized copper was observed on his nasal bone, which suggests, alas, that the replacement was neither gold nor silver, that Mother Nature gradually devoured it, and the mortician should not be slandered.

Enough speculation. Tycho's life both before and after

the duel indicates that he, not Parsbjerg, was the trouble-maker. Arrogant, conceited, avaricious, impatient, the typical son of an aristocrat, he seems to have understood quite early that most people were created inferior. He himself was studying Latin at the age of seven. Six years later, accompanied by a tutor named Vedel, he enrolled at Copenhagen University to study rhetoric and philosophy.

On August 21, 1560, he watched a solar eclipse. This eclipse had been predicted and the realization that such events could be foretold excited him. He bought a book of astronomical tables and for two thalers—talers, dalers, dollars—a copy of Ptolemy's *Almagest*.

After three years in Copenhagen he was sent to the University of Leipzig to study jurisprudence. Again he bought astronomical charts and books, as well as some instruments. He also bought a celestial globe about the size of an orange which he hid from his tutor, examining it late at night when Vedel was asleep.

He appears next at the University of Wittenberg, but only for a while. Plague broke out, so he moved to Rostock where the swift right hand of Manderup Parsbjerg short-ened his face.

In 1570 he returned to Denmark because his father was dying. He might have stayed there, seduced by the easy life at Helsingborg Castle, but on November 11, 1572, heaven intervened. He witnessed a supernova:

"One evening when I was contemplating, as usual, the celestial vault, whose aspect was so familiar to me, I saw, with inexpressible amazement, near the zenith, in Cassiopeia, a radiant star of extraordinary magnitude. . . ." He concludes his description by saying with a deplorable lack of originality: "I could hardly believe my eyes."

He thought it miraculous, the greatest miracle since the beginning of the world. Or at least equal to those miracles attested by Scripture: Joshua commanding the sun to halt, and the face of the sun darkening when Christ was crucified. "For all philosophers agree, and facts clearly prove it to be the case, that in the ethereal region of the celestial world no change, in the way either of generation or corruption, takes place; but that the heavens and the celestial bodies in the heavens are without increase or diminution, and that they undergo no alteration. . . ."

His amazement seems justified because supernova are uncommon. Only four—possibly six—have turned up in our galaxy. The brightest was seen by Oriental astronomers on July 4, 1054, although the light reaching the earth that day had been en route for 6,000 years. Yang Wei-te, chief astrologer at the Sung court, prostrated himself before this luminous spectacle and wrote: "I have observed the appearance of a guest star." It could be seen not only at night but during the day for three weeks, and he forecast good times because it was yellow. Yellow was the Sung imperial color.

Astronomers today believe that the supernova so respectfully acknowledged by Yang Wei-te gleamed with a brilliance equal to half a billion suns. Had it been as near to us as the nearest star, Alpha Centauri, it would have been brighter than a full moon. It is now referred to as the Crab nebula in Taurus and still is visible through a telescope because the explosion has not ended. The nebula, which is a cloud of turbulent gas, continues to expand at a speed of sixty million miles a day.

This supernova was also registered by Indians of the southwestern United States who drew symbolic pictures of it. On a cliff near Zuñi, New Mexico, is a pictograph showing a cross with a crescent moon just beneath it to the right. A similar design was found on the wall of Navajo Canyon in Arizona. The argument that they represent the

supernova is simple, but convincing: potsherds collected
at these sites date from the eleventh century, and astronomers know that the star appeared just above and to the
left of a crescent moon.

Medieval European intellectuals failed to report the
guest star; they may have been too busy squabbling over
neat theological distinctions.

By 1572, however, when Tycho's supernova materialized, Europe was ready. Stargazers across the continent
and in England tried to determine just what it was. A
German painter named Busch wrote two pamphlets about
the cosmic display in which he maintained that it was
created "by the ascension from Earth of human sins and
wickedness, making a sort of gas which was then set on
fire by the anger of God." This noxious gas, he continued,
drifted down on people's heads, causing "all kinds of un-
pleasant phenomena such as diseases, sudden death, bad
weather, and Frenchmen."

Tycho studiously observed the star. He fixed its position in the sky, just northwest of Cassiopeia's huge *W*,
measured its brilliance against that of other stars, and
charted the final diminution. He followed its progress for
seventeen months. He also tried to establish the star's parallax—parallax being a change in the apparent direction of
something when viewed from different points. Look at
your wife with your right eye shut, then with your left eye
shut, and she will appear to have moved slightly, which is
her parallax.

The exploding star showed no parallax. This was a surprise because most people thought it must be extremely
near the earth, closer than the moon. Brahe concluded
that since the star showed no displacement it must be
located on that remote celestial sphere which, according
to Aristotle, was perpetually changeless. In other words,

the infallible Greek—that supreme authority on just about everything—had to be wrong.

After much hesitation, because it seemed to him that writing for the public was undignified, he published *De Nova Stella*, a rather tasteless potpourri of letters, meteorological data, and astrological predictions. But *De Nova* did include twenty-seven pages of facts about the new star.

That same year he began living with Christine, who was a servant girl and/or a farmer's daughter. In any case she was not—socially speaking—a lady, and it has been suggested that he chose a lower-caste woman because of his unique nose. After "three winters," according to Danish law, they became man and wife, and they must have liked each other because they produced eight children.

Tycho's reputation at home increased speedily when the Danes learned that he was recognized abroad, which is the way it goes; and in 1576 King Frederik gave him the island of Hveen near Elsinore Castle on which to build an observatory. He was also granted money enough to build it however he pleased, and as landlord he would collect from every tenant and "servant of the Crown" on the island.

What he built was a Gothic complex protected by an eighteen-foot wall—an assemblage of turrets, spires, galleries, onion-shaped domes, gables, and balconies that might be described as an alliance between the Kremlin and the Copenhagen Glyptothek. It covered an acre of ground, and apart from the observatory there was a house for himself and his family, with sumptuously appointed rooms for distinguished guests, a library, an alchemical workshop, a paper mill, a printing press, servants' quarters, and a jail for Hveen citizens who got behind in the rent.

He named this singular growth Uraniborg. Its interior mechanism sounds like the work of da Vinci. Several rooms had running water pumped from a well in the basement. The printing press and paper mill were driven by water from a series of fish ponds. Hidden wires connected the banquet hall with the kitchen, enabling Tycho to evoke his servants by magic, and there were statues with concealed speaking tubes whose only purpose seems to be that they gave him a chance to terrify unsuspecting guests.

On the walls of Uraniborg hung portraits of history's eight supreme astronomers: Ptolemy, Hipparchus, Timocharis, al-Battani, King Alphonso of Castile, Copernicus, Tycho himself, and Tychonides—this last being Tycho's son and successor, who at that time had not been born.

Then there was a dwarf named Jeppe who crouched under the table during meals. Jeppe had the gift of second sight. If a citizen of Hveen fell sick the dwarf invariably foretold whether he would die or recover. Once he exclaimed: "Behold how your men wash themselves in the sea"—whereupon Tycho dispatched a servant to the roof. The servant returned quickly, saying he had seen a capsized boat and two men dripping wet on the shore.

The only thing Uraniborg lacked was Tycho's pet elk so he ordered the animal brought from his family estate at Knudstrup, but along the road the groom who was leading it decided to stay overnight at Landskroner Castle. Now what happened at Landskroner Castle sounds absurd. We are told that Tycho's elk climbed a flight of steps, entered a vacant apartment, got drunk on beer, then fell downstairs and broke a leg. However implausible this sounds, it must be true; nobody could make up such a story.

Uraniborg with all those gadgets may have impressed visitors, but the sixteenth-century peasants of Hveen failed to look upon their lord with respect and affection. The jail especially did not charm them. So, as years went by, while Tycho enjoyed himself at the observatory, at the laboratory, at the printing press, and at his magic dining table, a rustic muttering could be heard.

King Frederik died of booze in 1588. The new king, Christian IV, did not much care for stargazers; he thought the money Tycho was collecting and spending at Hveen could be better spent by the navy.

The wizard of Uraniborg, whose nature does not seem to have improved since the day he crossed swords with Manderup, finally packed up his globes and quadrants and notebooks and objets d'art and led his family and his private retainers out of Denmark into Germany. Apparently he thought the new king would ask him to come back. When this did not happen he wrote several obsequious letters to Christian, which made the situation worse. At last, dismayed and bewildered, he tried to express himself in rhetorical poems:

> *Denmark, have I deserved this ingratitude of yours?*
> *Have I, my native land, ever knowingly harmed you?*
> *Is not the fault you find with me after all one*
>   *and the same*
> *With the magnificent glory which through me alone*
>   *you have gained?*

This kind of verse did not win King Christian's approval either, so he moved to the court of Emperor Rudolph in Prague.

Rudolph, who could not surround himself with enough artists and scientists, installed Tycho and his entourage at Benatky Castle. But the humiliation of being squeezed out of Denmark must have weakened him; he died two years later, October 24, 1601, from some kind of gastrointestinal malfunction. Although long before his death Kepler had remarked: "The feebleness of old age was upon him." It sounds as though he was ninety, instead of fifty-four.

On the last night, delirious, he asked the same question several times: "Ne frustra vixisse videar?" Have I lived in vain?

Uraniborg disappeared. The peasants stole whatever was worth stealing as soon as their lord was on the road, and Christian saw no reason to preserve the extravagant buildings. Now, on the site of the fabulous workshop, there is only a grassy depression and some trees.

Tycho Brahe is not considered a genius. He made just one fruitful discovery and it doesn't sound like much: he realized that precise, continuous data was needed. Today this is such a scientific commonplace that we can't imagine a time when it was thought unnecessary. But because of this concept, and because he kept detailed records of his observations, his disgruntled associate Johannes Kepler was able to formulate those three great and tedious laws.

In Italy during this period lived another of the giants Newton was talking about—a chunky, rheumatic, red-headed individual with somewhat brutish features: Galileo. And how curious that three eminent astronomers should arrive almost simultaneously: Brahe in 1546, Galileo in 1564, Kepler in 1571. Marlowe and Shakespeare were born the same year as Galileo, proving beyond doubt a favorable planetary conjunction; though it's true, unfortunately, that 1564 also marked the deaths of Vesalius, Calvin, and Michelangelo.

At this same time lived two imaginative Dutchmen, Zacharias Janssen and Hans Lippershey. One or the other, or perhaps a Neapolitan named della Porta, invented the telescope. Janssen, a spectacles maker, is alleged to have seen a little telescope belonging to a traveler and copied it, but the story is vague. Lippershey's claim a few years later is documented. At any rate Galileo soon heard about the looking-device, constructed one for himself, and began inspecting the stars instead of women in the next block. He would have been better off with his telescope fixed in a horizontal position because what he found overhead disturbed the Church enormously and brought him to his knees before the Inquisition.

The sequence of events usually is regarded as inevitable. Given one nettlesome intellect, given a despotic religion, given a powerful new instrument and the mysterious sky at night, what would you expect?

Koestler, for one, disagrees: "The conflict between Church and Galileo . . . was not in the nature of a fatal collision between opposite philosophies of existence, which was bound to occur sooner or later, but rather a clash of individual temperaments aggravated by unlucky coincidences."

However the facts should be interpreted, Galileo did certainly strike at the sacred idea of an earth-centered universe when he observed Jupiter's four moons. Now, four moons on a Las Vegas slot machine wins the entire casino but in seventeenth-century Italy all it meant was trouble. Giovanni Magini, professor of mathematics at the University of Padua, declared that he would have Jupiter's satellites extirpated from the sky. Rome's leading mathematician, Father Clavius, peered through Galileo's diabolic instrument and insisted he could not see any moons. The professor of philosophy at Padua refused even to look.

And in December of that year, 1610, Galileo perceived that Venus underwent phases—from sickle to full disc—which was proof that it revolved around the sun. He made no public announcement of this; instead he contrived a baffling anagram:

"Haec immatura a me iam frustra leguntur o.y."

His purpose was to establish himself as the discoverer, but at the same time conceal what he had learned so that nobody else might profit by it. He filed this anagram with Giuliano de Medici, whom he trusted and who would be a powerful witness on his behalf.

Properly arranged the letters read:

"Cynthiae figuras aemulatur Mater Amorum."

Cynthia being the moon—a generally understood poetic metaphor—whose figures or shapes were emulated by Venus, Mother of Love.

This kind of business was not uncommon. The Dutch astronomer Huygens, for instance, protected an important discovery by writing in his book *Systema Saturnium:* "aaaaaaa ccccc d eeeee g h iiiiiii llll mm nnnnnnnnn oooo pp q rr s ttttt uuuuu."

A cryptographer might deduce that the letters should be organized as follows: "Annulo cingitur, tenui plano, nusquam cohaerente, ad eclipticam inclinato." In other words, obviously, Saturn is encircled by a flat ring inclined to the ecliptic and nowhere touching the planet.

Galileo himself decoded the Venus message somewhat later, and this revelation—that Venus sailed around the sun—brought him one step closer to the stake. Such telescopic observations might be real, said the professor of philosophy at Pisa, but it was heresy to suggest that the sun could be the center of the universe.

Galileo next antagonized the Jesuits. Father Scheiner, together with a young assistant named Cysat, had been studying the sky above Ingolstadt in Bavaria. In 1612 they reported sunspots. Cysat reputedly noticed them first and exclaimed, "Either the sun sheddeth tears or she is blemished!"

Father Scheiner's superior was not pleased by this news: "I have read all the works of Aristotle several times from beginning to end, and I assure you that I have not found anything in them which could be what you are telling me. Go, my son, and calm yourself. I assure you that what you took to be spots on the Sun are only flaws in your glasses or in your eyes."

But the spots did exist and Scheiner felt entitled to some credit.

It is now thought that four observers were aware of sunspots at that time: Fabricius in Holland, Harriot in England, Scheiner-Cysat in Bavaria, and Galileo. Who saw them first is an academic point, but the abrasive Italian loudly claimed them for himself and then proceeded to disparage Father Scheiner. It is almost as though he wanted to challenge the full strength and majesty of the Church.

Cardinal Dini cautioned him: "One may write freely as long as one keeps out of the sacristy."

Cardinal Bellarmine wrote to a priest who supported Galileo: "To affirm that the Sun is really fixed in the center of the Heavens, and merely turns upon itself without traveling from east to west, and that the Earth is situated in the third sphere and revolves very swiftly about the Sun, is a very dangerous thing, not only because it irritates all the theologians and scholastic philosophers, but also because it injures our holy faith and makes the sacred Scriptures false."

Pope Paul then spoke up: Galileo was admonished for the publication of heretical ideas.

This ominous charge worried him, as well it might; still he persisted, commenting in a letter: "I believe there is no greater hatred in the world than the hatred of ignorance for knowledge."

And before long he managed to irritate the next pope, Urban VIII.

On June 22, 1633, after ten weeks of trial, Galileo was "vehemently suspected of heresy" for having advocated Copernicus' theory of a moving earth "which is false and contrary to the sacred and divine Scriptures."

He knelt, a tired old man wearing the white shirt of a penitent, in the Dominican monastery of Santa Maria Sopra Minerva, and confessed under threat of torture that he abjured, cursed, and detested his previous belief: "I, Galileo, son of the late Vincenzo Galilei, Florentine, aged seventy years, arraigned personally before this tribunal and kneeling before you, Most Eminent and Reverend Lord Cardinals Inquisitors-General against heretical pravity throughout the entire Christian commonwealth, having before my eyes and touching with my hands the Holy Gospels, swear that I have always believed, do believe, and by God's help will in the future believe all that is held, preached, and taught. . . ."

He was confined to his villa Il Giojello in Arcetri, near Florence, not far from the convent where his two daughters lived. Until 1639, by which time he was blind, no visitors were allowed without permission of the Holy Office. After that he had all the company he wanted, such guests as Milton, Descartes, and Hobbes.

Milton reflected with little pleasure upon this visit to Italy: "I have sat among their learned men, and been counted happy to be born in such a place of philosophic freedom as they supposed England was, while they themselves did nothing but bemoan the servile condition into which learning amongst them was brought. . . . There it was that I found and visited the famous Galileo, grown old, a prisoner of the Inquisition for thinking in Astronomy otherwise than the Franciscan and Dominican licencers of thought."

Kepler, to some slight degree, may have been responsible for this. Galileo wrote to him on August 4, 1597, thanking him for a book and remarking on the fate of Copernicus who was jeered and mocked by an ignorant public. "I have written many direct and indirect arguments for the Copernican view, but until now I have not dared to publish them. . . . I would dare to come forward publicly with my views if there were more people of your way of thinking. As this is not the case, I shall refrain."

Kepler replied on October 13, saying that he himself would rather be criticized by one intelligent man than be praised by the masses. After the great work Copernicus had initiated, he went on, would it not be appropriate for those who understood the truth to join forces? "Be of good cheer," he suggested, "and come out publicly."

How much Galileo was influenced by this advice is impossible to estimate, but he could not have forgotten it. At last he did venture from his closet, and for revealing unacceptable facts the Inquisition drove him to his knees.

In 1642, when the crusty old heretic died, Grand Duke Ferdinand proposed a monument in his honor. Urban VIII objected, claiming that such a monument would insult papal dignity.

According to legend Galileo muttered "E pur si muove!" as he stood up after confessing to the Inquisitors, meaning that in spite of his formal abjuration he knew the earth did move. Scholars insist this is a fable. Just the same, he might have said it, even if nobody was close enough to hear. The story appeared first in *The Italian Library* by Giuseppe Baretti, published in 1757. However, there is a painting of the trial by Murillo, circa 1650, which includes those words, so the story goes back at least that far.

The other Galileo legend—dropping cannonballs from the tower of Pisa—makes scholars grind their teeth. It started when he began to question Aristotle: "Aristotle says: 'An iron ball of 100 pounds, falling from a height of 100 cubits, reaches the ground before a one-pound ball has fallen a single cubit.' "

Aristotle said no such thing, but that's irrelevant; Galileo thought he had, and suspected the statement was untrue, and set out to demonstrate its untruth. What Aristotle did say about moving bodies was less specific and depends on how you translate Greek. For instance, *rhopé* can mean speed or momentum or trend or tendency or impulse.

But the quarrel revolves around the experiment. Did Galileo, or did he not, drop anything from the tower?

Thiel: "His doubts led him to the famous climb up the leaning tower, from which he dropped balls of all sorts."

Ronan: "Unfortunately the story seems untrue, dramatic and to the point though it is: Galileo *may* have dropped weights in this fashion but he probably gave no public demonstration. . . ."

Dickson: "What Galileo did was to let the balls roll down an incline, which in principle is the same as letting them drop vertically. . . ."

Hawkins: "On several occasions he dropped weights from the leaning tower. . . ."

Moore: "He did not, incidentally, drop any stones off the Leaning Tower of Pisa; this is a story of the Canute-and-the-Waves type."

Ley: "Wohlwill was perfectly correct in denying that 'the event' described by popularizers ever took place. But that does not mean that Galileo did not drop things from the Campanile. . . ."

One of Galileo's pupils, Vincenzio Viviani, wrote that the master had disproved Aristotle's statement: ". . . demonstrating this with repeated experiments from the height of the Campanile at Pisa in the presence of the other teachers and philosophers, and the whole assembly of students. . . ."

Columbia Encyclopedia: ". . . the story has been disputed."

So he did or he didn't. Choose your scholar. Myself, I'll take Viviani because he brings to mind our recent campus spectaculars. You can practically see a bearded young teacher haranguing the crowd from the top of that old grain silo, whipping his students into a frenzy with scurrilous remarks about Aristotle and rolling cannonballs off the parapet while an FBI agent in a cassock sniffs the wind for heresy.

Well, not only was an autocratic Church shocked by the outrageous Florentine; he seems to have distressed the most sophisticated minds of the day. Johannes Kepler himself exclaimed again and again, with stark anguish, that the idea of infinity was unthinkable.

Galileo died the year Newton was born, which is either a meaningless coincidence or indisputable proof of reincarnation, according to your outlook. He, Newton, arrived on Christmas Day, a farmer's son, so unimpressive that he was not expected to survive. He lasted eighty-four years—lonely, arrogant, irascible—beyond doubt one of the most perceptive men who ever lived. He coordinated the work of that eccentric triumvirate Brahe-Kepler-Galileo and gave us a view of the universe that worked elegantly for three centuries—until the discovery of quasars, black holes, and so forth, when Newtonian laws had to be supplemented by Einsteinian laws.

He also invented the reflecting telescope—the Dutch device had been a refractor—and he created fluxions, which sounds like an indisposition suffered by eighteenth-century ladies, maybe a prelude to the vapors, but is in fact the science of calculus. The German mathematician-philosopher Leibniz invented calculus at exactly the same time, a development as strange as Wallace and Darwin independently and simultaneously comprehending evolution. In brief it's said that, with the possible exception of Darwin, or Wallace-Darwin, or maybe Copernicus, Newton has influenced our view of life more than any other man.

The Swiss physicist Bernoulli once sent the most redoubtable mathematicians of Europe a problem which he challenged any of them to solve within six months. Why he failed to notify the English genius is rather odd, but apparently Newton only learned of it six months later when Bernoulli renewed the challenge. Newton was at this time in poor health, physically and mentally, yet he solved the problem before going to bed. The next day, without identifying himself, he submitted his answer to the Royal Academy. And we are told that Bernoulli, upon receiving the answer, exclaimed "Ex unque leonem!" One knows the lion by its claws.

Leibniz must have felt a bit scratched by this performance because a number of years later he, too, concocted a puzzle—directing it especially at Newton who was then in his seventies:

Find the orthogonal trajectories of any one-parameter family of curves.

Sir Isaac was handed this exercise at five o'clock one evening. Naturally he picked it apart before blowing out the lamp.

Yet this same man, whose intellect may never have been equaled, argued that the Egyptian pyramids were built in 808, 824, and 838 B.C., and that in 989 B.C. the art of carpentry was invented by Daedalus. He also thought Bohemian alchemists were transmuting iron into copper—

though any high school chemistry student can explain what happens when iron is combined with copper vitriol. It does make you wonder.

Life's little amenities failed to seduce him, even after he had been appointed Master of the Mint and his income jumped from 60 to 500 pounds. By ordinary standards his house was plain—even austere—except for crimson curtains and crimson upholstery. Most of us could tolerate one or the other, but that combination sounds excessive, practically Byzantine. Crimson, crimson everywhere. Just thinking about it is enough to turn your stomach.

He lived without women. When he was a boy he pursued the village apothecary's stepdaughter so passionately that several years later they became engaged. Luckily for science, perhaps, something went wrong and she married a Mr. Vincent. Never again did young Isaac approach a female.

Nor was he fatally attracted to such bourgeois temptations as playing cards and drinking rum. During undergraduate days at Cambridge he closely watched expenses. His account book does register an occasional session at the pub, but only two gambling losses. Two. Just two. That was enough gambling. And you begin to wonder if he never—ever—lost his head.

He squandered no time on music, art, or dancing. He didn't keep a pet. As for rich food, vintage wine, stylish garments—well, our twentieth-century genius Albert Einstein was less than celebrated as a fashion plate and somebody once asked what governed his taste in clothes. Said Einstein: "Indifference." Sir Isaac evidently felt the same. The abbé Alari, having been invited to supper at Newton's home, later confided that the meal was "detestable." The great man seems to have been satisfied with a leg of mutton, a glass of cider, a game of chess, and time enough to harvest that prodigious brain.

Years after his death a retired officer of the Royal Engineers who was writing a biography of him turned up an old document: *True and Perfect Inventory of all and Singular the Goods Chattels of Sir Isaac Newton*. It listed 362 books in folio, 477 in quarto, 1,057 smaller books, and "above one hundred weight of pamphlets." There were a few histories, a few books on commerce and travel. Everything else was science.

A longtime friend and associate, Dr. Edmond Halley— the astronomer for whom the comet is named—once essayed a little joke about some theological or scientific matter and Newton rebuked him. The subject of the joke is unimportant; what matters is Newton's austerity. And those Edgar Allan Poe curtains! But such irregular patterns must be expected, of course, if you know anything about human behavior.

Still, you can't help liking the man, no matter how sick you might be of the falling apple story. They say that when he was a boy on the farm he was very good at making kites, lanterns, and water clocks; and during a storm, instead of leading the cows to the barn, he was observed jumping against the wind in order to measure its force. And when he was president of the Royal Society he caused a newly designed cannon to be rejected because, he said, "This diabolic instrument will only multiply mass killing." How times change.

Ever since he deduced the existence of gravity we have been accumulating splinters of confirmation, which now and again become unexpectedly relevant. Newton's celebrated law states that all things in the universe, from the heavenly bodies to the least particles, hold some attraction for one another. Now, the strength of this attraction is in direct proportion to the product of the masses of the bodies concerned and varies inversely as the square of the distance between them. Very well, you say, but what has that to do with me? In personal terms it means this much: two people standing at arm's length from one another experience an attraction that has been calculated at one-millionth of an ounce. The implications, as you see, are stupendous.

Newton's friend Halley, a natural man, had no trouble understanding this; he fell in love, which Newton never did—unless you count that interlude of madness with the apothecary's daughter. Halley fell in love with Miss Mary Tooke, whom he married, with whom he spent fifty-five years "happily and in great contentment."

Halley seems not only to have recognized but to have taken pleasure in the genius of Newton, though that must have been difficult for a man as outstanding as himself. Indeed, it was while trying to relieve Newton of some tedious work concerning the paths of comets that Dr. Halley made the discovery for which he himself is famous.

"I am more and more confirmed that we have seen that comet now three times since ye year of 1531," he wrote to Newton.

Somewhat later he was able to present the Royal Society with a table showing the orbits of twenty-four comets.

This sounds like the magnum opus of a dilettante, but Halley's table meant that comets were predictable. Consequently they shouldn't be frightening; and we know how erratically people behave when an unfamiliar light streams overhead. For instance, we are told by the great surgeon Ambroise Paré that in 1528 a hideous apparition bloomed in the sky above France: ". . . so horrible and dreadful . . . some died of fear, others fell sick. . . ." It was the color of blood, Paré insists. It was shaped like a human arm holding a sword, while on either side could be seen axes, knives, and monstrous faces with beards and tangled hair.

Now, we take it for granted that Ambroise Paré was a man with reasonably good eyesight. We assume furthermore that no such phenomenon as he describes could possibly have materialized in the sky. So it's a little troubling. If Ambroise Paré could misrepresent a cloud to this extent—well then, consider what panic must have addled the wits of ordinary men. Some died of fear. Others fell sick. Sinister tidings, my friend.

And in 1664 when a comet was pointed out to Alphonsus VI of Portugal—not to be confused with Alphonso of Castile who hung in Tycho's hall of fame—when Alphonsus of Portugal beheld this luminous visitor he rushed across the palace grounds threatening it with a pistol.

Theologians, one might suppose, would display better sense than common folk or kings. Do you think so? Listen. Bishop Gislebert of Lisieux, having reflected upon a radiant shower of meteorites in 1095, interpreted it as a signal calling for a militant invasion of the East: God must be urging young men to join the First Crusade.

The bishop's interpretation sounds positively Etruscan, but let it go.

Now consider the following:

On the night of November 12, 1883, a Carolina cotton planter was awakened by appeals for mercy and shrieks of horror from the plantation Negroes. While lying in bed wondering about the cause, he tells us, "I heard a faint voice near the door calling my name. I arose, and taking my sword, stood at the door. At this moment I heard the same voice beseeching me to rise, saying, 'Oh, my God! the world is on fire!' I then opened the door. . . . The scene was truly awful; for never did rain fall much thicker than the meteors fell toward the earth,—east, west, north, and south, it was the same!"

In other words, the annual Leonid shower had arrived, brighter than usual.

Planets, too, are capable of raising blisters on the brain. Once in a while they coalesce—which is to say, occasionally they form clusters because they travel at different speeds in different orbits, thereby overtaking each other. And when this happens, so that from earth the planets appear to have congregated, God Himself has trouble predicting how His inconstant children will react. For example, in the year 1186 an awesome sevenfold conjunction was observed. What else could this foretell but some incomprehensible calamity? As a result thousands of underground shelters were built, which should remind you of more recent alarums. And the Byzantine emperor Isaac II ordered his palace windows boarded up. And the Archbishop of Canterbury declared a three-day fast.

You might feel entitled to ask what occurred. If anything.

Let me put it like this. At that time the chronicles of York were kept by a rather droll clerk who wrote: "We have experienced nothing but the tempest emitted from the pulpit by His Eminence."

In 1524 another portentous conjunction developed. Being in the sign of the Fish it advised humanity to prepare for a disastrous flood. President Auriol of Toulouse University therefore recommended the immediate construction of an ark. The Margrave of Brandenburg shepherded weeping members of his court to the top of a little hill in Berlin. Et cetera.

Again we might ask what happened. Well, that particular year was noted throughout Europe for unusually cool temperatures and frequent rains. Whether this fulfilled the prophecy and justified the hysterics—who can say? It depends on your evaluation of singular events.

Here's one more. Dr. Halley's table of orbits accurately forecast the brilliant comet of 1773, and because of this scientific accomplishment nobody got upset when the thing materialized. True or false?

Listen. So many people thought the world must be coming to an end in 1773 that clergymen sold seats in Paradise for the twentieth of May, that being the date it was expected to strike and demolish the earth. Skeptics who asked how these tickets had been acquired, and to whom they should be presented, were denounced as atheists.

What next?

Suppose we let a couple of generations go by.

Biela's comet approaches. It, too, is on schedule, which means the universe has not slipped a cog. So far so good. But here we meet Dr. Heinrich Wilhelm Olbers who—after some narrow calculating—predicts that the glowing tail of this comet will brush the earth. And with that announcement Dr. Olbers absolutely electrified his fellow men. Artists sketched the forthcoming holocaust, journalists described it. Millions would die. Cities would burn. Very possibly everybody on earth would suffocate or be poisoned by noxious gases.

And if you think we have grown more sophisticated, my friend, read your paper the next time a planetary conjunction, a shower of meteorites, or a handsome comet favors us. You will learn that in some farmhouse or on some green Mississippi hilltop a tight knot of zealots, disposing of all earthly possessions, has gathered to await the Day of Judgment.

Many remarkable things may be explained, but why we are so faintly instructed by the past does not seem to be among them.

Well, one thinks of Dr. Halley—assuming one does think of him—as somebody who, like Biela, contrived to get his name in front of a comet. Other than that he may be remembered as Sir Isaac Newton's devoted amanuensis: a polite, timid, modest fellow. But this fails to coincide with seventeenth-century memoirs. We are told that Edmond Halley sopped up brandy like an old sea captain. And in 1691 when he applied for the job of professor of astronomy at Oxford the authorities refused even to consider him, partly because John Flamsteed, the first Astronomer Royal of Britain, feared that he might "corrupt the youth of the University with his lewd discourse." As anyone with any sense knows, such a thing is impossible, but Flamsteed's remark does bring the man into focus. Actually it brings both men into focus.

Then one fine day Czar Peter came to town. Ultimately he would be known as Peter the Great, but in those days he was a young prince touring western Europe more or less incognito to study industrial methods. He had worked awhile as a ship's carpenter in Holland and now he was in England to study boat building. He leased Sayes Court, a property owned by the diarist John Evelyn—who subsequently put in a heavy claim for breakage. Among other outrages, we are informed, the youthful czar mutilated Evelyn's bowling green, destroyed fruit trees, and had himself carried in a wheelbarrow back and forth through the holly hedge. All of which is irrelevant. Somehow, perhaps at a pub, young Peter got acquainted with Edmond Halley. They became friends. They ate together, talked science until late at night, merrily addressed themselves to the keg, and threw a number of undignified parties.

Halley's portrait gives no indication that he was such a bon vivant. He appears to be a discreet eighteenth-century gentleman. His periwig has not slid askew, his mouth is controlled, his eyes are large, dark, and lustrous. The impression is of intelligence and sobriety. He resembles his critic Flamsteed, although Flamsteed does not look refined.

Halley did at last make it to Oxford and we have no evidence that his students were corrupted. However, he was teaching geometry instead of astronomy, which perhaps moderated his lewd discourse. In any event, during the Oxford years he established himself as a distinguished astronomer, quite apart from Newton's blinding radiance. He suggested that those indistinct fields of light visible through a telescope might be clouds of gas, which some of them are. He thought the lovely shimmering polar aurora might be associated with earth's magnetic field, which it is. He argued that the universe could be infinite—a matter still troubling us. And he proposed a way to measure the distance from the earth to the sun.

This could be accomplished, he said, when Venus passed across the sun's disc. Observations would have to be made simultaneously from different points on earth.

Now it so happens that Venus does not very often travel between us and the sun. She makes the trip twice within a period of eight years, then there is a lapse of more than a century. It may not sound reasonable, but that's how things are.

The next transit of Venus would not occur until June 6, 1761, at which time Halley would be 105 years old and therefore unlikely to appreciate it; but he lobbied insistently for his idea, knowing that if you want the government to finance something you must plan well ahead. And it came about after much discussion by various European bigwigs, all of whom wanted to know how far away the sun was, because of course this might have military significance—it came about finally, years after Dr. Halley died, that several expeditions were dispatched to observe the transit of Venus.

The French detachment consisted of one astronomer.

Guillaume Joseph Hyacinthe Jean Baptiste Le Gentil de

La Galaisière was not a lucky man. Pondicherry, at that time a French enclave, was his destination, so in March of 1760 he sailed from Brest. Good students of the human circus will recall that a war was in progress—the Seven Years' War—and one fine day our hero was quite naturally troubled to perceive a British fleet on the horizon. His ship escaped, though, and reached Mauritius where Le Gentil learned that Pondicherry was besieged. However, a French fleet was about to embark with the intention of liberating Pondicherry and he obtained permission to sail on one of the gunboats.

Scarcely had he settled himself in his new quarters when a hurricane struck. He almost drowned. And because the expedition would need to be reorganized—in other words, postponed—it occurred to him that perhaps he would be able to observe the transit of Venus from Batavia. He therefore wrote to the French Academy in Paris and explained his plan.

While waiting for an answer he was afflicted with a disgusting malady known to many tourists.

Up again, still without word from Paris, he decided that after all he should go to Pondicherry. And because the troopship *La Sylphide* was just about to depart he hurried aboard.

As they were approaching Pondicherry the captain of *La Sylphide* received word that it had surrendered to the British. Who but a fool proceeds on a useless mission? *La Sylphide*'s captain wisely reversed course.

June 6, 1761, proved to be an excellent day for viewing and Le Gentil could see a little black dot on the face of the sun, but with *La Sylphide* rocking over the Indian Ocean he could not take measurements.

Once again in Mauritius he attempted to book passage home.

Unfortunately, no ships were going to France.

Le Gentil was not a man to waste time: he resolved to study the geography, geology, and folklore of the island.

In those days, of course, very few ships bound for Europe put in at Mauritius, and at last M. Le Gentil decided that since he had come this far he might as well wait for the 1769 transit. He therefore began to make preparations. And it occurred to him that possibly he could get a better view from Manila—4,000 miles east—so he wrote to Paris explaining his desire to change the program. He requested the academy to obtain permission from Spain, which governed Manila.

Then a Spanish warship bound for Manila put in at Mauritius. Le Gentil, having heard nothing from the academy, persuaded the Spanish captain to take him along.

In August of 1766 he reached Manila where at last, three years after the war ended, a letter from Paris caught up with him. Pondicherry no longer was besieged. The academy would prefer that he stick to the original plan.

M. Le Gentil, that obedient servant of science, packed up his instruments and sailed once more, although he left a telescope with a missionary in Manila and showed him how to operate it when the great day arrived.

The British, who now ruled Pondicherry, welcomed the French astronomer. They provided everything he asked for. They even constructed a little observatory in the ruins of the old fort. And here, with everything arranged, he settled down to wait.

On the eve of the big event he was too excited to sleep; he remained beside his telescope all night. It had been calculated that Venus would touch the sun's rim at 7:00 A.M.

At 6:50 A.M. in a clear sky one small cloud materialized. As though upon command it drifted over Le Gentil's observatory.

There it stopped.

In his diary he wrote: "Such is the fate which often awaits astronomers. I have wandered almost 10,000 leagues over great stretches of sea, exiling myself from my home country, only to watch a fatal cloud which came to disport itself in front of the sun at the exact moment of my observations, robbing me of the fruit of my troubles and labors."

And because Venus would not again visit the sun for more than a century Le Gentil started back to Paris. He arrived after a difficult journey, having been gone almost twelve years.

You might think that after so many tribulations Providence would look favorably upon M. Le Gentil de La Galaisière. Wrong. Such a long time had elapsed since anybody had heard from him that the courts adjudged him dead. His estate was in the process of liquidation, and it is said that he did not have an easy job recovering his property.

Later he heard from the missionary. The sky above Manila that day was perfect.

Le Gentil cannot be blamed for the fact that in all those years he accomplished nothing. If this malignant cloud had not blown over Pondicherry he would have lived to see his name wedged into the astronomy books as a contributor to the determination of the position of the planet Venus during the solar transit of June 3, 1769. Well, these things happen.

It's good to learn that eventually M. Le Gentil fell in love, got married, and became the father of a charming daughter.

Meanwhile, investigation of the solar system continued. Mercury, Venus, Mars, Jupiter, and Saturn, all being obvious and obviously traveling through the constellations, had long since been identified as planets. There seemed to be nothing else revolving around the sun.

Then one brisk evening in 1781 the organist of the Octagon Chapel at Bath, the German-born Mr. William Herschel, who resembled one of Hogarth's massive squires and whose hobby was stargazing, noticed something in the constellation of Taurus:

"On Tuesday the 13th of March, between ten and eleven in the evening, while I was examining the small stars in the Neighbourhood of H Geminorum . . ."

Organist Herschel—whose status can be judged by the fact that when he first stepped into the limelight his name was spelled Herthel, Mersthel, and Herrschel—Mr. Herschel thought he had spotted a comet in H Geminorum. Later observations by professional astronomers proved the traveling speck of light to be a planet. King George III, much impressed, created a new job—King's Astronomer—for the organist of Bath, quite a plum for one who started his career as an oboist in the band of the Hanoverian Foot Guards. And because the discoverer of a celestial object is entitled to name it Herschel proposed "Georgium Sidus" in honor of his benefactor. The Royal Society disapproved of this because it violated classical tradition, and scientists on the Continent objected for political reasons, so the new member of the system was named after the sky god Uranus.

Herschel had not been the first to see this planet, nor the first to catalogue it. Flamsteed observed it in 1690 but thought he was looking at a dim star; in fact he noticed Uranus on five occasions and charted the position each time. Lemonnier in France observed it thirteen times without realizing what it was.

Beyond Uranus lies Neptune, which was located before anybody saw it. This sounds implausible, if not impossible, but the explanation shows how thoughtfully men had begun to plot the firmament.

Between 1800 and 1820 Uranus did not perform quite

as expected. It seemed to be lagging. Several mathematicians attacked this puzzle, using Newton's gravitational theory, and concluded that some unknown object must be acting as a brake. They then plotted this object's hypothetical orbit. A young mathematician named John Couch Adams was the first to complete the work, which surprised nobody familiar with the situation because Adams was rather good at mathematics. During final examinations at Cambridge he accumulated twice as many marks as the runner-up—a certain Bashford who was himself no slouch, subsequently being appointed to a chair of mathematics. There was, indeed, a wider gap between the scores of Adams and Bashford than between Bashford and the lowest man on the scale, which tells you a bit about John Couch Adams.

This nascent genius called on Sir George Airy of the Greenwich Observatory, but Sir George had been summoned to France because of the "Cherbourg breakwater investigation"—whatever that was.

Adams went home, continued work on the problem, revised his calculations, and tried once more.

Sir George chanced to be out. He was attending a meeting of the Railway Gauge Commission.

Adams tried again. Sir George was at supper; he could not be disturbed. Adams seems to have become a trifle weary. He had brought along a paper concerning the hypothetical object and he gave this to a servant.

In due course Sir George got around to reading Adams' paper but the calculations failed to arouse him. Then he got a letter from a French mathematician, Urbain J. J. Leverrier, whose arithmetic was almost identical. Sir George now requested a Cambridge astronomer named Challis to look into the business.

Challis could not get started for several weeks, and then

he did not concentrate on the area pointed out by Adams and Leverrier. If he had, he undoubtedly would have charted the planet.

In Paris, meanwhile, Leverrier grew impatient. He already was disgusted with the somnolence of French astronomers; now it appeared that the British were no more alert. So he wrote to Professor Johann Galle at the Berlin Observatory: "Train your telescope on the point of the ecliptic in the constellation of Aquarius (longitude 326°) and within a degree of that point you will find a new planet, looking like a 9th magnitude star and showing a small disk."

This letter was delivered to Professor Galle at home on his birthday. That evening he went to the observatory where he asked to use the telescope.

"Tun wir doch den Herren in Paris den Gefallen," said the director. Let us accommodate the French gentlemen.

Galle located Neptune within an hour.

Challis may possibly have seen it before news of Galle's discovery reached England because he mentioned to a friend named Kingsley, with whom he was having supper, that he thought he had noticed a disc among the stars. Kingsley was so excited that he suggested they visit the observatory at once. Challis agreed, but Mrs. Challis prevailed upon them to have a cup of tea before starting out, the night being rather chilly. And by the time they finished tea the sky had grown overcast. And before it cleared up there came tidings from Johann Galle.

M. Leverrier was pleased when told that his theoretical object actually existed, but he never bothered to look at it. The mathematics of the problem interested him, the reality did not. One suspects that Leverrier and Newton would have enjoyed a glass of cider together, and perhaps a rousing game of chess.

Those phlegmatic villains Airy and Challis live forever in a kind of scientific purgatory; Adams now shares a marble niche with Leverrier and Galle. So the mills do grind—neither rapidly nor invariably to the right degree, but one shouldn't ask too much.

Soon after Neptune had been bracketed Leverrier theorized that there could be yet another planet. Various astronomers were thinking the same, and presently they determined that Neptune, like Uranus, was dragging his feet. Thus the lord of darkness, Pluto, stood revealed—smaller even than the earth, so small that it, or he, may be only an escaped satellite of Neptune, cruising in a slow elliptical orbit four billion miles from the sun.

Yet here, again, discrepancies in the predicted course hinted at something beyond.

Just where, one may ask, does our solar system end?

The most celebrated planet always has been Mars because of its sanguine color. Greeks called it Ares, which derives from a word that means vengeance or disaster or killing. Persians called it Pahlavani Siphir, the celestial warrior. Chaldeans named it for the god of battle, Nergal. And the earliest symbolic representation consists of a spear and a shield. So the military implications grow like red roots into our half-remembered past.

Even when people were able to look at Mars through a telescope they continued to see it through the filter of imagination. In 1664 the Jesuit Father Kircher reported: "The surface is extremely hard, rough, sooty, and sulphurous, but incombustible, sweating tar and naphtha, surrounded by poisonous vapors. From mountain gorges brownish flames burst forth with a frightful stench; the seas are viscous sulphurous mud." Clearly a parable of summer in New York.

The idea that it might be inhabited is not new, nor is

the desire to communicate with Martians. In the nine-teenth century many schemes were debated, not only by imaginative hod carriers but by such eminent personages as the director of the Vienna Observatory, Joseph von Lit-trow, and the mathematician Karl Friedrich Gauss.

Dig a geometric pattern of canals in the Sahara, fill these canals with water, pour kerosene on top, and set the network afire.

Plant a stupendous triangle of wheat in Siberia—wheat because of its uniform color.

Build a complex of mirrors to reflect earth's sunlight.

An ingenious Frenchman, Charles Cros, proposed that a gigantic mirror be used as a magnifying glass to focus the sun's heat, thereby making it possible to etch blazing words on the Martian surface. M. Cros did not specify what words should be written, though undoubtedly they would be French; nor did he suggest what to do if, in response, enormous Martian words suddenly began to scorch the Luxembourg Gardens.

One evening in 1877 when the seeing was good, as as-tronomers say, and Mars spun close to the earth—less than thirty-five million miles away—Giovanni Schiaparelli peered through his 8.5-inch refractor at the Milan Obser-vatory and noticed on the Martian disc a pattern of lines which he referred to as *canali,* meaning channels.

What happened next can be ascribed either to sloppy translation or a deliberate attempt by journalists to sell newspapers. The *canali* became canals, implying artificial construction. Canals also imply irrigation. Ergo: not only were there intelligent beings on Mars, they must be pro-gressive farmers. Probably Socialists, but never mind; the important thing was to find out what they were up to. An engineer calculated how much energy would be needed to pump water from the Martian polar cap to its equator and people began asking where the capital city might be located.

Schiaparelli seems to have been dismayed by the excitement:

"It is not necessary to suppose them the work of intelligent beings, and notwithstanding the almost geometrical appearance of all of their system, we are now inclined to believe them to be produced by the evolution of the planet, just as on earth we have the English Channel and the Channel of Mozambique."

Nobody listened to these cautionary words. A dialogue with Mars was expected to begin at any moment.

Madame Clara Goguet, a rich widow, promised 100,000 gold francs "à celui qui aura trouvé le moyen de communiquer avec un astre autre que la planète Mars." Conversation with Mars being practically a fait accompli, in Madame's opinion, the prize should be awarded for something truly difficult: a method of communicating with more distant beings.

At this point we meet Percival Lowell of the Lowells, who dressed like a banker, whose brother Abbott was president of Harvard, and whose sister was cigar-smoking verse-writing Amy. The existence of life on Mars seemed to him quite possible and when he heard that Schiaparelli's eyesight was failing he built an observatory near Flagstaff, Arizona, in order to continue the investigation.

One does not associate the Lowells of Massachusetts with Flagstaff, a place where a cowboy is not apt to remove his Stetson while having lunch, but the air was clean and dry in 1894 just as it is today. Lowell's observatory stands on a hill west of town. The neat buildings—if you except one monstrous silver bubble—suggest a Baptist summer retreat, the paths between them irregularly decorated with old pinecones as hard as hand grenades. The astronomer, who died in 1916, has been entombed near his telescope under a Persian blue dome, and almost every day the desert wind rushes around his vault with soft insistence.

Guided by Schiaparelli's map, Lowell and his associate William Pickering had no trouble identifying the canals, which radiated from dark regions into lighter areas like the spokes of a wheel. Calculations indicated that they were at least twenty miles wide, so it was thought they might be strips of irrigated land with an aqueduct in the center. Some of these spokes appeared to be double, which might mean that one of them functioned as a return conduit. Thus the water could circulate to and from the Pole. Yet how could water flow across a relatively flat surface for 2,500 miles? The Martians must have contrived some sort of pumping apparatus.

"Irrigation, unscientifically conducted, would not give us such truly wonderful mathematical fitness. . . . A mind of no mean order would seem to have presided over the system we see—a mind certainly of considerably more comprehensiveness than that which presides over the various departments of our own public works."

It's hard to tell, reading that last sentence, whether Lowell was attempting a touch of academic humor.

Because of the pumping stations and the double-barreled canals he is easily ridiculed, but he was not just an odd millionaire. Mars obsessed him, causing him to believe what he wished to believe, yet he did carefully observe the planet for a long time—eleven years—accumulating a formidable amount of data. If only he had not insisted on the public works. Eleven years of reputable work almost forgotten because of one spectacular mistake. But sometimes that happens. Who cares about Casey's batting average?

In any event, Lowell was neither the first nor the last scientist to visit Wonderland. Consider old William Herschel, King George's private eye. Look at Herschel's credits. The man was internationally recognized for his study of nebulae and for his great star catalogue. He charted not only Uranus but the sixth and seventh satellites of Saturn. His research into the nature of double stars, which are called binaries, demonstrated that these very distant systems are held together by gravitation and that they revolve about a common center. All of which should emphasize Herschel's scientific respectability as well as his analytic mind. Yet this lucid, sober gentleman managed to persuade himself that civilized beings were living on the surface of the sun.

Then we have the German selenographer, J. H. Schröter, who inspected the moon night after night for thirty years—until 1813 when French soldiers, who had nothing particular in mind, burned his drawings and his books and smashed his equipment. Schröter thought he had detected industrial activity on the moon. He believed he had seen factories with smokestacks. And so impressed by his observations were French astronomers that they petitioned Louis XVI for a telescope 10,000 feet long which would enable them to take a closer look.

How can it be? How is it possible? Schröter, Herschel, Lowell, the astronomers of King Louis, and any number of others—these must all have been intelligent, judicious men.

There's no answer. No answer except that we live in a world of drifting shadows.

Today, squinting backward, we feel remotely amused by such preposterous misapprehensions. We feel smug. Given those circumstances, we believe, we would have done better. But this is a slippery conceit. Given our present universe of quasars, pulsars, black holes, white dwarfs, neutrinos, photons, and so forth, only a grinning thumping fool would interpret the news with much assurance.

Try neutrinos. This is not a breakfast food. A neutrino is a ghost, a moment of spin, a particle of nothingness formed at the core of a star. It has no electrical charge and no substance, yet it flies through everything with the greatest of ease. It flies through space, it flies through earth. Our bodies are riddled by neutrinos: perhaps 50,000 a second flit through us. Perhaps many times that number. Now, we assume that in the sinister basement laboratories of places like MIT and the University of California there are solid lead walls designed to stop mysterious particles from escaping and killing everybody, and we imagine these walls to be a couple of inches thick, maybe a foot thick. Such walls naturally would stop neutrinos. You think so? Listen.

Neutrinos dance through lead walls the way mosquitos dance through a chicken-wire fence. Of course the analogy isn't strictly accurate, but never mind. Theoretically a lead wall could stop a neutrino, and physicists very much would like to stop one at least long enough to skin it. The problem is the wall. For example, the yellow star Arcturus is about forty light-years away, which, as most people know, means that light traveling from Arcturus at 186,000 miles a second takes forty years to get here. Now listen. A lead wall forty light years thick would almost stop a neutrino. Not quite, but almost. Obviously this makes no sense. Theoretically, you may argue, it does. Yes. All right. But still, something like that is inconceivable.

Pulsars. A pulsar is a source of radio waves emanating from whatever is left of a massive stellar explosion. You might think all stellar explosions are massive, as indeed they are, but everything is relative. Some are more so than others. Our sun, less than a million miles in diameter, is too little to explode. One fine day six billion years hence the sun will expand until it becomes a red giant, enlarging until its surface touches the planet Mercury. By this time the oceans on earth will have boiled away, most of the rocks will have melted, and the atmosphere will have dissipated—which should eliminate the shysters, quacks, generals, and politicians. Next the sun will shrivel and change color, becoming a white dwarf. At last it will lose heat and color and become an invisible cinder coasting around the nucleus of the galaxy until the entire galaxy explodes.

Is that comprehensible? Can you understand it? If not, we might return to the relatively simple business of pulsars.

The core of these pulsing apples is magically small. Some are thought to be no more than a mile in diameter and they blink on and off as frequently as thirty times a second. As for weight, a chunk the size of a matchbox—if you put it down gently—would break through the crust of the earth and keep right on falling toward the center. Anybody can visualize a falling matchbox; the problem begins when we try to imagine material of such density. Expressed another way, a rock the size of a sugar cube would weigh more than a fleet of battleships. And this, we are told, is not science fiction.

That should take care of pulsars but the show is not over. The next act—provided we have a large pulsar—is, quite literally, a sensation. It manages to leave the universe. Nothing remains, only a black hole.

En route to this condition of negativeness—of turning into a hole—the material contracts further. Time slows down. A second becomes eternity. Space has no meaning. And so extreme is the pull of gravity that light itself is trapped. A ray of light could no more escape from one of these collapsing stars than a man could pitch a baseball into the stratosphere. Nor could any sort of electromagnetic radiation escape. And the only evidence that there used to be something where finally there is nothing would be the presence of gravity.

A spaceship cruising near a black hole would be swallowed. The earth itself, if it sailed past a good-sized hole, would be stretched out of shape like silly putty and inexorably devoured.

A miniature black hole may have been responsible for the 1908 Siberian cataclysm which annihilated two villages, barbecued a herd of reindeer, and flattened a forest. Witnesses agreed that something brighter than the sun arched over the southern horizon and hurtled northward. Then, said one who was near the site of the explosion, the ground rose and fell like a wave in the sea and a column of fire spiraled upward. Passengers on the Trans-Siberian express saw it; but the engineer, no doubt conscientiously watching the tracks ahead, only felt a tremendous shock and thought his train had exploded, so he braked to a stop. Whatever the thing was—black hole or meteorite—it had buried itself in the earth 300 miles away. The shock wave registered on microbarographs in England.

Many years later Professor Leonid Kulik of the Russian Academy of Science located the site: "The whole region of the river basins Kimchu and Khushmo is covered with windfallen trees lying fanwise in a circle, their tops pointing outward. . . . The peat marshes of this region are deformed and the whole place bears evidence of an immense catastrophe. . . ."

Another huge explosion in Siberia, in 1947, undoubtedly was caused by a meteorite because twenty-three tons of meteoric material have been collected. Russian scientists think it originally weighed seventy tons. In this case, too, an object as bright as the sun streaked across the sky, thousands of trees were crushed, and a fiery column boiled from the earth. In 1947, you may recall, the Russians and the Americans stood tiptoe to tiptoe, each waiting for the other to make one violent move before retaliating with a storm of nuclear bombs. Even now, after all these years, one doesn't like to think about what would have happened if that meteorite had curled over the horizon and exploded not in Siberia but in the suburbs of Moscow or Washington.

At any rate, because of similarities between these two Siberian spectaculars, both may have been caused by meteorites. However, not a single meteor fragment has been found in the Kimchu-Khushmo basin, which is strange. Consequently, the unthinkable is being thought not only by your basic science-fiction huckster but by serious academic types. That 1908 explosion, they argue, might have been created by a black hole no larger than a virus.

Opponents argue that a black hole would then have passed completely through the earth and emerged in the North Atlantic where it would have caused a tidal wave. No such wave was recorded.

Well then, suppose we try something else. How about a nuclear-powered vehicle from Messier 33? Say it burned a bearing and crashed. Yet this should have left a measurable degree of radiation.

Perhaps a small comet hit Siberia—your average little comet of no significance with a diameter of several hundred feet, weighing a million tons. Or let's imagine a fragment from a larger mass such as Encke's comet. The argument for this theory is persuasive. In 1965 a fearful concussion shook southwestern Canada. Witnesses described a fiery object approaching, illuminating the sky for hundreds of miles before the impact. Scientists who flew over that area in a helicopter could find no trace of a meteorite, but they did observe and collect some black dust; and this dust had the same composition as a particular sort of meteorite which, many astronomers believe, occurs in the heads of comets. All of which may sound irrelevant until we learn that people who saw the 1907 Siberian blast also reported black dust.

Sooner or later the lab technicians—our white-frocked alchemists—will deliver a verdict. Spaceship, comet, black hole, or something still more alarming. But that's not the point. The point is that, regardless of what blew up in a Russian river basin seventy years ago, we've come a long way from Isaac Newton physics.

If you studied physics in high school you were taught that matter and/or energy could not be destroyed.

Well, maybe. Now they are suggesting that such laws apply only to the observable universe. The next question, as you might guess, is what other universe could there be?

Listen. Here is what they are telling us about these incredible black holes—these "puckers in the fabric of space." They may be conduits through time. Say we dove into one: we might emerge not merely in a different universe but during another epoch.

Believe such absurdities if you want to. Myself, I'm dubious.

Inevitably there is talk of trying to build a black hole. Why? Because the energy potential is stupefying. The Pentagon, of course, would dearly love to have a few, or a warehouseful, and just about here we should note that Einstein's curious equation led to Hiroshima. Say a manufactured black hole on the order of 1,600 tons were to escape from the U. S. Army's Dugway Proving Ground— that place in Utah where several thousand sheep abruptly died of natural causes. All right, what would happen? This probably won't surprise you, but the thing would drop out of sight, so to speak: it would begin eating the earth. And nothing could stop it.

The trouble with knowledge is that, contrary to what we expect, as understanding increases so does ignorance.

If you'd like something more formidable than black holes, try quasars.

Nobody is certain what they are, as you might deduce from the word itself which is a contraction of "quasi-stellar"—meaning an apparently starlike object. Astrophysicists seem perplexed by the information they have been gathering from quasars because some of these objects emit 100 times more energy than the largest galaxies in the universe. In other words, to generate that amount of energy a quasar must annihilate a mass equivalent to one billion suns every second.

Suppose we try it again: a good quasar shines as brightly as 100 galaxies of 100 billion suns each. Furthermore, during a period of weeks or months the light flashes like a traffic signal. One of these things—3C-345—the 345th item in Cambridge Observatory's third catalogue, registered a fluctuation of 50 percent within twenty days. At present such data is unintelligible. But we do know that the objects radiating this light must be located at the edge of the observable universe several billion light-years distant, and they are not very big.

Unless, of course, the so-called "red shift" could be duplicated by other means, in which case they may not be as bright as they appear to be, nor as distant. The red shift is simple. If light shifts toward the rear of the spectrum the object emitting that light is receding, just as you determine whether the cops are coming or going by the pitch of the siren.

Now, statistics can be interpreted in various ways to

provide various answers; all that seems undeniable is that quasi-stellar objects exist, or else we are being confounded by a superlative magician. And if they do exist, unless there has been a gross misinterpretation of the facts, quasars must be drawing energy from some source or by some method about which our physicists know absolutely nothing.

Certain theorists have suggested that they could be ports of entry to our universe, just as black holes could be ports of exit.

They could be galaxies in the paroxysm of birth.

Of course there's always a chance that whatever they are, they no longer are; they may long since have winked out. But if indeed they are billions of light-years distant then we are looking billions of years backward in time.

One further aspect of the great quasar controversy should be mentioned. Radio astronomers at the big dish in California's Mojave Desert have found indications that quasar components may be flying apart at speeds exceeding the speed of light, which contradicts the law that nothing travels faster than light.

So tell me, if you can, confronted by a sky filled with quasars and multiple universes, where time has lost significance, what constitutes reason?

In words that we all understand, how do you grasp the wind?

Not long after Neil Armstrong went lumbering across the face of the moon I happened to be in New Orleans, and I happened to visit the city art museum while an exhibit of wood and tin sculpture by an old self-taught black man named David Butler was on display. A brochure published by the museum showed him standing in his backyard, unmistakably at peace with the universe, dressed in a comfortable sweater and a soiled felt hat which he probably had worn all day every day for at least ten years.

According to the brochure he was born in 1898 in Saint Mary Parish in the town of Good Hope, Louisiana. He was the eldest of eight children. His father was a carpenter, and his mother—when she could salvage a little time for herself—participated in neighborhood religious activities.

He built roads, mowed grass, and worked at the sawmill until a few years ago when he was injured and partly disabled. Since then he has depended on a government check. His check arrives the first of each month at a nearby post office, and after cashing it he fills a paper bag with candy and trinkets which he distributes to children he meets along the way. The neighbors used to think he was peculiar, but now that his art has been recognized they are proud of him.

His favorite subjects are dogs, snakes, rabbits, ducks, skunks, roosters, peacocks, alligators, sheep, fish, and so on; but occasionally he will construct a flying elephant, a dinosaur, a sea serpent, or possibly a mermaid. Sometimes he does arrows, stars, hearts, or mysterious abstract symbols. Or he may reproduce a familiar biblical scene: the wise men bearing gifts.

Ideas come to him while he lies in bed and he sketches them with chalk on old sheets of tin roofing. Then, with a nail punch, a hammer, and a knife, he cuts out various shapes which he wires together. Next he attaches light bulbs, bottle caps, reflector buttons, brass bells, plastic toys, umbrella handles, or whatever else seems appropriate. Usually he paints his creations black and silver, but once in a while he will paint them red, white, and blue out of respect for the American flag.

Accompanying the exhibit of David Butler's work was a documentary that had been filmed at his home. And as the camera slowly spiraled around this world of painted tin, whose features he had perceived while lying dreamily on his bed, he was asked what he thought about the astronauts' trip.

The interview went like this, more or less, partly in his soft black Louisiana dialect:

Aw, they ain't nobody on the moon.

You say those men weren't on the moon?

Wasn't on the moon, naw.

But you saw them, didn't you? Didn't you see them on television?

I seed them, yeah. Aw yeah. My grandson, he got a TV. Come git me, say he want me to see the mens on the moon. Aw yeah. I seed the picture. But wasn't nobody on the moon, naw.

Well, how do you explain that?

Do it in the stu-dio. Tha's how they do it. Make ev'body think they's lookin' at the moon. Fix it up in the stu-dio. Ev'body say "Whooee! Jes' look there! Walkin' round on the moon! What you think bout that?" Naw. Naw. It's a il-lusion. What they call a il-lusion.

You're telling me they weren't actually there? It was a trick? We never went to the moon?

Wasn't nothin' but a trick. Make folks think they's seed the mens up there, yeah. Tha's all. A trick, yeah.

But why? Why would anybody go to all that trouble to trick us?

Aw, sometime they do that. Jes' do it. Yeah. Yeah. Dunno why. I 'spect you have to aks them. Have to aks them folks in the stu-dio. But wasn't never no mens on the moon. Naw.

Bibliography

Alter, Dinsmore. *Pictorial Astronomy.* Los Angeles, 1948.

Anton, Ferdinand, and Dockstader, Frederick J. *Pre-Columbian Art.* New York, no date.

Arbman, Holger. *The Vikings.* Translated by Alan Binns. New York, 1961.

Ardrey, Robert. *African Genesis.* New York, 1967.

Armitage, Angus. *The World of Copernicus.* New York, 1947.

Ashe, Geoffrey. *The Quest for America.* New York, 1971.

————. *Land to the West.* New York, 1962.

Banti, Luisa. *The Etruscan Cities and Their Culture.* Translated by Erika Bizzarri. Berkeley, Calif., 1973.

Basham, A. L. *The Wonder That Was India.* London, 1954.

Berenguer, Magín. *Prehistoric Man and His Art.* Translated by Michael Heron. Park Ridge, N.J., 1973.

Berrill, N. J. *Journey into Wonder.* New York, 1952.

Bickel, Lennard. *Mawson's Will.* New York, 1977.

Blindheim, Joan. *Vinland the Good.* Oslo, 1970.

Bloch, Raymond. *Etruscan Art.* Greenwich, Conn., 1965.

————. *Etruscans.* New York, 1958.

Boland, Charles M. *They All Discovered America.* New York, 1963.

Brace, C. Loring. *The Stages of Human Evolution.* Englewood Cliffs, N.J., 1967.

Brandon, S. G. F., ed. *Ancient Empires.* New York, 1973.

Brent, Peter. *Captain Scott*. New York, 1974.

Brodrick, James. *Galileo*. New York, 1964.

Brown, Peter Lancaster. *Comets, Meteorites & Men*. New York, 1973.

Brunhouse, Robert. *In Search of the Maya*. New York, 1974.

Bushnell, G. H. S. *Ancient Arts of the Americas*. New York, 1967.

Cameron, Ian. *Antarctica*. Boston, 1974.

Ceram, C. W. *The First American*. Translated by Richard and Clara Winston. New York, 1971.

––––––. *The March of Archaeology*. Translated by Richard and Clara Winston. New York, 1970.

––––––. *Gods, Graves, and Scholars*. Translated by E. B. Garside and Sophie Wilkins. New York, 1967.

Chapman, Walker. *The Loneliest Continent*. Greenwich, Conn., 1964.

Christensen, Erwin O. *Primitive Art*. New York, 1955.

Clark, Wilfrid Le Gros. *Man-Apes or Ape-Men*. New York, 1973.

Cleator, P. E. *Lost Languages*. New York, 1962.

Cles-Reden, Sibylle von. *The Buried People*. Translated by C. M. Woodhouse. New York, 1955.

Coe, Michael. *The Maya*. New York, 1966.

Cohen, Daniel. *Mysterious Places*. New York, 1969.

Constable, George. *The Neanderthals*. New York, 1973.

Cottrell, Leonard. *Lost Worlds*. New York, 1964.

––––––. *Wonders of Antiquity*. London, 1964.

Crone, G. R. *The Explorers*. New York, 1962.

Daniel, Glyn. *Man Discovers His Past*. New York, 1968.

––––––. *Myth or Legend*. New York, 1968.

Dart, Raymond A. *Adventures with the Missing Link*. New York, 1959.

Debenham, Frank. *Antarctica*. New York, 1961.

––––––. *Discovery and Exploration*. Garden City, N.Y., 1960.

Deuel, Leo. *Testaments of Time*. New York, 1965.

––––––, ed. *The Treasures of Time*. New York, 1962.

Dickson, F. P. *The Bowl of Night*. Cambridge, Mass., 1968.

Diringer, David. *Writing*. New York, 1962.

Ditfurth, Hoimar von. *Children of the Universe*. Translated by Jan van Heurck. New York, 1974.

Doblehofer, Ernst. *Voices in Stone*. Translated by Mervyn Savill. New York, 1961.

Dunaway, Philip, and Evans, Mel, eds. *Great Diaries*. Garden City, N.Y., 1957.

Edey, Maitland. *The Missing Link*. New York, 1972.

Edson, Lee. *Worlds Around the Sun*. New York, 1969.

Eiseley, Loren. *Darwin's Century.* Garden City, N.Y., 1958.

Emmerich, André. *Art Before Columbus.* New York, 1963.

Eydoux, Henri-Paul. *History of Archaeological Discoveries.* Translated by Joan White. London, no date.

Finley, M. I. *Aspects of Antiquity.* New York, 1969.

Franzén, Anders. "Ghost from the Depths: The Warship *Vasa,*" *National Geographic,* vol. 121, no. 1. Washington, D.C., 1962.

Franzén, Greta. *The Great Ship Vasa.* New York, 1971.

Gardner, Martin. *Fads and Fallacies.* New York, 1957.

Ghiselin, Brewster, ed. *The Creative Process.* Berkeley, Calif., 1952.

Golden, Frederic. *Quasars, Pulsars & Black Holes.* New York, 1976.

Hamblin, Dora Jane, ed. *The Etruscans.* New York, 1975.

Hawkins, Gerald. *Splendor in the Sky.* New York, 1969.

Heizer, Robert F. *Man's Discovery of His Past.* Palo Alto, Calif., 1969.

Hencken, Hugh. *Tarquinia and Etruscan Origins.* New York, 1968.

Hermann, Paul. *Conquest by Man.* Translated by Michael Bullock. New York, 1954.

Herold, J. Christopher. *Bonaparte in Egypt.* New York, 1962.

Hibben, Frank C. *Digging up America.* New York, 1960.

Holand, Hjalmar. *A Pre-Columbian Crusade to America.* New York, 1962.

Howell, F. Clark. *Early Man.* New York, 1973.

Howells, William. *Mankind in the Making.* Garden City, N.Y., 1967.

Hoyle, Fred. *Nicolaus Copernicus.* New York, 1973.

Hus, Alain. *The Etruscans.* Translated by Jeanne Unger Duell. New York, 1961.

Ingstad, Helge. *Westward to Vinland.* Translated by Erik J. Friis. New York, 1969.

———. *Land under the Pole Star.* Translated by Naomi Walford. New York, 1966.

Jensen, Hans. *Sign, Symbol and Script.* Translated by George Unwin. New York, 1969.

Jones, Gwyn. *A History of the Vikings.* London, 1973.

———. *The Norse Atlantic Saga.* London, 1964.

Kearns, William. *The Silent Continent.* New York, 1955.

Keller, Werner. *The Etruscans.* Translated by Alexander and Elizabeth Henderson. New York, 1974.

Kendrick, T. D. *A History of the Vikings.* London, 1968.

Kesten, Hermann. *Copernicus and His World.* Translated by E. B. Ashton and Norbert Guterman. New York, 1945.

Kirwan, L. P. *A History of Polar Exploration.* New York, 1960.

Koestler, Arthur. *The Sleepwalkers*. New York, 1968.

Kühn, Herbert. *On the Track of Prehistoric Man*. Translated by Alan Houghton Brodrick. New York, 1955.

La Fay, Howard. "The Maya, Children of Time," *National Geographic*, vol. 148, no. 6. Washington, D.C., 1975.

———. *The Vikings*. Washington, D.C., 1972.

Lawrence, D. H. *Etruscan Places*. New York, 1932.

Leakey, Louis. *By the Evidence*. New York, 1974.

———. *The Progress and Evolution of Man in Africa*. London, 1961.

———, and Vanne Morris Goodall. *Unveiling Man's Origins*. Cambridge, Mass., 1969.

Lear, John. *Kepler's Dream*. Translated by Patricia Frueh Kirkwood. Berkeley, Calif., 1965.

Leithäuser, Joachim. *Worlds Beyond the Horizon*. Translated by Hugh Merrick. New York, 1955.

Levitt, Israel. *Beyond the Known Universe*. New York, 1974.

Lewinsohn, Richard. *Animals, Men, and Myths*. New York, 1954.

Lewis, Richard S. *A Continent for Science*. New York, 1965.

Ley, Willy. *Watchers of the Skies*. New York, 1963.

———. *On Earth and in the Sky*. New York, 1958.

Macnamara, Ellen. *The Etruscans*. New York, 1973.

Macvey, John. *Whispers from Space*. New York, 1973.

Magnusson, Magnus, and Hermann Pálsson. *The Vinland Sagas*. New York, 1965.

Manley, Sean, and Lewis, Gago, eds. *Polar Secrets*. Garden City, N.Y., 1968.

Marx, Robert. *The Lure of Sunken Treasure*. New York, 1973.

Meyer, Karl E. *The Pleasures of Archaeology*. New York, 1971.

Millar, Ronald. *The Piltdown Man*. New York, 1972.

Montague, Ashley. *Man: His First 2 Million Years*. New York, 1969.

Moore, Patrick. *Watchers of the Stars*. London, 1974.

———. *Suns, Myths & Men*. New York, 1968.

Mountfield, David. *A History of Polar Exploration*. New York, 1974.

Mowatt, Farley. *Westviking*. Boston, 1965.

———. *Ordeal by Ice*. Boston, 1961.

Neider, Charles. *Man Against Nature*. New York, 1954.

———, ed. *Antarctica*. New York, 1972.

Norman, James. *Ancestral Voices*. New York, 1975.

Nylander, Carl. *The Deep Well*. Translated by Joan Tate. London, 1969.

Ohrelius, Bengt. *The Vasa*. Philadelphia, 1963.

Oxenstierna, Eric. *The Norsemen*. Translated by Catherine Hutter. Greenwich, Conn., 1965.

————. *The World of the Norsemen*. Translated by Janet Sondheimer. Cleveland, 1957.

Page, Thornton, and Williams, Lou, eds. *Wanderers in the Sky*. New York, 1967.

Pallottino, Massimo. *Etruscans*. Translated by J. Cremona. Bloomington, Ind., 1975.

Pericot-Garcia, Luis. *Prehistoric and Primitive Art*. Translated by Henry Mins. New York, 1967.

Pfeiffer, John. *The Emergence of Man*. New York, 1969.

Piggott, Stuart. *Prehistoric India*. London, 1961.

Pohl, Frederick J. *Atlantic Crossings Before Columbus*. New York, 1961.

Pope, Maurice. *Decipherment*. New York, 1975.

Quinn, David B. *North America from Earliest Discovery to First Settlements*. New York, 1977.

Rackl, Hanns-Wolf. *Diving into the Past*. Translated by Ronald J. Floyd. New York, 1968.

Ramsay, Raymond. *No Longer on the Map*. New York, 1972.

Rapport, Samuel, and Wright, Helen, eds. *Archaeology*. New York, 1964.

————. *Astronomy*. New York, 1964.

Rasky, Frank. *The Polar Voyagers*. New York, 1976.

Reith, Adolf. *Archaeological Fakes*. Translated by Diana Imber. London, 1970.

Richardson, Emeline. *The Etruscans*. Chicago, 1964.

Richardson, Robert. *The Stars and Serendipity*. New York, 1971.

————. *The Star Lovers*. New York, 1967.

Ronan, Colin. *Astronomers Royal*. New York, 1969.

————. *Astronomers*. London, 1964.

Ross, James Bruce, and McLaughlin, Mary Martin, eds. *The Renaissance Reader*. New York, 1953.

Ruz, Alberto. *Palenque*. Mexico City, 1947.

Sagan, Carl. *The Cosmic Connection*. New York, 1973.

de Santillana, Giorgio. *The Age of Adventure*. New York, 1956.

Savours, Ann, ed. *Scott's Last Voyage*. New York, 1975.

Schanche, Don. "The Vasa Affair," *Saturday Evening Post*, Philadelphia, October 21, 1961.

Schreiber, Herman. *Vanished Cities*. Translated by Richard and Clara Winston. New York, 1957.

Scott, Robert. *Scott's Last Expedition*. New York, 1923.
Scullard, H. H. *The Etruscan Cities and Rome*. Ithaca, N.Y., 1967.
Shapiro, Harry L. *Peking Man*. New York, 1974.
Silverberg, Robert. *Empires in the Dust*. New York, 1966.
————. *Sunken History*. New York, 1964.
————. *Man Before Adam*. Philadelphia, 1964.
Smith, Vincent. *The Oxford History of India*. Oxford, England, 1967.
Sprague, L., and de Camp, Catherine. *Citadels of Mystery*. New York, 1963.
Stefansson, Vilhjalmur. *Great Adventures and Explorations*. New York, 1952.
————. *Unsolved Mysteries of the Arctic*. New York, 1937.
Strong, Donald. *The Early Etruscans*. New York, 1968.
Sullivan, Walter. *We Are Not Alone*. New York, 1964.
————. *Quest for a Continent*. New York, 1957.
Sykes, Percy. *A History of Exploration*. New York, 1961.
Taylor, John. *Black Holes*. Glasgow, 1974.
Thiel, Rudolph. *And There Was Light*. Translated by Richard and Clara Winston. New York, 1957.
Thorndike, Joseph, ed. *Mysteries of the Past*. New York, 1977.
Time-Life. *The First Men*. New York, 1973.
————. *Cro-Magnon*. Edited by Tom Prideaux. New York, 1973.
Toulmin, Stephen, and Goodfield, June. *The Fabric of the Heavens*. New York, 1961.
Vaughan, Agnes. *Those Mysterious Etruscans*. New York, 1964.
Waechter, John. *Man Before History*. London, 1976.
Ward, Anne. *Adventures in Archaeology*. New York, 1977.
Wauchope, Robert. *Lost Tribes & Sunken Continents*. Chicago, 1962.
Wellard, James. *The Search for the Etruscans*. New York, 1973.
Wendt, Herbert. *The First Men*. Translated by Edmund White and Dale Brown. New York, 1973.
————. *From Ape to Adam*. No translator listed. New York, 1972.
————. *Before the Deluge*. Translated by Richard and Clara Winston. Garden City, N.Y., 1968.
————. *In Search of Adam*. Translated by James Cleugh. Boston, 1956.
Wheeler, Sir Mortimer. *Civilizations of the Indus Valley and Beyond*. London, 1966.
White, Peter. *The Past Is Human*. New York, 1976.
Whitney, Charles. *The Discovery of Our Galaxy*. New York, 1971.
Wichler, Gerhard. *Charles Darwin*. London, 1961.